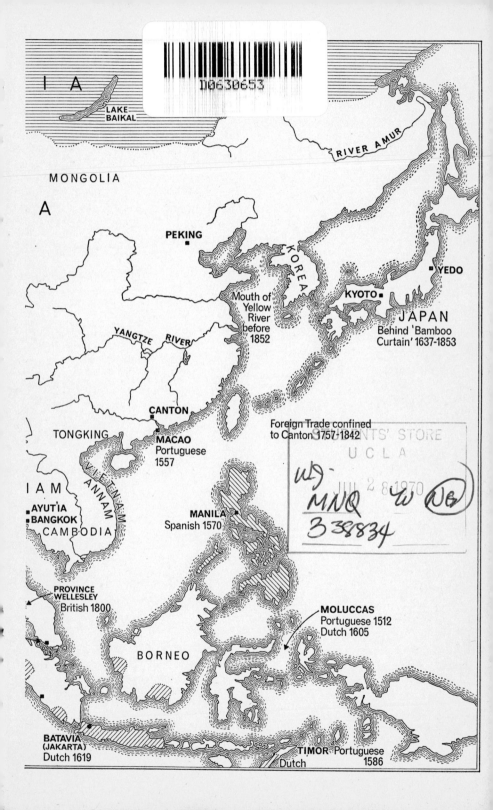

I A

LAKE BAIKAL

RIVER AMUR

MONGOLIA

A

PEKING

KOREA

YEDO

KYOTO

Mouth of
Yellow
River
before
1852

JAPAN
Behind 'Bamboo
Curtain' 1637-1853

YANGTZE RIVER

CANTON

TONGKING

MACAO
Portuguese
1557

Foreign Trade confined
to Canton 1757-1842

VIETNAM

ANNAM

I A M

AYUT'IA
BANGKOK
CAMBODIA

MANILA
Spanish 1570

PROVINCE
WELLESLEY
British 1800

MOLUCCAS
Portuguese 1512
Dutch 1605

BORNEO

BATAVIA
(JAKARTA)
Dutch 1619

TIMOR Portuguese
1586
Dutch

SOUTH AND
EAST ASIA SINCE
1800

SOUTH AND EAST ASIA SINCE 1800

BY

VICTOR PURCELL
C.M.G., LITT.D.

CAMBRIDGE

AT THE UNIVERSITY PRESS

1965

PUBLISHED BY

THE SYNDICS OF THE CAMBRIDGE UNIVERSITY PRESS

Bentley House, 200 Euston Road, London, N.W.1

American Branch: 32 East 57th Street, New York, N.Y. 10022

West African Office: P.O. Box 33, Ibadan, Nigeria

©

CAMBRIDGE UNIVERSITY PRESS

1965

Printed in Great Britain at the University Printing House, Cambridge
(Brooke Crutchley, University Printer)

CONTENTS

List of Maps   *page*   vii

Preface   ix

1   Southeast Asia, its Peoples, its Culture, and its History
    to 1800   1
    Description of the Region;   The Unity of Southeast Asia;
    Indian and Chinese Influences;   The Spread of Islam;   The
    Coming of the Europeans;   The Beginnings of the European
    Empires;   Effects of the Scientific and Industrial Revolutions

2   Southeast Asia, 1800–69   18
    The Region in 1800;   Anglo-Dutch Rivalry;   Raffles Founds
    Singapore;   The Anglo-Dutch Treaty of 1824;   India and
    Burma;   The 'Dutch East Indies' (Indonesia) 1818–69;
    British Relations with the Malay States and Siam;   Opening
    of the Suez Canal (1869)

3   European Colonial Expansion in Southeast Asia, 1869–
    1900   45
    New Attitudes towards Colonial Acquisition;   British Inter-
    vention in the Malay States;   The 'Resident' System on Trial;
    The British in Borneo: the 'White Rajas' of Sarawak, the North
    Borneo Company;   The rest of Burma brought under British
    Rule;   The French in Indochina;   Developments in Siam
    and the Philippines

4   South and East Asia in the Nineteenth Century   70
    The British Empire in India—the Indian Mutiny (1857)—
    Post-Mutiny India;   The Opium War;   China's resistance
    to change;   Commodore Perry reaches Japan (1853);   The
    Meiji Restoration (1868–1912);   The Sino-Japanese War
    (1894–5), the Reform Movement in China, and the Boxer Up-
    rising (1900);   The Influence of Events in India and China
    and Japan on Southeast Asia

5   The Colonial Régime at its Zenith, 1900–39   91
    Tin and Rubber in Malaya;   Progress in transport, public
    works, hygiene, and education;   A 'Plural Society' arises in
    Southeast Asia;   Dutch Colonial policy;   Siam's gradual
    transformation: the revolution of 1932;   British policy in
    Burma;   The French in Indochina;   America replaces Spain
    in the Philippines;   The Colonial Period in perspective

Contents

6 The Rise of Nationalism in East and South Asia,
   1900–31   *page* 119
   China after the Boxer Protocol; The Russo-Japanese War
   (1904–5) and its effects; The Chinese Revolution of 1911;
   Reforms in India and the rise of the Congress Party; The
   revival of the Kuomintang and the reunification of China;
   The growth of Japanese imperialism

7 Nationalism Extends to Southeast Asia, 1908–39   141
   Sarekat Islam and Nationalism in Java; Burmese Nationalism
   and the British; Vietnamese Nationalism and the French;
   The Filipinos press for independence; The impact of the
   Kuomintang on the Overseas Chinese—Malaya—Siam (Thai-
   land)

8 South and East Asia in the 1930s   158
   Mass disobedience in India; Chiang Kai-Shek and the ascend-
   ancy of the Kuomintang; Japan takes the plunge; Southeast
   Asia on the eve of the Pacific War

9 The Pacific War and its Aftermath   176
   The Japanese invade Southeast Asia; The Japanese occupation; The Japanese defeat; The surrender, and the Allied
   occupation of Japan; The post-war situation in Southeast
   Asia; India and Pakistan become independent; Civil War
   in China

10 South, East, and Southeast Asia since 1945   195
   Outstanding events of the period; The People's Republic of
   China is established; The Korean War, 1950–53; Dien Bien
   Phu and the Geneva Conference; The Afro-Asian Conference
   at Bandung; Malaya becomes independent; The Sino-
   Indian boundary question; The establishment of Malaysia

Appendix   215

Index   219

LIST OF MAPS

South and East Asia in 1800 (showing European possessions)   *on page* xii *and front endpapers*

South and East Asia in 1964 (showing European withdrawal)   *on page* xiv *and back endpapers*

1   Earlier Indian and Chinese influences on Southeast Asia

                                                                          page 5

2   The British conquest of Burma   35

3   British intervention in Malaya 1874–1909 (with references to earlier intervention)   49

4   French advance in Indochina 1859–1907   65

5   The extension of Dutch control in the East Indies   104

6   South and East Asia in 1939 (showing maximum Euro-
pean expansion)   116 and 117

7   Japanese conquests in the Pacific War at their greatest
extent   181

8   Southeast Asia; economics and population *c.* 1961   210

9   The Federation of Malaysia (created 16 September 1963)   211

The maps were drawn by Regmarad

PREFACE

The expression, 'the Far East', has long been in use in the West to describe the countries of Asia from India to Japan, and indeed it correctly represents their geographical relationship with Europe and America. But it is unreasonable to expect persons living in these countries or in a different geographical relationship to them to be satisfied with this description. In Asian usage, therefore, and increasingly in Western usage, Asia as a whole is now commonly divided into South, East, and West Asia.

But where does South Asia end and East Asia begin? Burma, Vietnam, Cambodia, Laos, Siam (Thailand), Malaysia, Brunei, Indonesia, and the Philippines can be said to belong to South Asia, and they can also be said to belong to East Asia. In fact, they together form Southeast Asia, which (as I shall hope to demonstrate) is a unity on its own. It would be better, therefore, to regard the expression South Asia as having an emphasis on the Indian Subcontinent, and East Asia as meaning, above all, China and Japan.

If this is accepted, how is the history of South and East Asia (considering them in their united sense) to be written? There is no single logical way of doing it. Such a history would have to depend for its proportions largely on the viewpoint of the observer. This book is intended primarily for the use of persons living in Southeast Asia, and more particularly in Malaysia, so that it would be appropriate if the history were written from this centre. And this is what I have attempted to do.

There is one further point I should like to stress, and that is the fact that whereas the Indian Subcontinent (India, Pakistan, and Ceylon) had a greater influence on most of Southeast Asia than China and Japan in ancient times, China and Japan have had a greater influence upon it in recent times (as witness the numerous communities of Overseas Chinese and the Japanese invasion of 1940–45). Nevertheless the earlier Indian contacts as well as Islam have left an indelible imprint on the larger part of Southeast Asia, and the modern history of the region since 1800 is not fully intelligible without recognition of these facts. For this reason I have provided an introductory chapter on the history of the area up to that date.

I am much indebted to Professor Tregonning for his valuable advice and assistance, and (once again) to Dr C. L. Wayper for his penetrating criticisms of the text which I have done my best to profit from in revising it.

VICTOR PURCELL

CAMBRIDGE
1964

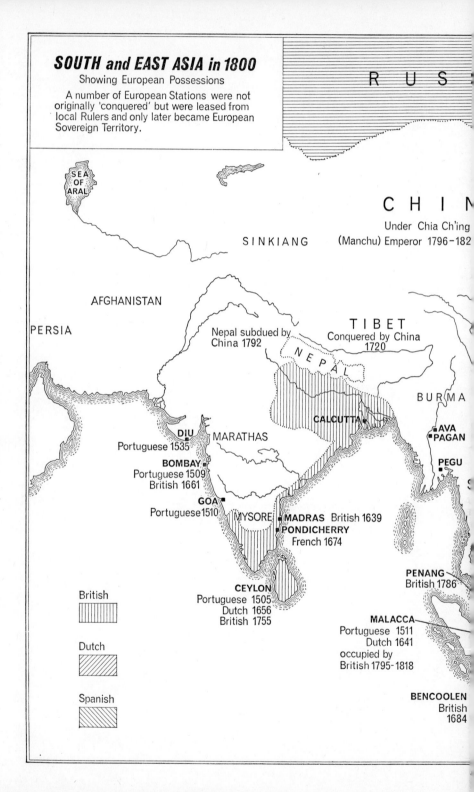

SOUTH and EAST ASIA in 1800

Showing European Possessions

A number of European Stations were not originally 'conquered' but were leased from local Rulers and only later became European Sovereign Territory.

R U S

SEA OF ARAL

C H I N

Under Chia Ch'ing
(Manchu) Emperor 1796–182

SINKIANG

AFGHANISTAN

PERSIA

TIBET
Conquered by China
1720

Nepal subdued by
China 1792

N E P A L

BURMA

CALCUTTA

AVA
PAGAN

DIU
Portuguese 1535

MARATHAS

PEGU

BOMBAY
Portuguese 1509
British 1661

GOA
Portuguese 1510

MYSORE

MADRAS British 1639
PONDICHERRY
French 1674

PENANG
British 1786

British

Dutch

Spanish

CEYLON
Portuguese 1505
Dutch 1656
British 1755

MALACCA
Portuguese 1511
Dutch 1641
occupied by
British 1795-1818

BENCOOLEN
British
1684

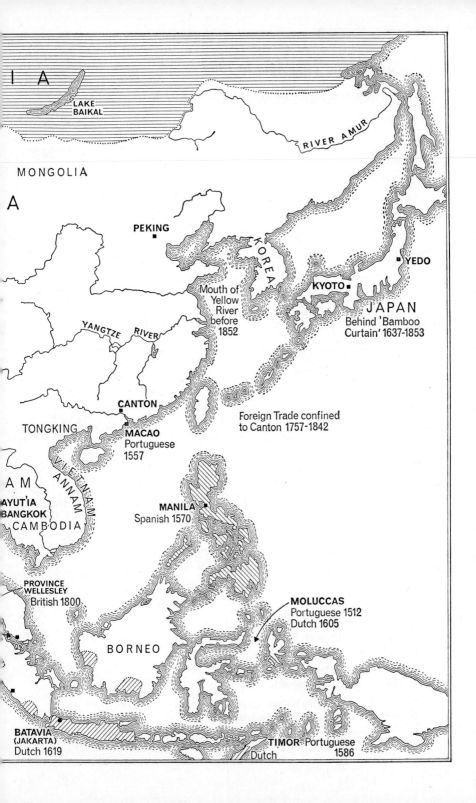

I A

LAKE
BAIKAL

RIVER AMUR

MONGOLIA

A

PEKING

KOREA

YEDO

KYOTO

JAPAN
Behind 'Bamboo
Curtain' 1637-1853

Mouth of
Yellow
River
before
1852

YANGTZE RIVER

CANTON

Foreign Trade confined
to Canton 1757-1842

TONGKING

MACAO
Portuguese
1557

A M

VIETNAM

ANNAM

AYUT'IA
BANGKOK
CAMBODIA

MANILA
Spanish 1570

PROVINCE
WELLESLEY
British 1800

MOLUCCAS
Portuguese 1512
Dutch 1605

BORNEO

BATAVIA
(JAKARTA)
Dutch 1619

TIMOR Portuguese
Dutch   1586

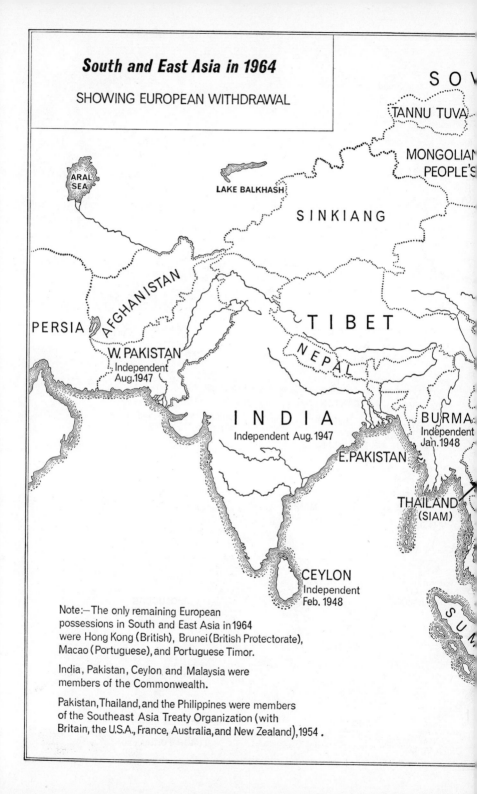

South and East Asia in 1964

SHOWING EUROPEAN WITHDRAWAL

S O V

TANNU TUVA

MONGOLIAN
PEOPLE'S

ARAL
SEA

LAKE BALKHASH

S I N K I A N G

AFGHANISTAN

PERSIA

W. PAKISTAN
Independent
Aug. 1947

T I B E T

N E P A L

I N D I A
Independent Aug. 1947

BURMA
Independent
Jan. 1948

E. PAKISTAN

THAILAND
(SIAM)

CEYLON
Independent
Feb. 1948

SUM

Note:— The only remaining European
possessions in South and East Asia in 1964
were Hong Kong (British), Brunei (British Protectorate),
Macao (Portuguese), and Portuguese Timor.

India, Pakistan, Ceylon and Malaysia were
members of the Commonwealth.

Pakistan, Thailand, and the Philippines were members
of the Southeast Asia Treaty Organization (with
Britain, the U.S.A., France, Australia, and New Zealand), 1954.

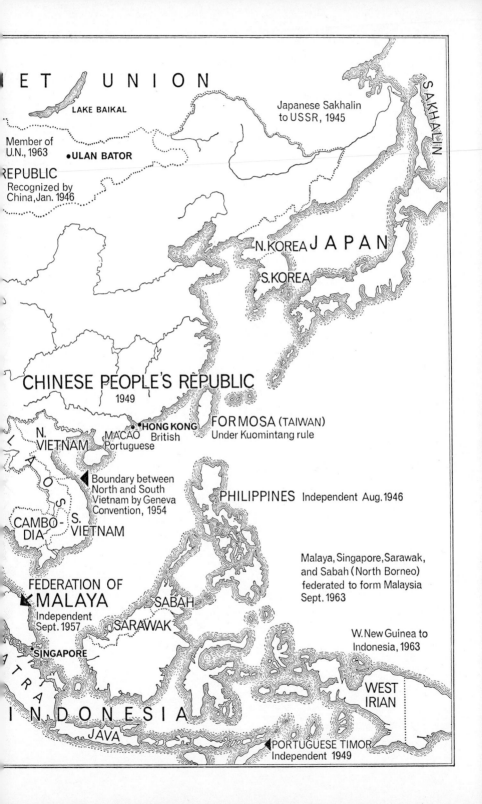

ET UNION

LAKE BAIKAL

Japanese Sakhalin
to USSR, 1945

SAKHALIN

Member of
U.N., 1963 • ULAN BATOR

REPUBLIC
Recognized by
China, Jan. 1946

N. KOREA J A P A N

S. KOREA

CHINESE PEOPLE'S REPUBLIC
1949

FORMOSA (TAIWAN)
Under Kuomintang rule

N.
VIETNAM
MACAO
Portuguese
British

HONG KONG

Boundary between
North and South
Vietnam by Geneva
Convention, 1954

PHILIPPINES Independent Aug. 1946

CAMBO-
DIA
S.
VIETNAM

LAOS

Malaya, Singapore, Sarawak,
and Sabah (North Borneo)
federated to form Malaysia
Sept. 1963

FEDERATION OF
MALAYA
Independent
Sept. 1957

SABAH

SARAWAK

W. New Guinea to
Indonesia, 1963

SINGAPORE

SUMATRA

INDONESIA

WEST
IRIAN

JAVA

PORTUGUESE TIMOR
Independent 1949

I

SOUTHEAST ASIA, ITS PEOPLES, ITS CULTURE, AND ITS HISTORY TO 1800

DESCRIPTION OF THE REGION

What is Southeast Asia, and what entitles us to consider it as a unity?

As a term to describe the whole region between India and China 'Southeast (or South-East) Asia' came into general use only during the Pacific War of 1941–45. Before then it had been used by geographers as a name for the region in general, but its boundaries were not yet precise, and only within the last twenty years or so has it been internationally accepted as comprising what are now Burma, Thailand, North and South Vietnam, Cambodia, Laos, the Federation of Malaysia, Brunei, Indonesia, and the Philippines.

The groups of countries which make up present-day Southern Asia have been given different names at different times, and this is sometimes confusing when we read old history books. 'East Indies' was a term long used for the Malay Archipelago, as opposed to the 'West Indies', the name given by early explorers to islands in the Atlantic which they believed to be off the coast of India ('the Indies'). The great naturalist Alfred Russel Wallace (1823–1913) included the Malay Peninsula in the Malay Archipelago, but recent geographers confine the latter to the vast group of islands known as 'Netherlands India' (Nederlandsch Indië) to the Dutch who ruled them for over three centuries, and, since independence, as Indonesia. The name 'Indonesia' is a nineteenth-century coinage, and was adopted by the Indonesian nationalists as a name for their country.

The name 'Malaya' is also of fairly modern origin. In the British period it included Singapore, but nowadays it is generally understood to refer to the Federation of Malaya alone. 'Malay' (*Melayu* in Malay) describes the peoples of the Malay race or their language, and is also used in the geographical expression 'The Malay Peninsula'. 'Malaysia' was originally a geographical term used to describe Indonesia and the Malay Peninsula together, but from 16 September 1963 it was officially applied to the new Federation of Malaysia, comprising the Federation of Malaya, Singapore, Sarawak, and Sabah (North Borneo).

One term that came into use during the period of the extension of British power eastwards from India in the nineteenth century was 'Further India', which was used to describe Burma and Malaya together, now that they had been brought under British rule or protection. So 'India-minded' were the British at one time that 'Ultra-Gangetic' (that is, 'beyond the River Ganges') was sometimes used by them to describe any region to the eastward of India. But this, and 'Further India', are nowadays terms with only a historical significance.

'Indo-China', too, was originally an expression coined to describe that part of the Asian mainland between India and China, but with the extension of French power in that area it was adopted by the French as a collective name for their possessions and protectorates in the Indo-Chinese Peninsula (i.e. Cochin-China, Annam, Tongking, Cambodia, and Laos). They spelt it usually as one word—*Indochine*. But although the French have now withdrawn from the country, Indochina can still be correctly used in a historical sense.

Thailand was known as 'Siam' to the West for some centuries, and although the name was officially changed to Thailand in 1950, Siam is still current as an alternative name for the country.

The names used for Southeast Asia and the countries composing it at various times were often an indication of the political influences of the period and therefore have significance to the study of history.

THE UNITY OF SOUTHEAST ASIA

The reasons for regarding Southeast Asia as a unity are numerous. They can be summarized as being geographical, cultural, and historical. The region is, in general, separated from its neighbouring regions by wide seas, mountains, or forests, and the fact that the greater part of the region has a tropical climate and that rice is the basic food means that the inhabitants of Southeast Asia share broadly similar ways of life. West Irian (ex-Netherlands New Guinea) marks the eastern boundary of Southeast Asia, for although politically it is now part of Indonesia, it is connected geographically with Australia, its inhabitants are closely related to the Australian aborigines, and its animals, birds, and plants are of the type found in the Australian Continent.

Although there are hundreds of racial types in Southeast Asia, the great majority of the people have a strong racial similarity and the only real gulf is that between this majority and the few tens of thousands of aborigines, represented in Malaya by the primitive negritos. But more important than racial diversity is cultural similarity.

Coedès, the French authority who has perhaps done more than anyone to demonstrate the unity of Southeast Asian history, sums up the characteristics of the region under the following headings— on the material side, the cultivation of irrigated rice-fields, the domestication of the ox and buffalo, the rudimentary use of metals, and skill in navigation; on the social side, the importance of women and descent by the maternal line, and the organization arising from irrigated cultivation; on the religious side, animism (the attribution of a soul to natural objects), the worship of ancestors and of the god of the soil, the location of shrines in high places, the burial of the dead in jars or at dolmens (graves of unhewn stones), and a mythology imbued with a dualism of mountain *versus* sea, winged beings *versus* water beings, and men of the mountain *versus* men of the sea coast. Winstedt adds to this list uniformity of race modified by different admixtures of Negrito, Indonesian, and Mongol blood, one language family, haruspicy (taking of omens from the entrails of animals), a god-king, respect for the number 7, the incantation, the pyramid, and so on, and one material culture (bronze, textiles, etc.). Krom, the Dutch historian of ancient Java, adds the *wayang*, or puppet shadow theatre, the *gamelan* orchestra, and *batik* work (the painted ornamentation of textiles). D. G. E. Hall insists that the unity of Southeast Asia is above all demonstrated by the high

status that women enjoy in society throughout the region as con-
trasted with that in some adjacent civilizations. 'Woman', he
writes, 'has largely maintained the high place accorded to her
before the earliest impact of Indian culture, a far higher one than
she has ever occupied in India in recorded history.'

Long before India and China began to exert their cultural influences on Southeast Asia, the great migrations of prehistoric times
were over. Nevertheless, pressures set up by the extension of
Chinese civilization and power southwards from the Yangtze still
caused some of the tribes settled in this region to migrate in an
effort to preserve their individuality. The result was a series of new
waves of immigration widely separated in time over the last two
thousand years, penetrating into Southeast Asia by the different
routes provided by nature. For example, one wave moved down
the Annam plain between the mountains and the sea, a second wave
followed the valleys further inland, and a third wave the valleys
still further to the north. Here the newcomers found peoples already long established—the Chams in central and Southern Annam,
the Khmers of the Mekong delta, the Mons (closely related to the
Khmers) in the Menam Valley and Lower Burma, the Pyus in the
Irrawaddy and Sittang basins—and eventually the three waves, by
conquest and intermarriage with the conquered, resulted in the
establishment of what are now respectively Vietnam, Thailand, and
Burma.

INDIAN AND CHINESE INFLUENCES

Meanwhile, in the first centuries of the Christian era (now adopted
as a convenient measurement of time by many Asian countries)
long before Burma and Siam came into being, the two major civilizations of the Far East, India and China, had made their indelible
imprint on the earlier states of Southeast Asia, and by the end of
the Middle Ages (in the Western sense) they had divided up the
region between them. The 'Indianized' division was much the
larger, consisting of what are now Burma, Thailand, Laos, Cambodia, Malaya, and Indonesia; the sinicized (i.e. China-influenced)
division comprising Tongking, Annam, and Cochin-China after

4

Indian and Chinese Influences

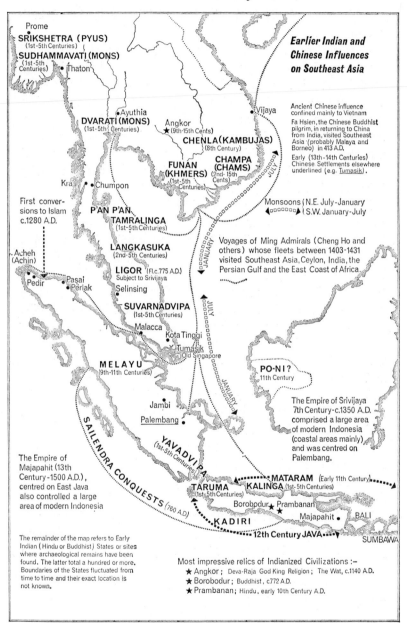

Prome
SRIKSHETRA (PYUS)
(1st-5th Centuries)
SUDHAMMAVATI (MONS)
(1st-5th
Centuries)   •Thaton

**Earlier Indian and
Chinese Influences
on Southeast Asia**

•Ayuthia
DVARATI (MONS)
(1st-5th Centuries)

Angkor
★ (9th-15th Cents)
CHENLA (KAMBUJAS)
(8th Century)

•Vijaya

Ancient Chinese influence
confined mainly to Vietnam

Fa Hsien, the Chinese Buddhist
pilgrim, in returning to China
from India, visited Southeast
Asia (probably Malaya and
Borneo) in 413 A.D.

Early (13th-14th Centuries)
Chinese Settlements elsewhere
underlined (e.g. Tumasik).

**FUNAN
(KHMERS)**
(1st-5th
Centuries)

**CHAMPA
(CHAMS)**
(2nd-15th
Cents)

Kra   •Chumpon

First conver-
sions to Islam
c.1280 A.D.

P'AN P'AN
TAMRALINGA
(1st-5th Centuries)

Monsoons { N.E. July-January
◄□□□□□► S.W. January-July

•Acheh
(Achin)

LANGKASUKA
(2nd-5th Centuries)

Voyages of Ming Admirals (Cheng Ho and
others) whose fleets between 1403-1431
visited Southeast Asia, Ceylon, India, the
Persian Gulf and the East Coast of Africa.

Pedir   •Pasai
•Periak

LIGOR (Fl.c.775 A.D.)
Subject to Srivijaya
Selinsing

SUVARNADVIPA
(1st-5th Centuries)
Malacca

Kota Tinggi
•Tumasik
Old Singapore

MELAYU
(9th-11th Centuries)

PO-NI?
11th Century

Jambi
Palembang •

The Empire of Srivijaya
7th Century-c.1350 A.D.
comprised a large area
of modern Indonesia
(coastal areas mainly)
and was centred on
Palembang.

The Empire of
Majapahit (13th
Century-1500 A.D.),
centred on East Java
also controlled a large
area of modern Indonesia

YAVADVIPA
(1st-5th Centuries)

SAILENDRA CONQUESTS (760 A.D)

MATARAM (Early 11th Century)
TARUMA **KALINGA** (1st-5th Centuries)
(1st-5th Centuries)
Borobodur★ Prambanan
★   ★
KADIRI Majapahit • BALI
•••••12th Century JAVA••••▼
SUMBAWA

The remainder of the map refers to Early
Indian (Hindu or Buddhist) States or sites
where archaeological remains have been
found. The latter total a hundred or more.
Boundaries of the States fluctuated from
time to time and their exact location is
not known.

Most impressive relics of Indianized Civilizations :–
★ Angkor ; Deva-Raja God King Religion ; The Wat, c.1140 A.D.
★ Borobodur ; Buddhist, c772 A.D.
★ Prambanan ; Hindu, early 10th Century A.D.

Map I

5

the fall of the 'Indianized' kingdom of Champa in the fifteenth century.

Nevertheless, care must be taken not to exaggerate these external influences, for the peoples of Southeast Asia had already long-established cultures of their own, and they borrowed from India or China without losing the basic structure of their societies. For example, the caste system, which was fundamental to Hinduism, has made very little impression on the regions of Southern Asia that were 'Hinduized'. The high status of women (stressed by Hall) was one notable feature of Southeast Asian society not removed by 'Hinduization'.

In the same way, the more primitive beliefs of the peoples of the region were not displaced by the introduction of Hinduism, Buddhism (usually Theravada[1]) and Islam into the Indianized countries, nor by that of Confucianism, Taoism, and Mahayana Buddhism into Vietnam—they were merely overlaid and obscured by the new teachings. Just as paganism underlies Christianity in the Western world, animism and magic, as well as the later Hinduism, persist among Southeast Asian peoples long ago converted to Islam—even though Islam, of comparatively recent introduction into the region, was more intolerant of primitive beliefs than were the other religions and its establishment raised the one real barrier among Southeast Asian peoples. Anthropologists have remarked that throughout the monsoon lands there is a unity of culture, with seasonal festivals, which preceded the civilization of Aryan India and left its mark on the civilization of China. Of the survival of this culture there is, for example, striking evidence in modern Malay magic and the ancient shadow-play (which is still performed in the east-coast states of Malaya).

What has been said of Southeast Asian religion and custom is equally true of Southeast Asian art. The architectural master-pieces of Borobodur (A.D. 772) and Angkor (twelfth–fourteenth centuries) (Buddhist and Hindu inspired respectively) are completely distinct from anything in India and are as original in essential respects as foreign-influenced art can possibly be.

---

[1] As distinguished from the Mahayana (Greater Vehicle) Buddhism. (Theravadists object to their School being called the Hinayana (Lesser Vehicle).)

6

Indian and Chinese Influences

The first Indianized states were in existence before A.D. 200 along the lower Mekong River and its delta, in the neighbourhood of Hué in modern Annam, and in the Malay Peninsula. One of these was Funan, with its capital in modern Cambodia, many of whose cults and traditions were adopted and carried on after its fall by the Khmers. Champa, immediately to the east of Funan, has been traced back (under another name) to the second century A.D. and was not overthrown finally until the fifteenth. The first Indianized island 'empire', however, was that of Sri Vijaya, which arose in Western Indonesia sometime in the seventh century A.D., and its capital was at Palembang in Sumatra. Sri Vijaya was the successor in power in Southeast Asia to Funan, and until it succumbed to the raids of the Cholas of Tanjore in the eleventh century, it dominated a large part of Indonesia and the Malay Peninsula. The influences shaping this empire were first of all Brahmanism and then Mahayana Buddhism.

Sri Vijaya lingered on for a century or two after the fatal Chola raids, and its place was eventually taken in a lesser way by Majapahit, the last of the Hindu-Javanese kingdoms, in the middle years of the fourteenth century. But although Majapahit was very inferior culturally to Sri Vijaya, being destructive rather than creative, in addition to its undoubted sway over most of Sumatra and as far north as Kedah in Malaya, it could even claim a protectorate over the countries of the Indo-China Peninsula.

Meanwhile, another civilization had made its appearance in Cambodia. This was the Khmer, in some respects the most remarkable of all the Southeast Asian 'empires'. Like Sri Vijaya, it was first based on Brahmanism, but King Jayavarman II, who came from Java to found the Angkor kingdom, revived an ancient cult, giving it a new form. It was that of Deva-Raja, a form of Hinduism which centred on sex-and-mountain worship, both of even earlier origin than Hinduism. The king himself was worshipped as a god, and after death he became Siva or Vishnu, or even Buddha, according to his own preference. Angkor subdued its neighbours, the Mon people, and, for a time, Champa, and reached the height of its glory with the building of Angkor Wat (c. A.D. 1140). It was the attacks of the Thais which caused the desertion of Angkor as the capital,

7

but Cambodia was never conquered and three years after the sack of Angkor by the Thais, the Cambodians transferred their capital to Phnom Penh, where it still remains.

These Indianized kingdoms of Southeast Asia now belong to the remote past. It is true that the cultural traditions they bequeathed still remain beneath the surface in the modern life of the region, but their history is very shadowy in the minds of the mass of the people. The monuments of Cambodia and Central Java remain as splendid reminders of the past, but these are hidden away far from the main centres of population. The histories of Funan, Sri Vijaya, Cambodia, etc., are largely the recreation of historians and archaeologists, and through the medium of modern books the educated Southeast Asian can summon up before him these ancient states as they were in their early days at the height of their careers and in their decline and fall.

THE SPREAD OF ISLAM

There now ensued an event which transformed a large section of Southeast Asia and whose effects are still before our eyes in Southeast Asia today—namely the coming of Islam. Brought hither by Arab and Indian Muslim traders and seamen, Islam took root in the coastal states of Sumatra in the late thirteenth and early fourteenth centuries and then began to fan eastward across the Malay Peninsula and Indonesia, bringing the collapse of Majapahit in its train. Within a space of two hundred years the whole of the Indonesian islands, except the small pocket of Bali where Hinduism still survives, became Muslim, and the religion was also established in the Philippines. It was not until the arrival of the Spanish in the Philippines in 1570, with their vigorous campaigns to convert the peoples to Catholicism, that the advance of Islam was arrested, and today Muslims are to be found in large numbers only in the southern island of Mindanao.

But although, in historical terms, the expansion of Islam into Southeast Asia was rapid, there was considerable resistance to its advance from the existing religions and cults, and it was long before it was fully accepted by the mass of the people. This fact is well illustrated by the history of the Malay kingdom of Malacca, which flourished from about A.D. 1400 to 1511, and which at the height of its power controlled the whole of the Malay Peninsula as well as an extension of its territory into Sumatra. The founder of the kingdom, Parameswara, was a prince of Palembang who married a princess of Majapahit in eastern Java. When he allied Malacca with Pasai he took a Muslim wife, adopting the religion of Islam and the name of Iskandar Shah. Yet his successor bore a Hindu title, Sri Maharajah, and it was not until the accession of Muzaffir Shah after a palace revolution in 1445 that a Muslim accession was assured, and only very gradually did Islam spread from the royal court to the mass of the people. Hindu tradition lives on in the court ceremonial of the Malay States where Sanskrit (the language of the Hindu Scriptures) is still used for announcements at investitures, and the titles of certain Malay high officials are still Hindu (e.g. Bendahara and Laksamana). Hinduism, as has already been remarked, survives in Malay society as a whole in the shape of numerous customs and beliefs.

The early years of the Malacca kingdom were marked by the appearance of an embassy from China. In 1403 (says the *Ming History*) the emperor of China sent the eunuch Yin Ching as envoy to Malacca with presents of silk brocade. Then in 1409 the famous Chinese eunuch-admiral Cheng Ho visited Malacca on one of the famous voyages which carried Chinese arms as far as the coast of Africa and the Persian Gulf, and in 1411 the first King of Malacca returned the compliment by making a personal visit to Peking.

Although so much of Southeast Asian history is known only through the Chinese annals (usually based on information at secondhand), the Chinese were tardy in establishing sea contacts with Southeast Asia and in making settlements there. Kublai Khan had sent a Chinese army against King Kertanagara of Java in 1292, but after some initial successes it was forced to take to its ships again and to sail back to China. A small Chinese settlement existed at Tumasik, or Old Singapore, in the fourteenth century, and on one of his voyages Cheng Ho (or one of his admirals) seized Ch'en Tsu-Yi, the chief of a Chinese pirate settlement at Palembang, and carried him back to China for execution. But Chinese settlement in Southeast Asia on any scale still lay in the future.

THE COMING OF THE EUROPEANS

From what has been said above it will be clear that for several thousands of years Southeast Asia was shaped by successive migrations bringing different sets of cultural influences, and then for the first millennium and a half of the historical period (from about the first century A.D.) by the impress upon it of India and China. In the last four and a half centuries Europe has made an impact on the region, resulting in a vast change in attitudes. Moreover, because of something that was happening to Europe itself, transforming its own outlook and way of life, this impact has had revolutionary effects in the twentieth century.

The germ of these changes is to be found in a new spirit that arose in Europe from about the middle of the fifteenth century onwards. Its inspiration was the belief that 'knowledge is power', and it manifested itself in curiosity and enterprise. Why this new spirit should have arisen in Europe and not elsewhere at this time is still a matter of discussion among historians, but it was undoubtedly connected with economic and commercial factors. The consequence was an outburst of energy which resulted first of all in a rebirth of literature, learning, and art (the 'Renaissance') and, a century or so later, in a surge of scientific enquiry (the 'Scientific Revolution'). The same spirit of curiosity and enterprise carried European seamen, soldiers, and merchants to the Eastern Seas.

First of all came the Portuguese, whose pioneer commander, Vasco da Gama, on his arrival in Calicut in India in 1498, declared that what the Portuguese sought was 'Christians and spices'— namely the conversion of Asians to Christianity on the spiritual level, and the obtaining of pepper, nutmegs, and cloves, so greatly in demand in Europe for flavouring food, on the material one.

Portugal was a small country, with no great economic resources, and, having few articles of commerce that were exchangeable for the rich and varied Asian products, had to rely on sea power to maintain its position in Asia. The Portuguese first established bases on the west coast of India, at Goa (1510) and elsewhere, and from these they reached out further to the east. At this time Malacca was the greatest entrepôt of Southeast Asian trade, and was annually resorted to by thousands of merchants from all over the Far East. To gain the control of this trade and to obtain easy access to the spices of the Moluccas, the Portuguese, in 1511, attacked Malacca and, after an initial repulse, conquered it. The last king of Malacca, Mahmud, and his son Ahmad, fled from the field and the Malay kingdom came to an end.

For nearly a century the Portuguese had the Asian trade largely to themselves, though the Spanish established themselves in the Philippines in the last three decades of the sixteenth century. But as the Portuguese power waned, the English and the Dutch took their place. The latter were traders pure and simple, and the conversion of the Asians to Christianity was to have no place in the programme of these nations for centuries to come.

How then did it come about that the British, the Dutch, and the French established 'empires' in the Far East whither they originally had come only for trade? The reply can be over-simplified, since the motives and pressures were various, but the origin of this extension of political power is to be found in a few basic facts. In order to keep their trading stations secure from attack, the Europeans had to ensure that they had a peaceful interior ('hinterland') behind them. Since the surrounding territory was often in a state of disorder, this at times involved military intervention. In the sixteenth and seventeenth centuries the position of these European outposts was very precarious, since they were dependent on the goodwill of the local princes for their survival. There were then two great empires in the Far East—the Mogul empire in Northern and Central India and the empire of China (conquered by the Manchus in 1644), and it was only as a favour that the Europeans were allowed to carry on trade with their subjects. As for Japan, fearing that the Spanish from the Philippines were planning to invade it and that the other European nations also had sinister designs on its independence, in the 1630s it withdrew behind what we today might call a 'bamboo curtain', forbidding all its subjects to go abroad or to build sea-going ships. The only foreign traders allowed to remain were the

Dutch, confined to a tiny artificial island in Nagasaki Bay, which served also as a Japanese peephole on the outer world. It was not until the arrival of the American Commodore Perry with his squadron of warships in 1853 that this 'bamboo curtain' was to be pierced.

THE BEGINNINGS OF THE EUROPEAN EMPIRES

Hitherto, the European incursions into the Far East had been politically unimportant, and had scarcely affected the age-old aspect of these Asian countries. But a transformation was in the making. The collapse of the Mogul empire after the death of the Emperor Aurangzeb in 1707 left a political vacuum in India which paved the way for European intervention. In their new participation in local disputes the Europeans made an important discovery, namely that small units of Indian troops under British or French officers could easily defeat the large, badly-disciplined armies of the Indian princes. The first attempt at 'empire-building' was made by Dupleix, Governor-General of French India, who by astute alliances with the princes made himself virtual master of the Carnatic in Southern India. Meanwhile the war of the Austrian Succession (1740–48) brought the French and British into conflict in the Far East, and in the Seven Years War (1756–63) they were engaged in a deadly struggle for supremacy in the Indian sub-continent. But within a few years the French were worsted in the contest and British power prevailed.

The British empire in India is usually dated from Clive's victory at Plassey in 1757 over the Nawab of Bengal, but it was Munro's triumph in 1764—when he defeated the combined armies of the Mogul emperor and the Nawab of Oudh at Buxar—which finally laid the way open for a large scale British advance. Yet 'imperialism' was never the single British motive, and there was always a ding-dong battle in progress between those governors-general who saw no alternative between complete conquest and complete withdrawal and the matter-of-fact directors of the East India Company in London who disliked wars which cost money and cut down their profits, and who wanted to incur no further responsibilities of government. But with the successive wars in Europe the strategical factor came repeatedly to the fore. European campaigns in Asia were now conducted with purely military aims in view, and the question of expense was relegated to the second place. This was very much the case during the British wars with France at the turn of the century (1793–1815) and it was scarcely an accident that the aggressive and ambitious Marquess Wellesley (the elder brother of the Duke of Wellington) was appointed Governor-General in 1797 and was replaced only when his rapid extension of British power was proving too expensive for the comfort of the East India Company Directors (1805).

The extension of British power in India was to be the eventual reason for their intervention in Burma—namely to safeguard the Indian frontiers—but this was not the only motive shaping British policy in Southeast Asia. Both the East India Company and the British Government attached very great importance to the trade with China, especially in tea, and the settlements that the British established in Malaya were regarded by them primarily as stations on the sea-route to China. The first of these was Penang (1786); Malacca was occupied by the British in the name of the Prince of Orange (1795); but Singapore (1819) had to wait until the conclusion of the Napoleonic Wars for its foundation.

In the seventeenth and eighteenth centuries, however, it was the Netherlands and not Britain which was the paramount European power in Southeast Asia. In the first part of the seventeenth century the Dutch and English East India Companies had come into collision in Indonesia, but whereas the Dutch Company had the full support of the home government, the English Company was only a private venture financed by London merchants. Thus the resources in ships and money the two companies commanded were unequal, and the English Company eventually withdrew from the contest to devote its attention to India and China. The Dutch were therefore left with the field of enterprise in Indonesia to themselves.

The Dutch Governor-General of the Indies, Jan Pieterszoon Coen, who founded Batavia (Jakarta) in 1619, saw that the European Far Eastern trade was insufficient in value to justify by itself the existence of a great trading organization. What promised greater profits, however, was the inter-Asian trade, and this could, by means of sea power, be controlled by the Dutch and profited from at their discretion. For the remainder of the seventeenth century the Dutch East India Company was a trading company, pure and simple, but when by the 1690s the Dutch had lost their sea power to the British, it is likely that the Company would have shrunk to almost nothing or entirely disappeared had it not been for the discovery that certain crops could be grown in Java and exported at a profit. Sugar was the first of these export crops, but in 1725 coffee was added and later on became the most important export of all. Hitherto the Dutch had been content with the possession of Batavia and its hinterland, the Preanger, but now brought pressure on the Javanese princes of the adjoining territories to compel their peasants to produce export crops, and appointed officials called 'coffee sergeants' to enforce and supervise the deliveries.

But although the Dutch East India Company continued to pay high dividends to its shareholders, it was based on unsound foundations. Two sets of accounts were kept, one in Batavia and the other in Holland, and these were never balanced against one another; expenditure was financed by loans obtained at high interest in the Batavian (East Indian) money market; and corruption among the Company's officials was rife. The Company managed in spite of this to survive until near the end of the eighteenth century, but in 1798 it was declared bankrupt and dissolved and its assets were transferred to the newly-founded Batavian Republic—that is the government of the Netherlands established under French Revolutionary auspices.

This brings our introduction to the eve of the period which it is our intention to study in detail. Let us then summarize the situation in Southeast Asia as it was in the decade or so preceding 1800.

European power was now established in India, Java, and the Philippines, but although it had already had important effects on the economics of the region, most of Southeast Asia was scarcely aware of the presence of the Europeans. In Burma, in the middle of the eighteenth century, the rise of a new dynasty under Alaung-paya represented a new aggressive mood. This monarch conquered the Mons, the earlier masters of Lower Burma, and then he and

14

his successors marched against Arakan, which, however, did not fall until 1784—an event not without interest to the British in India since it brought the frontiers of Bengal and Assam into dispute. Alaungpaya's last personal exploit was the invasion of Siam (1760). But while the Burmese defeated the Siamese to begin with, they were not able to hold them in subjection, and were finally expelled from everywhere except Tenasserim after they had repeatedly invaded Siamese territories.

A new dynasty was founded in Siam by Rama I (1782–1809), which still reigns at Bangkok. Under Rama I, the kingdom was consolidated and reorganized, and although the Siamese failed to regain Tenasserim from the Burmese, for some years a Siamese army was undisputed master of Cambodia. Further to the east and north, the Nguyen empire was being established (1777–1820), reuniting what today are North and South Vietnam, the process being greatly assisted in the earlier stages by a French volunteer force; in the very month that the Bastille fell (July, 1789), a French bishop, Pigneau de Behaine, was helping Nguyen Anh, the founder of the new dynasty, to reduce Cochin-China to obedience. Thereafter, the French Revolution halted for many years the attempts at French empire-building in Indochina. In Java, the Dutch, with their home country ruled by the French and their sea-routes cut by the British navy, were in 1800 largely on the defensive, attempting to reorganize the trade and territories of their lately defunct East India Company. In the Malay Peninsula, the British in 1800 added a strip of territory on the mainland (Province Wellesley) to their settlement of Penang by a new treaty with Kedah, but the Malay States, though hopelessly weakened by a long period of intervention by the Bugis of the Celebes, were now left to their own devices with only occasional interference from outside.

The above selected facts are sufficient to show that at the beginning of the nineteenth century the greater part of Southeast Asia was still fully independent, was working out its own destiny, and paying only slight attention to the British empire in India which had arisen to the west and to the handful of Europeans who had established their stations on the fringes of the vast Southeast Asian territory.

EFFECTS OF THE SCIENTIFIC AND INDUSTRIAL
REVOLUTIONS

The interplay of indigenous forces was to continue for some decades to come without large-scale interference from the Europeans;
yet European intervention, when it did take place, was to be increasingly decisive. The explanation for this is again to be found
in the Scientific Revolution to which reference has already been
made. This Revolution took many forms—the transformation of
scientific theory by philosophers such as Bacon and Descartes, the
astonishing advance of astronomy in the hands of men like Galileo
and Kepler, and the introduction of the mathematical calculus by
Leibniz and Newton. It was Newton, too, who put forward a great
new theory of universal gravitation which was to be the basis of
physics for centuries to come. In the same century (the seventeenth)
there were equally important discoveries in other fields of knowledge, such as the beginnings of modern medicine and chemistry.

This revolution in science led to many inventions which had a
practical application, such as the telescope and the microscope
which revealed to the human eye for the first time the worlds of the
infinitely great and the infinitely small. The advance in astronomy,
too, led to great improvements in the art of navigation; by metallurgy
and other sciences ship-building was transformed; and European
weapons became increasingly more efficient than those of South and
East Asia.

Europe was now, in fact, technologically ahead of Asia, as well
as being more efficient in administration and strategy. Yet, up to
the end of the Middle Ages the advantage as regards techniques had
been with Asia. Indian textiles, for example, were better than
European, and Chinese techniques were superior to those of the
West in almost every respect. The change had been wrought by
the coming of modern science. By 1800, however, this turning of
the tables was only beginning to be felt, and it was not until the
latter half of the nineteenth century that it was to prove decisive.

One recent consequence of the Scientific Revolution in Europe,
namely the Industrial Revolution, was already, in the early years
of the nineteenth century, making itself felt in Southeast Asia. This

had taken place first of all in Britain, and can be said to have begun with the application of coal to smelting about 1750. Meanwhile a series of remarkable inventions (such as the 'flying-shuttle' in cloth manufacture (1738), Arkwright's 'water-frame' (1767—using water power) and Crompton's 'spinning mule' (1779)), paved the way for the transfer of industry from the home to factories. Steam-power was harnessed by engineers such as Newcomen and Watt. The consequence was that Britain, at least, by the early years of the nineteenth century could manufacture articles (cloth, pots and pans, etc.) in greater quantities than ever before and often of superior quality to the products of domestic industry, and had a surplus of these for export. The search for markets therefore was a prominent motive behind British foreign policy and in that of other European countries as they became industrialized. At the same time, the industrialized countries had to import from abroad raw materials for their factories and additional food to feed their workmen.

We discover, then, two main factors at work at the outset of the nineteenth century which were to decide the future course of Southeast Asian history. The first was the appearance of the new scientific age on the horizon which promised in the long run to transform the way of life of the whole region, and the second was the survival of the basic characteristics of the peoples, first established in pre-historic times, which ensured that however much their way of life was changed they would remain essentially themselves.

2

SOUTHEAST ASIA, 1800–69

In 1800 the countries of the Far East were little interested in one another's affairs. To the east, China, the 'Middle Kingdom', remained in deliberate isolation, intent on preserving its traditional way of life; its smaller neighbour, Japan, was still entrenched behind its 'bamboo curtain'; in India, to the West, the British were continuing their advance, assisted (and indeed led on) by the jealousies of the Indian princes among themselves. Southeast Asia, midway between the two great blocs, was split up into many states and principalities all absorbed with their local ambitions and seemingly unconscious of the larger unities that had once been theirs.

This lack of unity was especially the case in the territories of what are now Indonesia and Malaysia. The States of the Malay Peninsula, for example, situated in a small jungle-clad tongue of land reaching towards the equator, were a series of small and widely-separated settlements, confined to the coasts and the banks of the rivers. The previous half century had been one of uninterrupted strife. Johore, the last of the Malay empires, had been weakened beyond repair, first by the attacks of the Minangkabaus and of the Bugis from the Celebes, and after that of the Dutch. Under the Bugis ruler, Daing Kemboja, Johore had indeed temporarily revived its sway, for the military prowess of its general, Raja Haji, compelled Jambi and Indragiri to pay homage to it, thus for the time being renewing its influence in Sumatra. Raji Haji had then turned his attention to the subjection of Perak and Kedah. In Selangor, the Bugis created a new dynasty from which the present ruler is descended. In 1784 the Bugis attacked Malacca and Raji Haji was killed in the fighting and the Dutch, having repulsed the Bugis attack, occupied their capital at Rhio (Riau). Rhio was held by the Dutch until 1795, but their local base of Malacca having been occupied by the British, the Bugis were able to resume control of it.

Bugis intervention in the Malay Peninsula in the eighteenth century proved to be only a passing phase, but it had important consequences in that it destroyed what chances Johore had of becoming the unifier of Malaya, but at the same time it frustrated Dutch ambitions of controlling the Peninsula. Moreover, it created situations which were exploited by the British in founding Penang, and (later) Singapore.

The establishment of Penang, the first British Settlement, in 1786, was the consequence, first of the extension of the British Empire in India, and second of Anglo-Dutch rivalry. The Directors of the East India Company had for years been looking for a harbour on the eastern side of the Bay of Bengal where ships disabled in the northeast monsoon or in fights with the French could be repaired, and they sought at the same time a place where they could grow spices to compete with the Dutch monopoly. In 1786, through the instrumentality of Captain Francis Light, the Sultan of Kedah agreed to lease the island of Penang (108 square miles) to the Company. In making this cession, the Sultan's motive was to secure the support of the British against the Siamese. In 1800 a strip on the mainland was added (Province Wellesley, 290 square miles) and an annual rent was paid to Kedah in respect of both cessions of territory.

In 1800, however, the future of Penang was very uncertain. It had not provided the dockyard that had been hoped for (among other things, its timber turned out to be unsuitable for ship-building), it was proving only a qualified success as a spice-grower, and at one time there was talk of abandoning it. Yet only five years later, optimistic reports of Colonel Wellesley (later Duke of Wellington) and others as to its strategic value and commercial possibilities would decide the Directors to promote it to be the Fourth Presidency of India, on an equality with Bengal, Madras, and Bombay. An astonishing change from pessimism to optimism in a short space of time!

As the nineteenth century dawned, the political power in the Malay Peninsula was once more 'Malay' (as distinguished from

Bugis). The British, it is true, had gained a foothold at Penang and (temporarily at least) at Malacca, but they were now locked in their death struggle with the French in Europe and so far as possible avoided further local involvements. The Dutch influence in the Peninsula was eclipsed by British sea-power. To the north, the new Chakri dynasty in Bangkok was beginning to revive Siam's ancient claims to the Malay States, but its active intervention was still nearly two decades ahead.

If the British wished to avoid involvements in the Malay Peninsula, the Dutch were even more anxious to concentrate their energies on Java. The latter claimed the whole of the Malay Archipelago as being under their sovereignty and subject to their trade monopoly, but cut off from Europe and divided among themselves, they were in no position to make good these claims to control such a vast territory, only a fraction of which they (or anyone else) had even explored. Nevertheless, early in the eighteenth century they were at length masters of the whole of Java, they were the overlords of the remainder of the islands to the eastward, and only Bali and Lombok remained free from their rule. In Sumatra, most of the coastal states were their vassals, but Acheh, though no longer able to keep the Dutch out of the pepper trade in this sector, defied their claims to sovereignty and was able to maintain its independence of them until the beginning of the twentieth century. In the huge dark island of Borneo, the relations of the Dutch were for long mainly with the Sultan of Bandjermasin, while in the Sambas Sultanate of Borneo's west coast, a colony of Chinese, organized under their *Kongsis* (district or clan associations), were able to remain semi-independent while they mined the local gold.

So it is that the history of Southeast Asia is to be sought for in this period not only, or mainly, in the activities of the Europeans but in the separate annals of Burma, Siam, Annam, Tongking, Cambodia, and a score of other states, and in the mainly unrecorded tribal dissentions of the Dyaks, the Dusans, the Melanaus, and hundreds of other communities scattered over the great region. Nevertheless, the age of European influence on a major scale was dawning, and it is with this that a history of Southeast Asia must increasingly be concerned.

The Region in 1800

At the moment that the Dutch East India Company was dissolved (1798) the principles of the French Revolution, namely 'liberty, equality and fraternity',were to the forefront in the Batavian Republic at home, and it might have been expected therefore that these would have been extended to the Dutch colonies. Indeed, in keeping with this new revolutionary spirit, an ex-governor of the Northeast Coast Province of Java, Dirk Van Hogendorp, did urge the Dutch Government to abolish the forced deliveries of export crops and compulsory labour in Java, but this recommendation was in direct conflict with the official view that the first requirement of 'colonies' was that they should benefit the home country, and that in any case it was necessary to compel the native peoples (who were naturally lazy, it was believed) to work in their own interest. The Dutch policy, therefore, continued to be to keep them in strict subordination. Hence there was little promise in 1800 that the new administration of the Dutch possessions in the east would differ in any essential respect from that of the old East India Company. But the continuation of the war between Britain and France was to bring great changes for Java and for Indonesia in its train.

It would be wrong to imagine, meanwhile, that the monopolistic policy of the Dutch or, for that matter, the concentration of the British East India Company on its own mercantile and administrative interests, entailed the automatic hostility of the Indonesian or Malay rulers. This was by no means the case, as the native princes were also primarily concerned with their own interests, which often coincided with those of either the Dutch or the British. 'Nationalism' was yet to be born. Thus the Sultan of Bantam came to the assistance of the Dutch when the British attacked Batavia in 1800, and Surakarta and Jogjakarta also remained on good terms with their 'feudal overlord'—if such the Government at Batavia can be termed. Batavia, in 1800, it should be added, was an entrepôt for non-Dutch, especially American ships.

In 1800, the French wars were continuing. Napoleon was First Consul in France and was about to resume his career of conquest, to be interrupted only by the Peace of Amiens of 1802-3. His attempted conquest of Egypt as a first move against the British in

India had failed, and the British fleets sailed unchallenged through Southeast Asian waters. The Dutch were concentrating on the defence of Java (in case the British should decide to attack it) and on the production of coffee for export when the peace should come.

At this point we may leave the 'Malay world' for a moment to direct our attention to the contemporary situation in Burma, Siam, and the Indo-China Peninsula.

The concern of the British in Burma in the last two decades of the eighteenth century had been first to counter French plans to use Burma as a base of attack against their Indian empire and to secure the frontiers of Bengal. During the War of American Independence (1776–83) in which the French had joined America against Britain, Admiral de Suffren and Charles Castelnau de Bussy had tried to persuade the French king that there was a better chance for the French to expand their power in Burma than in South India, and that they could use Burma as a base from which to attack the British. In 1783 de Bussy was sent to conclude a commercial treaty with Burma, but nothing had come of it. Thereafter, the British command of the seas was to put further French attempts to establish themselves in Southeast Asia out of the question for many years to come. The only outstanding issues after 1800, therefore, were Anglo-Burmese relations over frontier matters and British trade with Burma.

In 1795 the Governor-General of India, Sir John Shore, sent Captain Michael Symes to Burma to attempt to remove the causes of misunderstanding that had arisen with the Court of Ava (the ruling Burmese house) over a frontier incident in Arakan, and to persuade the Burmese to close their ports to French ships of war. In addition, he was, if possible, to negotiate a commercial treaty permitting a British representative to reside in Rangoon to supervise British trade. Symes (says Hall) was 'treated with a mixture of studied rudeness and friendly hospitality', but was made to understand that it was beneath the dignity of the Court of Ava to treat on terms of equality with the representative of a mere governor-general. The Burmese king, however, made some vague concessions regarding the frontier and agreed that a British trade representative

22

might reside in Rangoon, but refused flatly to close his ports to French warships.

The British representative appointed by the Governor-General of India to reside in Rangoon was Captain Hiram Cox, who arrived the following year (1796). Cox was not given the status of an ambassador, either by his own government or the Court of Ava, and his attempts to behave as such led to his arrest. His attitude, moreover, received no countenance from the Governor-General whose letter to Ava requesting Cox's release was apologetic in tone. It might be true that the Burmese threatened to invade Bengal, but the Governor-General (now the ambitious Wellesley) was busy preparing to invade Mysore and wanted no distractions in remote Arakan.

Trouble again flared up on the Bengal-Arakan frontier. This time it was when some Arakanese, conscripted for service against the Siamese, fled to Chittagong in British India, and were pursued there by Burmese troops. When the Viceroy of Arakan demanded the expulsion of the fugitives, Wellesley, preoccupied with fighting Tipu Sultan in South India and with the anarchy in the Maratha dominions, again played for time. Tipu Sultan was defeated at Seringapatam, but the scourge of the Marathas was not to be checked until they were defeated by the Governor-General's brother, Arthur Wellesley (later Duke of Wellington) at Assaye (1803). The frontier differences with Burma were fated to continue, punctuated by wars, for some eighty-five years to come.

As regards Siam, mention has already been made in Chapter I of the recovery of the kingdom under Rama I from the devastation caused by the Burmese invasions and of Rama's own aggressive drive against his eastern neighbour, Cambodia. In 1795 he annexed the Cambodian provinces of Mongkolbaurey, Sisophon, and Korat, and that same year Battambang and Siemreap (Angkor), under the semi-independent mandarin Ben, were also transferred to Siam. This was to remain the situation for another two years until the foundation of the empire of Gia-Long (the dynastic title adopted by Nguyen Anh) in 1802 which presented Siam with a competitor for the control of Cambodia. To ward off the danger that what remained of their country might again become a battleground, the

Cambodians courted both Rama I and Gia-Long simultaneously by sending tribute to them, and both sovereigns found it expedient to wink at this duplicity.

The peoples of the Indo-China Peninsula were moving once again towards unity. In 1673 the partition of Vietnam into the two states of Tongking and Cochin-China had brought about a long series of dynastic quarrels which had given the French an opportunity to intervene. But for nearly two centuries this intervention was not powerful enough to be decisive, and merely entailed assistance to one or other of the warring factions.

The career of Pigneau de Behaine (1741–99) is notable because it represented the French pattern of 'colonialism' rather than the British or the Dutch. His motives were religious and cultural as well as political, whereas the ambitions of the British and Dutch colonial pioneers were usually confined to administration and the promotion of commerce. Trained at the Séminaire des Missions Etrangères in France, Pigneau went to Cochin-China in 1765 where he joined the missionary college at Hon-Dat in Ha-Tien. After many vicissitudes during which he and his colleagues were put in gaol, had their settlements burned by Chinese and Cambodian pirates, and were forced on occasion to seek refuge in India, Macao, or Siam, he became associated (1775) with the young prince Nguyen Anh, then a fugitive in Ha-Tien. In 1787 Pigneau returned to France on a visit, was received by Louis XVI, and submitted to the King's ministers a plan for an expedition to place Nguyen on the throne of Annam. France, however, was in no position at the time to finance such an adventure. Nevertheless, in 1787, in the name of Nguyen Anh, Pigneau concluded a treaty between France and Cochin-China. In return for ships, men, and arms, France was to receive Pulo Condore (later to be a French convict settlement) and territory in the Bay of Tourane. In point of fact, this project was some sixty years or so before its time, and the wars between France and Britain rendered it illusory at this period. However, in 1802, three years after Pigneau's death, Nguyen Anh proclaimed himself Emperor of Vietnam at Hué and assumed the title of Gia-Long. An embassy was then sent to Peking asking for the confirmation of this title, which was granted in 1803. The Nguyen dynasty survived, first of all under vague Chinese suzerainty, and then under protection of France until 1954 when the latter withdrew, but the following year, with Vietnam's independence, the last emperor, Bao Dai, was deposed.

This completes our outline survey of Southeast Asia in 1800, except for the Philippines whose isolation for so long from the remainder of the region was the consequence of Spanish rule. The Spanish, who were on the eve of losing all their South American colonies in the wars of independence, were resolved at least to retain their one Asian possession, and though isolated from it by war with Great Britain, during which the British naval victory at St Vincent (14 February 1797) cut off from Spain its colonial revenues, the Spanish governors kept the Philippines in jealous isolation. In 1797 the British proposed to send an expedition under Colonel Wellesley (later Duke of Wellington) to destroy Spanish shipping at Manila. This project brought Wellesley to Penang, intended as the rendezvous for the British forces, and though the expedition itself was not carried out Wellesley wrote a highly favourable report on Penang which undoubtedly carried weight with the Directors of the East India Company when in 1805 they decided to promote that small settlement to be the Fourth Presidency of India.

ANGLO-DUTCH RIVALRY

After the resumption of the war in 1803, events of world-shaking importance followed one another in quick succession. Quite a number of these events were battles on land and sea, but some were developments of a less bloody and more subtle kind but of equal importance to history.

One consequence of the placing of Napoleon's brother, Louis Bonaparte, on the throne of the Netherlands (1806) was the intensification of the age-long rivalry between the British and the Dutch in Southeast Asia. This rivalry was complicated by the fact that Britain had a traditional interest in maintaining a strong Holland (Netherlands) as a factor in the European balance of power. Thus the seizure of the Dutch possessions by the British in the course of the wars with France was always in the name of the Prince of Orange (an ally of the British, and the rightful ruler of the Netherlands according to British ideas of legality), not as 'conquests', and the declared intention was to return them to the Dutch at the peace. Nevertheless, the fight between the two nations was conducted with considerable bitterness.

The cutting of the sea-routes by the British navy put an end to all trade between the Netherlands and its colonies. Thus when Napoleon's nominee, Marshal Daendels (a Dutchman who had risen through service in the French army), was appointed Governor-General of the Dutch Indies in 1808, he had to run the British blockade by a long and adventurous voyage to reach his destination. His instructions were primarily to strengthen the defences of Java, but he was also authorized to examine the system of forced deliveries and to take measures to improve conditions among the native peoples. But though in pursuance of his strategic task he centralized the government and carried out administrative reforms, he not only omitted to abolish the forced deliveries (accepting the common Dutch view that the Javanese were naturally 'lazy') but increased the number of coffee trees from 27 to 72 million. His reforms, however, were so drastic, especially in the overhaul of the judiciary, that he made himself thoroughly unpopular with many local Dutchmen. On top of this, the British blockade was tightened to such an extent that his vast stocks of coffee became unsaleable. Daendels was recalled and General Janssens was appointed Governor-General in his stead. Janssens had as Governor of Cape Colony (South Africa) been compelled to surrender it when it fell for a second time to the British; it was not to be long before he would be forced to surrender Java to them in turn.

In August 1810 the British government (through the Indian Board of Control) instructed Lord Minto, Governor-General of India, to 'expel the enemy' from Java. This was in order to frustrate Napoleon's designs for the encirclement of India. In obedience to those instructions a large British expeditionary force appeared before Batavia in August 1811. After stout resistance by Janssens at the Battle of Meester Cornelis, the Dutch were forced to capitulate and Java, with all the other Dutch possessions in the archipelago, passed to the British. The administration was then placed by Lord

Anglo-Dutch Rivalry

Minto in the hands of Thomas Stamford Raffles, as Lieutenant-Governor of Java.

This appointment introduces us to an outstanding figure in the colonial history of Southeast Asia—perhaps *the* most outstanding among British colonial officials. Raffles was born at sea off Jamaica in 1781, the son of a sea captain. His father, however, fell on evil days, and young Raffles at fourteen years of age had to find work in the East India Company's headquarters in Leadenhall Street, London. His outstanding ability, however, attracted the attention of his superiors, and at the age of twenty-four he was offered a prize appointment, namely that of Assistant Secretary to the newly created Presidency of Penang. This he accepted, and on the voyage out (it took six months in 1805) he learnt the Malay language with such effect that upon arrival at his post he was employed as an interpreter in the Company's negotiations with the Malay States. In 1808 he was instrumental in deterring the East India Company Directors from demolishing Malacca (a move, Raffles considered, that was detrimental to British interests).

Raffles administered Java and its dependencies for five years (1811–16). His record in this capacity has naturally been subjected to searching criticism by the Dutch, whom he supplanted, and most of whom, as rivals of the British, he regarded as enemies. In Java he introduced scores of administrative reforms, his greatest innovation being a general tax on land as a substitute for all compulsory services and forced deliveries. It was levied on the *desa*,[1] or village, not on the individual peasant. The tax could be paid either in rice or money. On slavery Raffles had strong views and was an early 'abolitionist', but the system was too firmly established in Java to be abolished at a stroke of the pen, and Raffles had to be content with alleviating the lot of the slaves and facilitating their liberation. The ancient Indonesian practice whereby a creditor could seize the man in debt to him, together with his wife and children, and compel them to work for him for nothing, he forbade altogether. In legal procedure Raffles abolished torture, and reorganized the entire legal system. Raffles's financial reforms were

[1] Incidentally, a Sanskrit word, indicating the original 'Hinduized' organization of Javanese society.

such as would take a long time to mature, and the five and a half years in which he was in control was insufficient for them to bear fruit—indeed he was removed from his appointment in 1816 by the Directors because he had failed to make Java pay its way. Nevertheless his land revenue system was retained by the Dutch when they resumed the government of Java. Indeed, the Dutch retained most of his administrative and judicial reforms with certain modifications, and this by itself is a sufficient testimony to the soundness of the principles on which they were based.

On his replacement as Lieutenant-Governor of Java in March 1816, Raffles sailed for England via the Cape of Good Hope. At St Helena he had an interview with Napoleon who had been exiled there by the British after his defeat at Waterloo the previous year. Raffles found Napoleon rude and arrogant, and formed the opinion that he regarded all other human beings as his inferiors. On arrival in London, Raffles published his *History of Java*, a copy of which he presented to the Prince Regent on the occasion when the latter knighted him for his services at Carlton House.

RAFFLES FOUNDS SINGAPORE

Raffles had hoped to be able to persuade the British government to retain Java after the peace which followed Napoleon's defeat, but in this he was unsuccessful. In the interests of the policy of maintaining a strong Netherlands, Britain had already decided to return Java to the Dutch, and a promise to this effect had been given at the Congress of Vienna (at which the allies had laid down the terms of the peace two years before). In August 1816 the retransfer of the island and its dependencies to the Dutch was carried out by Raffles's successor, John Fendall.

The only appointment now available for Raffles was that of Lieutenant-Governor of the 'white elephant' settlement of Bencoolen in Sumatra, which the East India Company had held since 1684 with little profit to themselves. Raffles assumed the appointment in 1817, and from this point of vantage surveyed the post-war scene in the 'Malay world'. He saw that Penang, the only possession remaining to the British in the region except Bencoolen, was situated where the Straits of Malacca were too wide to be effectively patrolled by sailing-ships. He knew, too, from his previous experience that Penang was proving only a qualified success, even though it was now the Fourth Presidency of India (with an expensive administration). The obvious place, he felt, for a British settlement was some island to the south of the Peninsula where the Malacca Straits were narrow and could therefore more easily be patrolled, and which would be, moreover, at the conflux of many trade-routes.

In 1818 Raffles visited India and was able to persuade the Governor-General, the Marquess of Hastings, to authorize him to proceed with a small squadron of ships and a force of sepoys (Indian soldiers) to Malayan waters to carry out a diplomatic mission to the Sultan of Acheh and to look for a more suitable place than Penang as a British station in the Straits of Malacca.

Raffles sailed, but when he reached Penang, Colonel Bannerman, the Governor, who resented Raffles's intervention, raised objections to his proceeding to Acheh since he regarded it as being within his own province, and Raffles sailed straight on down the Straits of Malacca. This change of plans was, as it turned out, fortunate, since Hastings, fearing that the Dutch might resent the new move in what they regarded as their sphere of influence, had countermanded his orders to Raffles. But before the Governor-General's orders could reach him, Raffles had proceeded far towards the accomplishment of his mission. Having rejected other possible sites for his settlement (e.g. the Carimon Islands off Sumatra), he had reached Singapore and had entered into an agreement with the local authority, the Temenggong of Johore, permitting the East India Company to establish a station on Singapore Island.

When Raffles founded Singapore in 1819 (the 'preliminary agreement' with the Temenggong was signed on 30 January) the only inhabitants of the island were about 150 Malay followers of the Temenggong, a few pagan Malay fishermen, and about 40 Chinese cultivating gambier.

Raffles was perfectly aware that his agreement with the Temenggong was not sufficient to constitute a legal claim to Singapore, since the Temenggong was not a sovereign in his own right but only a subject. It was necessary, therefore, to obtain a treaty with the

Sultan of Johore before the Dutch could intervene. But who *was* the Sultan ? The answer was by no means clear, and the Dutch and the British had different ideas on the subject.

It is not practicable to go into the question of the Johore succession in any detail, but the following facts are sufficient to indicate the nature of the dispute.[1]

At the end of the eighteenth century the empire of Johore had been split into three main divisions. The Sultan had become a puppet of the Bugis and his effectual rule was limited to the Rhio-Lingga Archipelago. Johore's mainland territories were then divided between two great officers of state—namely the Temenggong of Johore and the Bendahara of Pahang. The elder son of the reigning Sultan, Hussein, had been designated as his father's heir, but his younger son, Tunku Abdur-Rahman ('Abdu'r-Rahman), had been installed as Sultan in his stead. In 1818, when the Dutch reoccupied Rhio, they ignored Hussein and made their treaty with Abdur-Rahman. Raffles, however, ascertained that the treaty applied only to Rhio and maintained therefore that the Dutch could lay no claim to Singapore. He thereupon recognized Hussein as Sultan and he was proclaimed as such by the Malays at Singapore on 6 February 1819. On the same day the Sultan and Temenggong signed a treaty with Raffles, confirming the 'Preliminary Agreement' of 30 January and granting the East India Company the right to set up 'factories' (i.e. warehouses) etc. on Singapore Island in return for an annual allowance of $5,000 to the Sultan and one of $3,000 to the Temenggong.

Raffles had anticipated that directly the Dutch became aware of his establishment of Singapore they would raise a great outcry—and he was not mistaken. From Batavia, and also from Malacca (which had been restored to them under the Treaty of Vienna in 1818) they demanded the complete withdrawal of the Singapore settlement, and, failing this, threatened to use force. If Van der Capellen, the Dutch Governor-General at Batavia, had decided to make this threat good by sending a military expedition against Singapore early in 1819, it is probable that the British would not

---

[1] For the details, see Winstedt, *History of Malaya*, pp. 159, 198. Also Hall, p. 433.

have risked an Anglo-Dutch war to retain this infant, unproved settlement.

When the news reached Europe, a diplomatic 'paper war' between the capitals ensued. Luckily for Raffles's new settlement, communications in those days were very slow, and before the British government felt compelled to come to a decision, Singapore had had time to give promise of its future value. Immigrants flocked in to take advantage of British protection, to receive grants of land, and to enjoy the fruits of the policy of free-trade. Raffles in the meantime did not allow the grass to grow under his feet. He organized the administration of his new settlement, planned a land-registry, and introduced a provisional code of law. He negotiated further treaties with Hussein and the Temenggong. He also conducted a vigorous publicity for Singapore in correspondence with some highly-placed persons whose friendship he had cultivated when in England in 1816–17, not without putting forward some exaggerated claims as to the population and trade of his settlement, for Raffles shone as a propagandist almost as much as an administrator.

By the time that the wrangle between the British and the Dutch had reached a point where a settlement seemed profitable for both sides, Singapore was well worth bargaining to retain.

THE ANGLO-DUTCH TREATY OF 1824

The anxiety of the British government was lest Raffles's activities in Southeast Asia should impair Anglo-Dutch relationships in Europe since a friendly and neutral Netherlands (Holland) was the key-stone of British policy in Europe. Thus the treaty negotiated between the two countries in 1824 was intended to put an end, once and for all, to their differences in the East. It is true that the trade rivalry continued and that the treaty allowed for discriminatory tariffs, and later there was to be conflict over James Brooke's activities in Sarawak, but in a broad sense the treaty did succeed in defining British and Dutch spheres of activity right to the end of the colonial period. It was in fact the logical consequence of the Vienna Treaty whereby Britain had restored Java to the Dutch.

Under the treaty, Holland (the name of a single province of the original seven by which the entire Netherlands has long been known to the British) ceded to Britain all the Dutch 'factories' in India and Malacca. At the same time, the Dutch withdrew their objections to the British establishment in Singapore. Britain, in return, surrendered Bencoolen to the Dutch. The Dutch undertook to make no more settlements in the Malay Peninsula and to enter into no further treaties with its rulers, and the British gave a similar undertaking with respect to Sumatra and the islands to the south of Singapore (i.e. the Carimons and the Rhio-Lingga Archipelago). None of the stations given up by either signatory to the treaty were to be ceded to any other power, and both countries agreed that neither should make any new settlement in the 'Eastern Seas' without previous authority from the home government in Europe. On the commercial side, the treaty provided that the Netherlands should make no attempt to establish a commercial monopoly, an exception being made of the spice trade of the Moluccas. As regards import and export duties, the rates charged on British goods entering Dutch ports was not to be more than double that imposed on Dutch goods, and *vice versa* in the case of British ports (a provision making it clear that the trade war was to continue).

The Anglo-Dutch Treaty of 1824 marks the end of a phase in the colonial history of the 'Malay World', and it is fitting therefore to append as a postscript a short (and tentative) assessment on the character of the outstanding personality of this phase, namely Sir Thomas Stamford Raffles (1781–1826).

Raffles represented the best aspects of 'colonialism' in the early nineteenth century. Though entirely self-educated, he became a botanist, zoologist, and historian of considerable attainments. He was a notable linguist in addition. He discovered in the forests of Sumatra the largest flower in the world which was named after him (*Rafflesia Arnoldi*). After his retirement he became the principal founder of the Zoological Society of London, and consequently of the London 'Zoo'. He was an opponent of slavery and an advocate of Free Trade long before it became British official policy. In education, he favoured a policy of educating the select few according to the theory that this education would (by some mysterious process it must be confessed) percolate down to the many. The reason for his success, however, was that in essential outlook he was a man of his own period of history—of his own 'age'—and as such he took the optimistic view that wherever commerce went enlightenment was bound to follow. Some of the innovations he introduced were failures, and in pursuit of his ambitions he occasionally stooped to dubious methods. Although he had read widely, his own prose style was often flowery and inflated. When in later years Malaya became very prosperous, those who benefited most from this prosperity tended to put Raffles on a pedestal—even to canonize him so to speak as the 'lay saint' of British Malaya. The fact is, nevertheless, that at this stage in history, the expansion of British trade, bringing with it cheaper and better manufactured goods, was a beneficial development for Southeast Asia. It was only later when the doctrine of uncontrolled private enterprise (*laisser faire*) held sway, that the limitations of trade as a benefactor of mankind became apparent.

INDIA AND BURMA

In the light of the prevailing trends, it is logical to consider the history of Southeast Asia in the nineteenth century within the framework of the pressures exercised upon it from outside. One of those was Anglo-Dutch rivalry; another was the series of clashes leading eventually to war, that were taking place much further to the north between the British in India and the Burmese.

Frontier incidents had continued to be common throughout the first decades of the nineteenth century, but the hands of the British in India had been tied by wars with the Marathas and with Nepal. But at length, in February 1824, the Burmese staged a full-scale invasion of the British protectorate of Cachar. This was a challenge which could not be avoided. On 5 March the government of India declared war on Burma. The British plan was to draw away the Burmese forces from the Indian frontier by a massive invasion of Lower Burma. This strategy was well conceived, and Rangoon was occupied without a blow. Thereafter, however, defects in the actual conduct of the campaign began to reveal themselves. In consequence of these, the British force of 11,000 men was held up for six months during the height of the rainy season, while dysentery and fever reduced their effective strength to a few hundreds. Nevertheless, the Burmese attack was repulsed and success was achieved in other theatres of war. But it was not until 26 February 1826, after nearly two years of fighting, that the Burmese admitted defeat by signing the treaty of Yandabo whereby they conceded Arakan, Tenasserim, Assam, and Manipur to the British and agreed to pay a crippling indemnity.

There can be no doubt that the government of India hoped to solve its frontier problems by peaceful negotiation. What it was slow to recognize was that once it had a foothold in the country sheer force of circumstances was bound ultimately to bring about complete annexation. A great obstacle in coming to terms with Burma was that the country was ruled by absolute monarchs, artificially protected in their sense of personal greatness by having little or no comprehension of the realities of the situation or of the relative size and strength of the parties engaged (a subject who dared to enlighten his sovereign in this regard would have found himself in grave danger). For example, when Crawfurd arrived as British envoy to the Court of Ava (the Burmese monarchy) in September 1826, the presents he bore from the Governor-General of India were represented to the king by his courtiers as a token of submission to the 'Golden Feet' (as the king was called) and of the desire on the part of the Governor-General for pardon for past 'offences' (i.e. the annexation of Arakan and Tenasserim). In the circumstances, it was not surprising that Crawfurd and the Burmese ministers haggled for weeks over an extremely simple and harmless commercial treaty so that only four of the original articles appeared in the final draft. Nor were the frontiers settled to the satisfaction either of the Indian government or the Burmese king.

To state that Burma was appallingly misgoverned under the Court of Ava is by no means to overstate the facts. Two rebellions (one in Lower Burma in 1830, and another in the Shan country in 1840) gave the king an excuse to get rid of anyone he found in his way—the ex-queen was trampled to death by elephants; her brother, Minthagi, was disposed of in an equally barbarous way. In 1846 King Thirawaddy died and was succeeded by an even greater

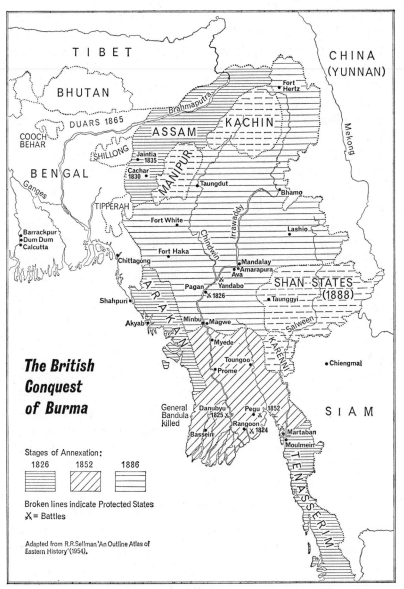

TIBET

BHUTAN

CHINA (YUNNAN)

COOCH BEHAR

DUARS 1865

SHILLONG

BENGAL

Ganges

Brahmaputra

ASSAM

KACHIN

Fort Hertz

Mekong

MANIPUR

Jaintia 1835

Cachar 1830

TIPPERAH

Taungdut

Bhamo

Fort White

Chindwin

Irrawaddy

Lashio

Barrackpur
Dum Dum
Calcutta

Chittagong

Fort Haka

Mandalay
Amarapura
Ava

Shahpuri

ARAKAN

Pagan

Yandabo
X 1826

SHAN STATES
(1888)

Taunggyi

Akyab

Minbu
Magwe

Salween

Myede

KARENNI

Chiengmaï

**The British
Conquest
of Burma**

Toungoo
Prome

General
Bandula
killed

Danubyu
1825 X

Pegu 1852
X

SIAM

Bassein

Rangoon
X 1824

Martaban

Moulmein

TENASSERIM

Stages of Annexation:

1826   1852   1886

Broken lines indicate Protected States
X = Battles

Adapted from R.R.Sellman 'An Outline Atlas of
Eastern History' (1954).

Map 2

35

ruffian, Pagan Min. Pagan Min's ministers carried out a systematic expropriation of his richer subjects by putting them to death on trumped-up charges and confiscating their belongings. During the two years of his power, six thousand persons perished in this way. But it was the breakdown of central control which eventually brought renewed war with the East India Company.

Matters came to a head again in 1851 over heavy fines imposed on two British sea-captains for alleged murder and embezzlement (charges that proved to be unfounded). This was only the latest of a long series of provocations, but it proved to be the last straw so far as Lord Dalhousie, the Governor-General of India, was concerned. Having recently defeated the Sikhs, and in any case not being the type of man to suffer indefinitely injuries inflicted on his countrymen, he despatched warships to Rangoon to demand redress. When the shore batteries opened fire on the ships, and the somewhat impetuous British Commodore retorted by destroying all Burmese war-boats within reach, Dalhousie followed this up by stepping up the compensation demanded to ten laks of rupees. In April 1852, when the ultimatum expired, Rangoon and Martaban were occupied and the Second Burma War had begun.

As it happened, Dalhousie's masterly conduct of the war was in striking contrast to that of the war of 1824 which (as we have seen) had been grossly mismanaged by the British. The British forces occupied Prome, Pegu was annexed, and King Pagan was deposed and succeeded by his half-brother, Mindon—a very different character, who was a sincere Buddhist and hated bloodshed. Pagan was allowed to retire, however, into honourable captivity in which he died many years later in 1881.

THE 'DUTCH EAST INDIES' (INDONESIA) 1818–69

While the British were, almost in spite of themselves, extending their Indian empire into Burma, the Dutch were creating an 'empire' of a different sort in the Archipelago far to the South.

The Dutch were in quite a different position from the British. It was all very well for Raffles to wax lyrical over the universal benefits conferred on humanity by trade, for Britain not only had

command of the sea but was now largely industrialized and flourished in proportion to the growth of its export trade. Holland, on the
other hand, was behind Britain industrially, and had, for example,
no piece-goods to offer to prospective customers of the quality that
England could produce. So when Holland recovered its colonies
after the Napoleonic Wars, it was scarcely surprising that it fell back
on the system of its old East India Company, monopolizing as
far as possible the primary products and raw materials of Indonesia.

The trading company (Nederlandsche Handelsmaatschappij)
formed by Van der Capellen in 1825, with the King of the Netherlands as the principal shareholder, and intended to deal a blow at
British competition, was a failure in its first years of existence, and
when the new Governor-General, Van den Bosch, landed in Java
in 1830 he proceeded at once to carry into effect a project which
became known as the 'Culture System'. In many ways it was only
the old Dutch East India Company's system of forced delivery of
export crops in a new guise. The Javanese peasant was held to be
too ignorant to make the best of his land and he was therefore to
be compelled to devote a portion of it to the cultivation of export
crops as directed by the government, and the latter would take the
produce in lieu of land-rent in cash. The supplies thus raised were
to be handled by Dutch merchants, shipped in Dutch vessels, and
sold in the Netherlands, which would in consequence once more
become a world market for tropical produce. At the same time,
Dutch home industry was to be stimulated by being given a closed
market in the colonies. Indigo and sugar were the first export crops
selected.

Financially, the Culture System was a success from the start.
The full application of the system lasted from 1830 to 1860 and
from beginning to end the Dutch exchequer benefited to the extent
of some 900 million guilders (say £43 million), and the treasury at
Batavia also shared in the proceeds. The system was condemned
later on by the Dutch Liberals as being altogether bad for the
Javanese native in its results, but then the Liberals were voicing
the claims of private enterprise as much as those of humanitarian-
ism, and the fact is that the system had both good and bad effects.
In some cases, notably in East Java, where the officials paid as much

attention to rice as to sugar, there was prosperity; in others, where they attended only to the cultivation of export crops and neglected rice, there was famine. One other bad result during the period that the Culture System was in full force was that the Dutch concentrated their attention more than ever on Java, an island with a natural land-drainage system and a rich volcanic soil, neglecting the Outer Islands (Sumatra, Borneo, etc.), and as a result did not pay due attention to the problem of the piracy which was rife there. The Culture System was never officially abolished, but from the 1870s onwards gradually gave way to private capitalist enterprise which undertook not only the development of the resources of Java but also those of the Outer Islands.

In the meantime the conscience of the Dutch people was awakened by the publication (1860) of a novel, *Max Havelaar*, written by E. Douwes Dekker under the pseudonym of 'Multatuli'. It dealt with the evils of the Culture System. Backed up by pamphlets by other Dutch writers, it stirred up wide support for the Liberal campaign in Holland against government control over agricultural production. But it was still much too early for the movement to find any response in 'Nationalist' feeling in Java.

BRITISH RELATIONS WITH THE MALAY STATES AND SIAM

Since the East India Company regarded Singapore, Penang, and Malacca (combined in 1830 to form the Straits Settlements) purely as ports of call en route to China and as trading stations, it was determined as far as possible to keep clear of involvement in Malay affairs. This policy, however, was complicated by the renewed attempts of the Siamese to absorb the northern states of the Peninsula, and the Company had to make up its mind to what extent, if any, it would resist this attempt. The treaty that was concluded at Bangkok in June 1826 by Captain Burney was an attempt to draw a line between British and Siamese spheres of influence in the Peninsula.

The Burney Treaty became the basis of the British position in the northern states of the Peninsula for the next fifty years. It fixed the southern boundary of Kedah as the limit of legitimate Siamese control, and secured the independence of Perak and Selangor. It needed, however, the despatch of a military expedition at an early stage to enforce the treaty as regards Perak. In the case of Kedah, the Burney Treaty had committed the British to preventing the Sultan-in-exile from attempting to recover his lost kingdom. In the end, the exiled Sultan made his submission to Siam and was restored to his throne as a vassal of that state in 1842.

Siam was an absolute monarchy which had been ruled by the Chakri dynasty since 1782 (a Chakri king still occupied the throne in the 1960s). The two kings of the dynasty to whom Siam owed its independence in great measure were father and son, Rama IV (Maha Mongkut) (1851–68), and Rama V (Chulalongkorn) (1868–1910). The first of these, who was the rightful heir to the throne when his father, Rama II, died in 1824, had been displaced as king by his brother, Rama III, and had remained in a Buddhist monastery for many years. Here he made himself a highly educated man, not only becoming deeply learned in the Pali scriptures, but learned Latin, mathematics, and astronomy from the scholarly French missionary, Bishop Pallegoix. Added to this, he became an enthusiast for the study of English, which he learned from American missionaries, and made it his second language. This study and contact with foreigners persuaded Mongkut that Siam must come to terms with the modern western forces that were now threatening its independence. Thus, when he eventually succeeded to the throne in 1851 he was well equipped to negotiate with the foreigners, having obtained some insight into what was in their minds.

But it must not be forgotten that Siam was in an extremely backward condition and the introduction of new methods, even on a limited scale, caused a double conflict—one between the king and the ruling classes and one in the king's own mind. Was it possible to combine absolutism with enlightenment, or to modify absolutism and still retain the throne?

A great and irrevocable step, however, was taken when in 1855 Mongkut concluded a Treaty of Friendship and Commerce with Britain. One provision of the treaty was to limit the duty payable on goods by British merchants to 3 per cent *ad valorem*, and export duties were to be according to a fixed scale. It can be seen from this that Siam had surrendered a measure of its sovereignty and was thus brought within the western economic system. Even more striking was the establishment under the treaty of the extra-territorial system for British subjects. This meant that a British consul was to reside at Bangkok to exercise civil and criminal juris-diction over all British subjects in Siam, who were thus made in-dependent of the Siamese courts and answerable to the Consul alone. This was not altogether a novelty, as the Dutch had obtained a similar concession in the seventeenth century, but when other Powers (beginning with the United States) demanded and obtained similar treaties, it was plain that Siam's independence was of a very qualified kind.

The backwardness which justified extraterritoriality was never-theless very great. Sir John Bowring (who negotiated the 1855 treaty for Britain)[1] wrote that 'on the whole, the Siamese laws must be deemed superior to the Chinese', but added that 'all rights in a country where a government is an absolutely despotic one are, of course, held on sufferance'. Prisoners were mostly employed on the public works, but at night were fastened together by a long chain and were so crowded in their cell that there was not room to lie down. The worst convicts carried an iron collar round their necks, handcuffs, leg-gyves, and an iron belt round their waist, to which a cangue (a portable pillory for head and arms) was sometimes added. Slaves were divided into seven classes, though Bowring found that only three of these classes were logically distinct—that is, slaves captured in war, slaves by purchase ('debt-slaves'), and slaves by birth. The number of prisoner-of-war slaves alone in Siam in 1855 was estimated at 46,000.

Some offences were treated with very barbarous punishments. For example, the penalty for melting down an idol of gold or silver stolen from a temple was to be burnt alive. Adulterers were pun-ished by marking with a hot iron on the cheeks, and the forehead was sometimes branded for other crimes.

Even in 1868 (says Malcolm Smith[2]) there was no fixed code of

---

[1] See J. Bowring, *The Kingdom and People of Siam*, London, 2 vols., 1857.
[2] Malcolm Smith, *A Physician at the Court of Siam*, London, 1946.

laws; no system of general education; no proper control of revenue and finance; no postal or telegraph service; no medical organization; no army on modern lines; no navy at all; no railways and almost no roads.

Facts such as these should always be brought into consideration in judging the rightness or otherwise of foreign intervention in the affairs of Southeast Asian countries.

Later in the century, Siamese influence in the northern Malay States of Kedah, Kelantan, and Trengganu was again to be the occasion of a forward move by the British, but in the first half of the century the British were concerned mainly with developments further to the south.

Malacca, after its final handing over to Britain by the Dutch under the 1824 treaty, became a quiet backwater. But its quietness did not save it from a minor frontier war. Its interior was inhabited largely by Minangkabau Malays from Sumatra who were divided into a confederacy of small independent states, later known as Negri Sembilan (the Nine States—though actually there were many more than nine). In the eighteenth century these states had begun the practice of bringing over a prince from Sumatra to be their head (the Yang di-pertuan) but this practice had now lapsed. This confederacy (which now existed only in name) became involved in 1831 in a war with the East India Company. The forces engaged were two battalions of the Company's troops against a few score Malays, and this campaign was conducted with extreme incompetence by the superior British forces. Nevertheless, the eventual outcome was never in question. Naning, one of the tiny border states, was subdued and embodied in Malacca territory. But there ensued a series of wars between these jealous little states themselves over an attempt to revive the Yang di-pertuanship, which kept the area in ferment for the next forty years and prevented Malacca merchants from exploiting the hinterland.

During the period covered by this chapter, the position of Singapore was somewhat more important than that of Penang and Malacca (as the largest settlement and, after 1830, the capital of the three) and its relations with the Malay world more complex.

One unexpected result of the treaties of 1814 and 1824 was the creation of a Malay State, Johore, which was in many respects a British dependency. The fact that Raffles had recognized Hussein as Sultan meant that henceforth the former Johore Empire was split into two parts—one with Sultan Abdur-Rahman under Dutch control over the islands south of Singapore and the other with Hussein as nominal overlord of Johore and Pahang on the mainland. The fact was that Hussein had no authority in either Johore or Pahang. Pahang was ruled by the Bendahara of the old empire. In the same way Johore was controlled by the Temenggong with whom Raffles had made his original treaty. Both he and Hussein lived in Singapore on pensions from the East India Company. The successor of Hussein (who died in 1835) remained like his father a pensioner with a small income and large debts, but the successor of the Temenggong (who died in 1827) found himself the possessor of a country of growing value. Singapore had advanced commercially by leaps and bounds, and when, with the impoverishment of the agricultural land of the island by over-cultivation, Chinese gambier and pepper planters moved into Johore to plant and the Temenggong's Malay subjects provided him with a valuable *gutta percha* monopoly, he became a rich man. Nevertheless he remained a British pensioner living in Singapore.

The connexion thus indirectly established between themselves and Johore was bound to involve the East India Company more and more in the affairs of the Peninsula. One complication was the dispute between the Temenggong and Sultan for the control of Johore, and the other was the Pahang civil war of 1857. The Johore dispute was ended by a compromise in 1855 by which the Sultan Ali recognized the Temenggong as sovereign of Johore in return for a fixed monthly pension and a small area in western Johore as his 'principality'. The Pahang war, however, was a much more difficult matter since Siam had a finger in Pahang affairs and Siamese soldiers were engaged in the hostilities.

Colonel Orfeur Cavanagh, who became Governor of the Straits Settlements in 1859, saw in these developments a Siamese threat to the independence of the Malay States. He was a man of energy and force of character and when in 1862 the Siamese temporized in removing two of their Malay agents from Pahang (as agreed in Bangkok) Cavanagh took the law into his own hands. Seeing that the Siamese were merely waiting for the approach of the north-east monsoon which would close the harbours and enable them to delay implementing their promise until the monsoon changed again in April 1863, he despatched two warships to Trengganu to present an ultimatum. Unless within twenty-four hours steps were taken to remove one agent and to stop helping the other, the capital would be bombarded. The ultimatum was ignored, and the capital *was* bombarded. The ultimate consequence was that there were no further attempts on the part of the Siamese to interfere in Pahang, though Cavanagh had to meet stern criticism from his superiors for the extreme measures he had adopted.

OPENING OF THE SUEZ CANAL (1869)

In the third quarter of the nineteenth century the European attitude towards the acquisition of colonial territory was undergoing a change which would amount to a transformation. This development, however, turns out on examination to be merely the latest phase in the same process that had been initiated a century or two before in the revolutions in European science and industry. The latter had taken place first of all in Britain, but the other countries of Europe had by the middle of the century become industrialized and were competing vigorously among themselves for markets and for supplies of raw materials. Meanwhile it was becoming increasingly clear that the old policy of intervention in local affairs only to the extent necessary to maintain the security of sea routes and trading stations was out of date since the operation of the new economic forces had caused the disruption of the local Asian systems and had led to political decay tending towards anarchy. European statesmen as well as the 'man on the spot' were realizing more and more that the process that their ancestors had set in train could not be arrested—it must be continued to its logical conclusion.

The British and the Dutch, however, were long reluctant to accept this view, but the French (influenced, perhaps, by their greater affection for logic?) accepted it with alacrity as justifying

43

the 'new imperialism' of the Emperor Napoleon III (1852–70). In 1859, with the capture of Saigon, they renewed a drive which had been interrupted by the Revolutionary and Napoleonic wars, and whose object was the annexation of Cochin-China, Annam, Tongking, and Cambodia. They were late in the colonial field and were making up for lost time. This operation, however, belongs mainly to the period covered by the next chapter of this history and for that chapter an account of it is reserved.

As regards Malaya, the British government long resisted physical intervention in the Malay States. That they did so, however, was scarcely the fault of the local British merchants who urged for years that intervention was inevitable for the protection of their trade and to stop piracy. The local British residents did eventually succeed, however, in persuading the home government to transfer the Straits Settlements from the India office to the Colonial office in 1867. Hereafter the Straits Settlements would be administered more in keeping with local requirements and not at the whim of a remote, and largely indifferent government in India. The change of political climate in Britain is often dated from Disraeli's Crystal Palace speech of 1872 in which he attacked the 'Little England' policy of the Liberals and urged a 'forward movement' in the colonies, but a ferment of new ideas was already affecting even Liberal statesmen. It is a strange fact that when the policy of non-intervention came to be abandoned it should be under a Liberal government, namely the first government of Mr Gladstone (1868–74). The way in which the change was effected will in due course be explained.

The year 1869 has been chosen as the ending of the present chapter since it saw the opening of the Suez Canal by the Empress Eugenie (Napoleon III's consort). The building of the Canal, on the initiative of a Frenchman, Ferdinand de Lesseps, is a landmark in the history of the Far East and of Southeast Asia. Henceforth the sea voyage by the Canal would be several weeks shorter than the old voyage via the Cape of Good Hope. The gain to trade need scarcely be stressed, and the Canal besides had great strategic value, as the early years of its operation coincided with the rapid development of the steam-ship. The opening of the Suez Canal, therefore, was an event of more than symbolic importance.

3

EUROPEAN COLONIAL EXPANSION IN SOUTHEAST ASIA, 1869–1900

NEW ATTITUDES TOWARDS COLONIAL ACQUISITION

With the rise of 'Nationalism' and the reaction against 'Colonialism' a picture of the last century or so in Southeast Asia has gained acceptance that is in many respects distorted. The expansion of European power and influence into the region is represented in this picture as pure aggression. No doubt among the European pioneers and advocates of expansion there were many who were unscrupulous or greedy, but the fact is that the British and Dutch *governments*, at least up to the 1870s, were reluctant to acquire any further possessions, if only for the reason that they cost money to defend and maintain. From the 1870s onwards, however, when intervention seemed necessary and inevitable, they accepted it more readily. But to depict the British or Dutch acquisition of protectorates over the Malay or Indonesian States, or even the extension of British and French control in Burma and Indochina, as being no different from the subjugation of Central Asia by the Mongol hordes in the thirteenth and fourteenth centuries or of North and Central India by the Moguls in the sixteenth and seventeenth (as is sometimes done) is to ignore all proportion. To realize this, one has only to compare the small expeditionary forces and even tinier garrisons of the Europeans in nineteenth-century Southern Asia with the vast armies of earlier Asian invasions, living like locusts on the land, and disciplined only by their appetites. The truth is that trade, treaties, persuasion, and legality were the usual instruments of European expansion—not fire and the sword. That there was an element of coercion in colonial policy does not alter this fact.

Basically, the impulse of the Europeans in the nineteenth century (whatever it may have been in earlier periods) was not to dominate other races but to find markets for the manufactures made available

45

for the first time in great abundance by the Industrial Revolution in Europe and to feed their factories with raw materials. The 'aggression', in the final analysis, was not so much by nations or individuals as by the superior skills with which the Europeans had now become possessed, and it was facilitated—indeed invited—by the increasing disunity of the Southeast Asian States.

The truism about nature 'abhorring a vacuum' holds equally for politics. If one power withdraws from a region, another power automatically moves in to occupy it. The Johore empire, as successor to the Malay empire of Malacca, inherited the nominal over-lording of all the Malay States south of Siam. Towards the end of the eighteenth century Johore lost its position to the Dutch. But the Dutch East India Company was itself decaying, and when the Revolutionary War of 1795 cut off Holland from the East, its ruin (as related in the previous chapter) was completed. The French Wars were the occasion for the seizure of Malacca and the conquest of Java by the British and during their continuance the whole area became a British trading preserve.

But great changes had taken place in the half century following the conclusion of the Napoleonic Wars. For one thing, other European countries besides Britain were now becoming industrialized and were more and more competing with Britain for markets in the East; for another, while the Europeans were consolidating their Settlements in Southeast Asia and extending their commercial system, the native states of the region were disintegrating politically. One by-product of this disintegration was the alarming increase in piracy.

'Piracy' is a word that has been used to describe acts ranging from ordinary robbery with violence on the high seas to seizure of the contraband of neutrals in a war. It was to a considerable extent a consequence of the breaking down of the traditional trade-routes and the disorganization of the native commerce due to the impact upon it of the Portuguese and Dutch in the sixteenth and seventeenth centuries. In the eighteenth century, the Bugis were both traders and pirates—in the latter role the terror of the Archipelago. But it was the Dutch who by destroying their base at Macassar and ruining their trade with the Spice Islands set them on their career of piracy. When they could find other outlets for their energies, the Bugis ceased to be pirates and in the nineteenth century no more is heard of them in that capacity.

The place of the Bugis was taken, however, by an even greater scourge of the seas—the Moros or Ilanos (Balanini) of the Sulu Archipelago which connects Borneo with the Philippines. Their enemies and rivals were the Malay pirates of the Rhio-Lingga Archipelago. Then, in the early part of the nineteenth century, the north-west coast of Borneo became a notorious pirate centre from which the Sea-Dyaks (the *Orang Laut*) sailed in their praus to prey on the commerce of the region, directed by Malay chiefs from on land and a few Arab leaders. It was in his campaign against the Lanun and Sea-Dyak pirates that Raja James Brooke (whose career is summarized later in this chapter) extended the territories he had obtained from Brunei to many times their original size.

The increase in the prosperity of Singapore's trade brought a corresponding increase in the prosperity of the pirates who preyed on it. The few naval vessels that the Singapore government had at its disposal were inadequate to deal with the threat to commerce, and it was not until the arrival of steam (paddle-driven) gunboats from 1837 onwards that the pirates began to be outclassed in speed as well as gun-power. But the problem of the complete suppression of piracy was not to be solved for many years to come.

Piracy in its intensified form was a by-product of the advance of the European commercial system, as was the political breakdown of the Southeast Asian States. But there could be no going back, no reversion to the old system of self-sufficiency. Thus the Colonial powers were faced with the necessity of intervention in the affairs of those states to restore order and to make international communications safe: similarly the Southeast Asian States were confronted with the necessity of modernization in their battle for survival. Hitherto, European intervention in Southeast Asian affairs had been local and intermittent; henceforth it was to be frequent and on a large scale.

BRITISH INTERVENTION IN THE MALAY STATES

Up to 1873 the British government was resolutely opposed to any active intervention in the Malay States. It might be true that the

47

States were weakly and badly governed, and the internal conflicts and confusion might on occasion amount to anarchy, but the British wanted no more territorial commitments in the region. But in that year a change of policy took place. What was the reason?

The answer to this question lies in the growth of the economic connexion between the Straits Settlements and the Malay States, and in international rivalry. Throughout the fifties and sixties the operations of Chinese planters in Johore and of Chinese tin-miners in the west-coast states opened up new avenues for investment. Chinese and European capital from Singapore and Penang financed tin-mining and the Malay princes who ruled the areas of development became partners in those undertakings. Warfare between rival Chinese factions among the tin-miners controlled by their secret societies increased the political confusion and the widespread lawlessness. Piracy, too (as we have seen), made Malayan waters unsafe for legitimate commerce and threatened life and limb into the bargain.

Many individuals and groups of merchants in the Straits Settlements and in England had for many years demanded intervention— but in vain. And when intervention was approved the strange thing is that this should have been during the first government of Mr Gladstone, the stubborn opponent of 'Imperialism'. The fact was, however, that the climate of opinion among Gladstone's ministers was undergoing a change, and a notable convert to the idea of intervention was Lord Kimberley, the Colonial Secretary. But no one in high authority contemplated *military* action, or annexation of any kind.

Reference has already been made to the new spirit abroad in Europe, in England signalized by Disraeli's Crystal Palace speech of 1872, which favoured a 'forward policy' and full assumption of responsibilities on the part of the Colonial Powers, and this was fundamentally responsible for the different outlook, but the transfer of the Straits Settlements from the India Office to the Colonial Office in 1867 facilitated the change of policy in Malaya. What, however, proved to be decisive was the fear that if Britain did not intervene in the Malay States some other European Power would be invited by some Malay State or other to do so.[1]

[1] This is the thesis put forward by C. D. Cowan, *Nineteenth Century Malaya: The Origins of British Political Control*, 1961, p. 175.

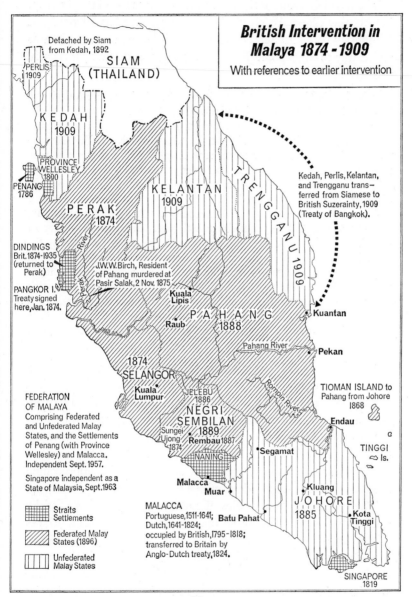

British Intervention in
Malaya 1874-1909
With references to earlier intervention

Detached by Siam
from Kedah, 1892

SIAM
(THAILAND)

PERLIS
1909

KEDAH
1909

PROVINCE
WELLESLEY
1890

PENANG
1786

DINDINGS
Brit.1874-1935
(returned to
Perak)

PANGKOR I.
Treaty signed
here,Jan. 1874.

PERAK
1874

KELANTAN
1909

TRENGGANU 1909

Kedah, Perlis, Kelantan,
and Trengganu trans—
ferred from Siamese to
British Suzerainty,1909
(Treaty of Bangkok).

J.W.W.Birch, Resident
of Pahang murdered at
Pasir Salak, 2 Nov. 1875

Kuala
Lipis

PAHANG
1888

Kuantan

Raub

Pahang River

Pekan

1874
SELANGOR

Kuala
Lumpur

JELEBU
1886

NEGRI
SEMBILAN
1889

Rompin River

TIOMAN ISLAND to
Pahang from Johore
1868

FEDERATION
OF MALAYA
Comprising Federated
and Unfederated Malay
States, and the Settlements
of Penang (with Province
Wellesley) and Malacca.
Independent Sept. 1957.

Singapore independent as a
State of Malaysia, Sept.1963

Sungei
Ujong
1874

Rembau1887

NANING

Segamat

Endau

TINGGI
Is.

Malacca

Muar

Kluang

JOHORE
1885

Kota
Tinggi

Straits
Settlements

Federated Malay
States (1896)

Unfederated
Malay States

MALACCA
Portuguese,1511-1641; Batu Pahat
Dutch,1641-1824;
occupied by British,1795-1818;
transferred to Britain by
Anglo-Dutch treaty,1824.

SINGAPORE
1819

Map 3

The new Governor of the Straits Settlements appointed in 1873, Sir Andrew Clarke, received his instructions in a letter from Lord Kimberley dated 20 September 1873 written to him while he was on his way to Singapore. Here are the more important passages in this letter:

Her Majesty's Government have, it need hardly be said, no desire to interfere in the internal affairs of the Malay States. But looking to the long and intimate connection between them and the British Government and to the wellbeing of the British Settlements themselves, H.M. Government find it incumbent upon them to employ such influence as they possess with the native princes to rescue, if possible, those fertile and productive countries from the ruin which must befall them if the present disorders continue unchecked.

I have to request that you will carefully ascertain, as far as you are able, the actual condition of affairs in each State, and that you will report to me whether in your opinion, any steps can properly be taken by the Colonial Government to promote the restoration of peace and order, and to secure protection to trade and commerce with the native territories. I should wish you especially to consider whether it would be advisable to appoint a British officer to reside in any of the States. Such appointment could, of course, only be made with the full consent of the Native Government, and the expenses connected with it would have to be defrayed by the Government of the Straits Settlements.

How were those instructions to be interpreted? Sir Andrew, a soldier by profession (he was an officer of the Royal Engineers), had already decided in his own mind that he would regard those instructions as authority to take a very positive line. It happened that the opportunity for this had arisen in the affairs of Perak, where a disputed succession to the throne as well as faction fighting among the Chinese miners had created a state of affairs approaching anarchy, and Clarke was determined to intervene.

The traditional Malay rules of succession can be simplified by stating that there was an order of ranks among the leading princes of the State—in Perak it was Sultan, Raja Muda, Raja Bendahara, etc. On the death of the sultan, the Raja Muda (usually the son of the last sultan but one) succeeded him and the others went up one step in rank. But the succession was subject to confirmation by election of all the princes of the State. The usual succession had been departed from in Perak, so that when Sultan Ali died in 1871

British Intervention in the Malay States

there were three possible candidates for the throne—Abdullah who could claim the normal succession as Raja Muda, Ismail as having been Bendahara during the previous two reigns, and Yusof who would have been Raja Muda if the proper succession had been observed. Ismail was elected. By the beginning of 1872 there were three *de facto* rulers in Perak—Ismail, the nominal sultan, acknowledged by the up-country chiefs, Abdullah, also styling himself sultan and supported by a number of chiefs on the lower Perak River, and the Mantri at Larut, the strongest of the three, who controlled the tin-miners and dealt with the Penang authorities as an independent chief.

Sir Andrew Clarke called a meeting of the Malay chiefs at Pangkor Island in January 1874 and persuaded those who attended to sign a treaty recognizing Abdullah as sultan. Another article in the treaty, which was to become the foundation of the 'Resident System' by which Malaya was to be governed right up to the Japanese invasion of 1941–42, was that the sultan should receive a British 'Resident' 'whose advice must be asked for and acted upon on all questions other than those touching Malay Religion and Custom'.

At the same meeting, the heads of the Chinese factions representing the rival secret societies, the Ghee Hin and Hai San, signed a bond, undertaking under a penalty of $50,000, to disarm, destroy their stockades, give up their rowing-boats, and not again to break the peace.

The first British Resident appointed to Perak was Mr J. W. W. Birch, the Colonial Secretary of the Straits Settlements, who had only been in Malaya for a few years but had had many years' experience as an administrator in Ceylon.

Sir Andrew Clarke next turned his attention to Selangor. At the time of his arrival in Singapore in November 1873, a civil war in Selangor was drawing towards an end, leaving the Viceroy, Tunku Zia'u'd-din (commonly called Kudin[1]), in possession of the field. (It is noteworthy that in this war, the 'Capitan China' of Selangor, Yap Ah Loy, took part in the recapture of Kuala Lumpur, which had been held for seven months by one of Zia'u'd-din's opponents.)

[1] The correct spelling is Zia'u'd-din, but in English books and documents he is referred to as Kudin, Udin, or Dia Oodin.

51

In February 1874, just a month after the Pangkor treaty, the Sultan of Selangor, the Viceroy, and Sir Andrew Clarke had a meeting which paved the way for the acceptance of a British Resident, for which post Mr J. G. Davidson, a Singapore lawyer and the Viceroy's personal adviser, was chosen.

The situation in Negri Sembilan was more difficult on account of the rivalries of Sungei Ujong and Rembau, and, in Sungei Ujong itself, of the Dato Klana and the Data Bandar. But by the end of 1874 British advisers and assistant advisers were at work in Larut, Lower Perak, Klang, Langat, and Sungei Ujong.

Thus it was that a momentous experiment in government was inaugurated in the Malay States. But it was only an experiment, and how it would work out in practice it was impossible to prophesy. The Malay rulers were autocrats by definition, and the chiefs were members of a proud aristocracy. What was the nature of the 'advice' to be tendered to them and how far would they find it acceptable? Everything must turn on the answers to these questions.

As it happens, the first application of the 'Resident' system, in Perak, was a tragic failure. J. W. W. Birch, the Resident, has been called 'an idealist in a hurry'. He was a person of strict principles who believed in firmness and speed—a man with a mission. His object was to divert the taxes considered as their perquisites by the local chiefs to the purposes of the State, and to remove crying abuses such as debt-slavery. Unfortunately he cut off their means of support from the chiefs without first providing for their salaries or pensions—with the inevitable result that they became his enemies. Moreover, he treated Abdullah, the British nominee as sultan, as a youthful delinquent. Abdullah undoubtedly was (as Swettenham said) 'weak, inordinately vain, and hopelessly extravagant', and an opium-smoker into the bargain, but he was nevertheless the sultan and as such resented Birch's schoolmasterly rebukes.

Sir Andrew Clarke had been succeeded by a new Governor, Sir William Jervois (also, like his two predecessors, a Royal Engineer) and it was he who had to bear the consequences of Sir Andrew Clarke's misjudgments—first in choosing Abdullah as sultan, and second in appointing Birch as Resident. Things went from bad to worse in Perak, and came to a head when Jervois decided to dispense with 'advice' and to rule the Malay States directly through 'Queen's Commissioners'. In the meantime the chiefs had met in secret and had resolved on Birch's murder.

The first attempt to dispose of Birch was by means of magic, but when this did not succeed, it was planned to waylay him when he was engaged in posting up proclamations of the appointment of Queen's Commissioners at places on the Perak River. On 2 November 1875 he was speared to death through the walls of a palm-leaf bathing-shed in the river at Pasir Salak. (Frank Swettenham, his assistant, who was also posting proclamations further up the river, only just escaped a like fate.)

British intervention now took place in earnest, and troops poured in from India and Hong Kong. As it turned out, these were not required, for a general rising of the Malays did not take place (as Jervois had feared). After a short campaign, all resistance ended. The Maharaja Lela, who had actually supervised the murder, was executed, and Abdullah, who had been a party to the plot, was exiled to the Seychelles.

What was now to happen to the 'Resident' system? Would the British attempt once more to make it work, or would they commit themselves to out-right annexation of the western Malay States? The short answer is that the Secretary of State for the Colonies, Lord Carnarvon, decided that the system should be given one more trial, and it was on this decision that the whole future of the British protectorate of the Malay States was to turn. It is somewhat strange that whereas a British Liberal government had decided on intervention in 1873, a British Conservative (and supposedly 'Imperialist') government decided against annexation in 1875.

THE 'RESIDENT' SYSTEM ON TRIAL

The 'Resident' system, as we have seen, started off badly. Yet the proposal for 'Queen's Commissioners' had produced a violent opposition from the Malays, and it was clear that direct rule by British officials in the name of the sultan was even more unacceptable than indirect rule by 'advice'. Unless the British were willing to run the risk of a rising of all the Malays against them, the only practicable alternative was to try to make the 'Resident' system work. This, at least, was how the Colonial Secretary, Lord Carnarvon, argued, and his instructions to the Governor of the Straits Settlements were in keeping with this view.

Everything would turn on the character of those who were chosen to be Residents, the kind of 'advice' they proffered, and the tact with which they did it. They had no easy task. The treaties excepted 'Malay religion and custom' from the subjects on which advice might be offered, yet the whole of Malay society was founded on religion and custom. In matters of relationship with other states, or even of the sultan and his subordinate princes, it might be possible to keep away from those forbidden subjects, but the collection of revenue could not be separated from the customary system by which the sultan and his chiefs derived their incomes. And even if the principle could be established that henceforth those personal incomes were to be applied to public purposes and that the ruler and his chiefs would receive only the allowances allotted to them, how and by whom were these revenues to be collected and administered?

Malay society in the 1870s has been described as 'feudal', though this description is not strictly correct. It was certainly 'authoritarian' and depended on the subordination of the common people to the aristocracy. There was so far no idea of 'public' interests, and if the Malay States were to be successfully modernized this idea must be implanted and encouraged to grow. At the same time a civil service must be created to collect and administer the newly separated revenues. At the beginning, the Residents were either entirely on their own or had only a single assistant and had yet to recruit a civil service to help them in their work. Nor had the Residents a military force to back them up. In Perak, Captain Speedy, as Assistant Resident, it is true, had a Residency Guard of twenty-five Sepoys and a police force of about 160 men, mainly Indian, which he had built up when he was in the service of the Mantri, but this was not a large force (nor a reliable one) and the other Residents or Assistants were not even in this comparatively advantageous position. The real military power lay in the hands of the Governor of the Straits Settlements, but he was a considerable distance away, and he would be unlikely to back a Resident in a serious dispute with a Ruler unless he felt he could justify his action with the home government. Nor could the Malays as a whole be expected to believe that the Residents were animated purely by altruistic motives. Unused to a chief who was only a civil servant acting under the orders of a remote superior, the Malays could be pardoned for believing that he was only seeking his private enrichment at their expense. Nor could they easily accept the story that the Resident was intended to limit himself to giving advice. In fact as the Malays told Frank Swettenham, they thought that he and the other Residents were only put where they were as bait—to tempt them to ignore or destroy them and thus give the British an excuse for conquest. 'If the Malay chiefs swallowed the bait', they told Swettenham, 'they would find themselves on the British hook; of course, no one would worry about the bait.'[1]

To removing this impression and to substituting an entirely new conception of British protection the energies of the next generations of British civil servants in the Malay States were to be devoted.

That the renewed experiment succeeded, and succeeded triumphantly, was due to the wise selection of men for appointment as Residents. Outstanding among the Residents of Perak was Sir Hugh Low who held the post from 1877 to 1889. He was not, by origin, a professional administrator but a botanist, and had served most of the previous thirty years in that capacity in Sarawak under Raja James Brooke and his successor. He spoke Malay with perfect fluency, and had a long experience of Malay customs. By nature he was tactful but firm, and the possession of a dignified presence with a long white beard was calculated to impress the people of Perak. His success was due in no small measure to the fact that he treated the latter as, so to speak, 'fellow aristocrats'—the only basis of intercourse which was acceptable in Malaya (if not among human beings in general).

The system that Low evolved (and which was simultaneously being worked out in the other States by the other Residents, notable

[1] F. Swettenham, *British Malaya*, p. 219.

among them J. P. Rodger and Swettenham himself) included the provision of compensation for chiefs deprived of their perquisites by their allocation to the general revenues. Many of the latter were appointed as tax-collectors who paid their own salaries out of their receipts and remitted the remainder to headquarters. To the penghulus (village headmen) were allotted police and administrative duties. A land-tax was substituted for the previous rights of the chiefs to forced labour, and as a money-economy was gradually substituted for the old customary relationships, and police, for example, took the place of armed retainers to a chief, local society began to be transformed. Slavery and debt-bondage similarly rapidly became out of date, and finally in 1884 were both abolished by law, the former masters receiving a money compensation.

But these changes were brought about, not on the direct authority of the Resident, but by the sultan acting on the Resident's advice. In practice, if a new measure was proposed, the sultan and the Malay chiefs were first consulted. If they approved, well and good; if they opposed, the measure was modified, and if the opposition was strong enough, abandoned altogether. This remained the policy throughout the whole period of British protection.

The working of the Resident system was greatly facilitated by the creation of the State Council, introduced first of all into Perak by Low. The Council was presided over by the sultan, and its members were the leading Malay chiefs, Chinese leaders, and the Resident himself. The Council was the legislative body of the State, approved the estimates of revenue of expenditure, and all the more important appointments and administrative measures. The Perak Council proved such a success that councils on similar lines were set up in the other States under British protection.

Now that civil war between the Malay States had ended and order had been established internally, a prerequisite for development was improved communications. Hitherto these had consisted entirely of the rivers and jungle-paths. Roads were now constructed to link up the tin-mines with the growing townships, and railways began to be built from 1885 onwards. To begin with, these were short lines joining the State capitals to the coast, but eventually a trunk line would join up Singapore and Penang, and, in the coming century, be extended to Siam with a new line to the east-coast States. Drainage, water-supplies, and medical services were established, and, on the economic side, in addition to the cultivation of coffee, pepper, sugar, gambier and tobacco, Liberian coffee was now grown in plantations established with European capital. Even more significant, as the foundation of the prosperity to come to Malaya early in the twentieth century, was the experimental cultivation of the Brazilian rubber-tree by Sir Hugh Low (a botanist, be it remembered) in the Residency gardens at Kuala Kangsar.

The reforms were soon reflected in improved State finances; the revenues increased many times within a decade or two, and money was increasingly available for the modernization of the country.

The Resident system, first applied to Perak and Selangor, was then extended to Negri Sembilan, and in 1888 to Pahang. All the Residents were following a similar policy in broad outline, but the time now seemed ripe for some form of centralization to help them coordinate their efforts. The idea for the federation of the four Malay States under British protection originated with Frank Swettenham; in 1895 the rulers of the States agreed to his plan, and the Federated Malay States (F.M.S.) came into being on 1 January 1896. Kuala Lumpur (in Selangor) was chosen as the federal capital, and Swettenham was appointed the first Resident-General. Each State, however, still retained control of its own internal affairs and each had its own British Resident. Johore, so closely linked with Singapore, remained outside the Federation, and at the turn of the century the four northern Malay States were still under the suzerainty of Siam.

THE BRITISH IN BORNEO: THE 'WHITE RAJAS' OF SARAWAK, THE NORTH BORNEO COMPANY

Attention must now be directed to what was happening in the meantime in other parts of what was eventually to become the Federation of Malaysia.

The clash between Birch and Abdullah is a reminder that personality plays as great a part in history as policy, and the remarkable story of the Brooke family in Sarawak is an even more striking example of this.

James Brooke (1803–68) was the son of an East India Company servant, and entered the East Indian Army in 1819. After being seriously wounded in the First Burma War he quitted this Service in 1830. One of his biographers writes of him—'while travelling in the East he conceived the idea of putting down the plague of piracy in the beautiful islands of the Eastern Archipelago and bringing the blessings of civilisation to the inhabitants.' This is a typically Victorian idealization of the man and his motives, and while the judgment of him (in 'anti-colonialist' books) as a 'ruthless imperialist' is even more off the mark, the historian is called upon to view his career somewhat more critically than do most of his biographers.

Inheriting £30,000 on his father's death, Brooke fitted out a yacht, carefully trained its crew, and in October 1838 sailed for Sarawak. He arrived at an opportune time, for a revolt was in progress against the Sultan of Brunei, and Brooke took the leading part in suppressing it. For this he was rewarded with the title of Raja of Sarawak and was given this province to administer. This was officially effected on 24 September 1841.

The fact is that Brooke was, to begin with, the agent and subordinate of the Sultan of Brunei and the original province governed by him was of only 3,000 square miles with a population of 8,000. Before the Brooke family finally ceded Sarawak to the Crown in 1946, it had grown to a country of 47,500 square miles with a population of some 600,000. Brunei, on the other hand, which originally had claimed vague overlordship over most of North Borneo, had shrunk to a state of only just over 2,000 square miles. Sarawak's territorial gain had been entirely at the expense of Brunei, Brooke's original overlord.

On the face of it, those figures suggest that acquisitiveness on the part of the Brookes was the reason for the phenomenal growth of Sarawak, but this simple explanation is not enough. James Brooke, it is true, did not contemplate accepting permanently the nominal overlordship of an old but effete dynasty, and in 1846 he declared his independence, which was confirmed by Brunei. He also sought some official recognition of his position from the British Crown,

and in this same year gained this to a certain extent when he persuaded Britain to accept the cession of Labuan from Brunei and
himself became its Governor and British Consul-General for Brunei
at the same time. But the accretion of territory must not be regarded as 'conquest'. By far the greater part of it was virgin forest
and unadministered. Moreover, pirate settlements were scattered
along its coasts. The application to this huge area of a measure of
settled government can only be regarded, in twentieth-century
terms, as a necessary prelude to the creation of a modern state. To
accomplish this was utterly beyond Brunei's ambition and resources.

As might have been expected, the annexation of Labuan—and
indeed the whole of Brooke's career to date—evoked strong remon-
strances from Holland. The Dutch contended that the British action
in Borneo was a breach of the Anglo-Dutch Treaty of 1824, but the
British government warmly defended Brooke and would not agree
that any interpretation of the treaty could mean that the British
were denied the right to establish a station on any island on which
the Dutch already had one, in this case huge Borneo, the third
largest island in the world. In replying to the Dutch note, the
British cabinet took the opportunity of reminding the Dutch of their
own transgressions, including breaches of the commercial agreements of 1824.

Brooke had set out his policy in a pamphlet he sent to England in
1842 in the hope of rousing interest and support there. He said
that he would insist on a just administration; he would defend the
oppressed Dyaks; he would encourage the Chinese merchants, and
would welcome any commerce that was not detrimental to the
natives' interests. He would like British trading houses to take an
interest in Sarawak and the Church to send a mission there (though
he privately believed that the Americans made better missionaries
than the English). All the same, he undoubtedly made 'the suppression of piracy' the occasion for the extension of dominion, and in
the middle of the century he was subjected to a prolonged campaign
of attack by British Liberals and humanitarians. The publication of Captain Munday's Journals in 1848 revealed an enthusi-
astic bellicosity on the part of Brooke and Admiral Keppel in their
bombardments of 'pirate lairs'—£20 for every pirate killed was

paid to the armed forces under an Act of George IV, and £12,000 was paid to a Captain Belcher, R.N., on this account in 1849, and over £20,000 to a Captain Farquhar and his men for the battle of Batang Maru. (Killing pirates, it seemed, had become quite an industry.) Brooke's opponents said that many of the 'murdered Dyaks' were not pirates at all, and Cobden declared at Birmingham that 'his atrocities threw those of the Austrian General Haynau (the champion rebel-queller of the age) into the shade. Nevertheless, Brooke had more friends than enemies. In a debate in Parliament on 10 July 1851, when an M.P. named Hume demanded that a Royal Commission be appointed to investigate Brooke's acts, Cobden declared that Brooke fought his neighbours for the purpose of obtaining their land; Gladstone described him as 'a truly Christian philanthropist' but felt, all the same, that the question of piracy and suppression should be examined; while Palmerston, winding up, quoted laudatory reports on Brooke from the consuls in the Dutch and Spanish colonies, and declared that he 'emerged from the discussion with his character untarnished and his honour unblemished'. Hume's motion was negatived by 230 votes to 19.

In 1857, Brooke's troubles were added to by a Chinese rising in Kuching. In some ways it was an overflow of the Second War between China and Britain, then in progress, but it was also a plot engineered by the Chinese secret societies to get rid of the 'red-haired devils'. The rebels set fire to the Raja's house and he only escaped by diving into the creek and swimming to safety under the Chinese boats moored there. The revolt was suppressed, but Brooke had lost most of his possessions, and what remained of his private fortune went to re-equip himself and his officials. Had it not been for advances of money from Brooke's friend, the Baroness Burdett-Coutts, Sarawak might have become bankrupt.

Sir Steven Runciman, his most recent biographer summing up James Brooke's character, says of him:

If there is any meaning in the word greatness, James Brooke was a great man. He had his faults and his weaknesses. He was touchy, impatient, inconsistent and imprudent; and in his later years his mental balance did not always seem secure. He was a poor administrator and incompetent at finance. His judgment of men was often poor. . . . For simple races he felt an instinctive sympathy and affection. It was by a series of accidents that he found himself the ruler of an oriental state. . . . His burning sense of justice came as a blessing to the miserable Land Dyaks and all other poor folk oppressed by extortion and raiding, whose lives he so profoundly changed.[1]

So Brooke remains a hero to many and a villain to some. He was succeeded by his nephew, the Tuan Muda, born Charles Johnson, who had adopted the surname Brooke on his succession and who later became Sir Charles Brooke, G.C.M.G. Charles Brooke was also an outstanding character, but his reputation is overshadowed by that of the first 'White Raja'.

Brunei became a British protectorate in 1888, having reached a condition even nearer complete anarchy than any of the Malay States, and the creation of Sabah (British North Borneo—another unit of Malaysia) dates from 1881.

Because of the lateness of its formation, the history of the British North Borneo Company belongs more to the next phase of Malaysian history than that here described. It is sufficient to remark that the Charter was said to have been granted in a fit of absence of mind by Mr Gladstone—who repented of it when it was too late. The acquisition by a shadowy British concern of North Borneo, or Sabah (Saba), to give the territory its Brunei and perhaps Biblical name,[2] aroused the protests of Spain, Holland, and the United States of America, and the protests of Spain and the U.S.A. have been echoed over the proposals for Malaysia. Even more protesting was the Raja of Sarawak, for the Brookes, both James and Charles, had the great ambition to possess all north and west Borneo as a national park for their Dyaks to roam about in at their ease. The Company became a competitor with Sarawak for unclaimed territory. It survived and achieved, for the inhabitants of the country, a quiet success, but paid very meagre dividends. From 1899 to 1905 it was 2 per cent; in 1905, 3 per cent; at times dividends were paid out of capital or ceased altogether; in 1938, it was 4 per cent. Whatever its lasting value as a State, North Borneo (for the Company's shareholders) was scarcely a money-making concern.

[1] Steven Runciman, *The White Rajahs*, 1960, p. 156.
[2] Psalm 72, Verse 10, vide Tregonning, *Under Chartered Company rule: North Borneo, 1881–1946*, p. 16.

THE REST OF BURMA BROUGHT UNDER BRITISH RULE

The British acquisition of Burma was a process of a somewhat different character from that of the extension of British influence and protection in the Malay Peninsula and Borneo. The former arose from the necessity of consolidating the frontiers of an empire which had grown rapidly in a short period of years, whereas the latter was mainly in the course of securing a peaceful 'hinterland' (a protective buffer of territory lying to the back of a settlement) for the British stations on the way to China. One consequence of this difference was that much greater military force had to be employed at times in the case of Burma than in the case of Malaya and Borneo, with the result that the British acquisition of Burma is more easily represented as 'aggression' than the peaceful treaty-making which for the most part marked the development of British influence in Malaysia.

So far, Arakan, Tenasserim, and Lower Burma had been added to India: the swallowing-up of the remainder of Burma came in 1885. The mistake made by the reigning king, Thibaw (spelt Thee-baw in old books), was to try to play off the French against the British. The period of tacit understanding among the European Powers regarding their 'spheres of influence' was now over, and there was bitter rivalry between them. While piling up arms, Thibaw made extensive concessions to the French, agreeing by treaty to allow them to finance the construction of a railway from Mandalay to Toungoo in British Burma. The French, it was rumoured, were further negotiating to take over the management of the royal mono-polies and of the postal system, to run river steamers in competition with the British-owned Irrawaddy Flotilla Company, obtain a lease of the ruby mines, and open up the overland trade with Tongking. This was bad enough from the British point of view, though scarcely an excuse for war by itself, but what was insupportable was that Thibaw, pressed by his creditors for money, simultaneously began to squeeze the Bombay Burmah Trading Company (another British concern) for what he thought he could get out of them.

Even had there been no threat to British interests, it is certain that the British would have eventually intervened in upper Burma if only to keep their frontiers intact. Under Thibaw's weak and capricious rule, the country was in a condition little short of chaos. 'Dacoity' (gang-robbery) was rife, the Kachins rebelled, Chinese guerillas burnt Bhamo, and most of the feudatory Shan tribes threw off their allegiance to Ava. Plots were hatched to dethrone Thibaw, and the ensuing massacre of suspected plotters made a blood-bath of the capital. In the middle of all this came an ultimatum from Lord Dufferin, the Viceroy, demanding that the case in which it was proposed to deprive the Bombay Burmah Company of its rights to exploit teak forests should be submitted to arbitration. Relying on French support, the Court of Ava summarily rejected the proposal. War then ensued—but France kept aloof. Operations began on 14 November, and a fortnight later, after an almost bloodless campaign, Mandalay was occupied and Thibaw surrendered. The government of India would have preferred to place the country under a protectorate, with an approved member of the royal family on the throne. But there was no suitable candidate. Hence on 1 January 1886 a proclamation was issued annexing the former territories of King Thibaw to the British dominions. But the real struggle was yet to come.

The process by which Burma was brought under British administration was very different from that which marked the development of the 'Resident' system in the Malay States—and much more painful. In 1886 the annexation of Upper Burma was followed by disorder, for the Burmese army disregarded the order to surrender and melted away to carry on guerilla warfare from the jungle villages. It took five more years of hard campaigning by a government force which at one time amounted to 32,000 troops and 8500 military police before the resistance was finally broken.

The treatment of Burma as part of the Indian empire was, looked at in retrospect, an error, for the Indian pattern of government that was applied to it was not consistent with Burmese custom. Sir Charles Crosthwaite, who was charged with the pacification of Upper Burma after the annexation, brought with him from India a ready-made scheme for making the village, as in India, the administrative and social unit. To bring this about he destroyed the traditional Burmese system of 'circle headmen'. In the view of

J. S. Furnivall (a British civil servant with many years' experience of Burma) the effect was to impose duties on the villages without any compensating rights; the village was a mere artificial administrative unit, and the disappearance of the circle headman (the *myothugyi*) meant that the habit of referring serious disputes between adjacent villages to his arbitration lapsed and was replaced by 'the mechanical logic of the courts'. Burmese society remained unsettled and therefore fertile soil for rebellion. But whether the semi-feudal power of the *myothugyi* could be rightly termed 'popular self-government' (as Furnivall seemed to think) is another question, and it seems certain that even if he had been retained he would not have been able to meet the vastly changed conditions of the coming century.

THE FRENCH IN INDOCHINA

France came into the colonial field in Southeast Asia later than Holland and Britain, and the area it chose for its activities was the Peninsula of Indochina and neighbouring lands. This was not the first time (as has already been seen) that the French had taken a hand in the affairs of this region. But the Revolutionary and Napoleonic wars had drawn French attention from Southeast Asia, and when peace in Europe had been restored, France had other preoccupations, such as the colonization of North Africa and the revolutions in Europe of 1830 and 1848. Min-Mang, who succeeded Gia-Long as emperor in 1820, hated the 'barbarians from the West' and refused to conclude a commercial treaty with the French. In 1826, he broke off official relations with France altogether.

Unlike the British and Dutch of the period, who were reluctant to acquire new responsibilities, the French sought an opportunity to start a colonial empire of their own in Southeast Asia—no doubt because they felt that the wars and revolutions in Europe had denied them their 'place in the sun'.

It was the persecution of French missionaries which gave France an opportunity to intervene in Annam. On several occasions in the 1840s French warships appeared off the coast to demand the release of imprisoned missionaries under threat of bombardment—and

The French in Indochina

French Advance in Indochina 1859 – 1907

CHINA

TONGKING (French Protectorate 1884)

Lang Son

(French defeated here by Chinese 1885)

Hanoi

Haiphong

Kwangchow-wan (Leased by French from China 1898)

HAINAN

Luang Prabang

Mekong River

Vientiane

French Protectorate (1893)

Mekong River

SIAM

ANNAM

Hué

Tourane

Regions ceded by Siam
1907   1904

Binh Dinh

French Protectorate 1884

CAMBODIA (French Protectorate 1863)

Phnom Penh

COCHIN-CHINA

Saigon (1859)

COCHIN-CHINA
Declared a French 'Colony' 1867
(Other Indochinese States were French 'Protectorates')

UNION OF INDOCHINA (Created 17th Oct. 1887)

P. Condore Convict Settlement 1862

Map 4

usually with success. But it was not until 1859 that the murder of a missionary caused a Franco-Spanish force under Admiral Regault de Genouilly to put the Annamese forts out of action and to occupy Saigon.

The capture of Saigon in February 1859 was the start of the French empire in Indochina. By the peace, the Emperor of Annam ceded to France the three eastern provinces of Cochin-China. Two years later, Cambodia, where Siamese influence had been strong, became a French protectorate, and the French were launched on a career of conquest that would eventually carry them to the frontiers of China.

A great opportunity afforded the French in their acquisition of territory was in Tongking which was in a state of grave disorder consequent on the flight of rebels from China following on the suppression of the Taiping Rebellion (1850–64). The Emperor Tu-Duc, unable to cope with them, had called on the Viceroy of Canton to help, but when the latter sent regular Chinese troops into Tongking, instead of helping to suppress the rebellion, they had joined the rebels in pillaging the country. To the French the combined forces of robbers became known as the Black Flags. Admiral Dupré, the Governor of Cochin-China, saw in this state of affairs the opportunity for intervention he was looking for. France had been overwhelmingly defeated in the Prussian war in Europe in 1870–71, resulting in a dangerous decline of French prestige in Asia, and Dupré and other Frenchmen regarded expansion in Indochina as the best way to revive it.

The French government at home, however, was not at this time in a position to back up this, and repudiated the seizure of the citadel of Hanoi by Dupré's friend Francis Garnier, and the French contented themselves for the time being with treaties with Tongking by which the Emperor Tu-Duc recognized French sovereignty over Cochin-China, received a French Resident at his capital Hué, opened the ports of Qui-nonh, Tourane, and Hanoi to French trade, and agreed to the appointment of a French consul to each port accompanied by a bodyguard.

Tongking, however, was a vassal of the Chinese emperor, and this forward movement was bound to bring the French and the

Chinese into collision. China was very weak after its two wars with the West, but was resolved to do its best to retain its position in this region. War broke out in 1885. The French were successful at sea (destroying the Chinese fleet as it lay at anchor at Foochow) but suffered a great defeat on land at Langson on 28 March. The French troops panicked, abandoned all their baggage and guns, and fled to the mountains. Nevertheless, by successful diplomacy, the French were able to secure a peace with China which left their position in Indochina unaffected. In spite of several rebellions, they were able to consolidate their gains. In October 1887, their 'colony' of Cochin-China, and their protectorates of Cambodia, Annam, and Tongking were brought together to form the *Union Indochinoise*. By 'Boxer Year' (1900), China's hour of greatest weakness, the French Governor-General, Paul Doumer, had brought the Union under a French Colonial administration 'on the Napoleonic pattern' which eliminated the last vestiges of local autonomy and turned Indochina into a highly centralized dependency of France.

French colonial policy and aims were in many respects different from those of the British or Dutch. Whereas the British and Dutch both tended to establish their rule over their colonies without radically changing the native societies, the French strove to 'gallicize' (frenchify) their possessions and to regard them as extensions of France itself. These differences will become clearer when the different colonial systems are compared in the next chapter.

DEVELOPMENTS IN SIAM AND THE PHILIPPINES

In the course of reviewing Southeast Asian history in terms of the pressures on the region from outside, notice has been taken of the Dutch pressures in Indonesia, the British pressures on Malaya, Borneo, and Burma, and of the French pressure on Indochina. This treatment accounts for the whole of Southeast Asia except Siam and the Philippines, and to these countries attention must, in conclusion, be directed.

Sandwiched in between British-occupied Burma to the north and west and French Indo-China to the north, and those Malay States which had come under British protection to the south, the

Kingdom of Siam nevertheless managed to retain its independence throughout the colonial period. How did this come about? The answer lies first in the rivalry between Britain and France who found it advantageous to have a buffer between their spheres of influence, and second in the diplomatic skill of the Siamese monarchs, Mongkut and Chulalongkorn.

But while Siam remained independent, it was not without the loss of a certain amount of sovereignty and of actual territory, first when the French sphere expanded at its expense with the annexation in 1888 of twelve Siamese cantons to the French empire, and later (in 1909) when the four Northern Malay States were transferred to British protection.

The Bowring Treaty of 1855 with Britain set up a chain-reaction resulting in similar treaties with France, the United States, Denmark and the Hanseatic cities, Portugal, Holland, Prussia, Belgium, Italy, Norway, Sweden, and Japan, and by each treaty extra territorial rights were conceded to the country in question. Europeans were now employed as advisers and teachers and to reorganize the public services. Trade began to boom and of this the British had the biggest share.

If Siam were to retain its independence it was certain that it must modernize itself, and modernize itself swiftly. Chulalongkorn (Rama V, 1868–1910), who succeeded to the throne on attaining his majority in 1873, saw this more clearly than anybody. As a child, he had received the groundings of a European education from a remarkable English governess, Anna Leonowens, which was continued in his youth under an English tutor named Robert Morant. Before assuming the reins of government, Chulalongkorn went on a long foreign tour, studying on the way the methods of administration employed by the Dutch in Java and the British in India, and returned to Siam with his mind and outlook still further broadened. Then, in the years that followed, he instituted a long series of reforms.

Since the extraterritorial privileges of the foreigner derived from the backwardness of the Siamese law and the administration of justice, reform in this sphere was an essential before the treaty countries could be persuaded to surrender their extraterritorial rights. But this took a long time, and it was not until the early years of the twentieth century that the foreign countries began to give up their extraterritorial privileges one by one.

The situation of the Philippines was quite different from that of Siam. These islands had been under direct European control for over three centuries, and their culture now bore the deep imprint of Spain. Unlike the remainder of Southeast Asia, the inhabitants of these numerous islands had not come under the influence of India or (to any extent) of China, and Islam had established itself permanently only in Mindanao. Therefore when the Spanish arrived they found the people still living in a primitive 'Indonesian' stage of culture which could not effectively oppose that which they themselves had brought. Hence conversion to Roman Catholicism was general, and the Philippines became the single christianized Far Eastern State.

Upon the native system of the villages (*barrios*) the Spanish superimposed an administration which they had developed in Spanish America. Under this, the governor had almost despotic powers, restricted only by the existence of an *audiencia* or Supreme Court. Economically, the basis of Spanish rule was the landed estate held in feudal tenure by a privileged class of *caciques* or chiefs, and so strongly was this system entrenched that, in spite of some land reform under the American régime, and rather more extensive measures since independence, in its essential features it survives to the present day. The effect of the long period of Spanish rule was to develop a highly Spanish—and Church—influenced society but at the same time to freeze it into immobility.

Nevertheless, a sense of Philippine separateness and nationality had germinated and began to grow in the long years of Spain's decline as a world power, and when the American forces arrived in the Philippines in 1898 in the course of the Spanish-American war, a Filipino insurrectionary force was in the field against the Philippine government. But it was to be many years before nationalism developed in the islands sufficiently to bring about independence.

4

SOUTH AND EAST ASIA IN THE NINETEENTH CENTURY

THE BRITISH EMPIRE IN INDIA

Southeast Asia has two great neighbours—China, Japan, and Korea (of the same cultural family) to the north and east, and the Indian subcontinent (now divided into India and Pakistan) and Ceylon[1] to the west. In the nineteenth century it was the former that was more influential politically than the latter in Southeast Asia, which justifies priority being given to its history in this period.

It has already been seen in Chapter 2 how the growth of the British empire in India resulted in conflict with, and the eventual absorption of, Burma and in the establishment of British settlements in the Malay Peninsula, with far-reaching consequences, and to make the picture clearer an account must be given of developments in India itself during the passage of the century.

The great drive for the expansion of the British 'Raj' (rule, sovereignty) in India was initiated by Wellesley. When he arrived in 1798 the Company's possessions were limited to the island of Bombay and to strips of land round Calcutta and Madras. His policy was to induce the Indian States to enter into what was known as 'subsidiary alliances' with the British, by which the ruler retained control of internal affairs but handed over the care of defence and external relations to the British. Wellesley, having struck and destroyed Tipu, the 'Tiger of Mysore', opened the way for the annexation of the Carnatic to the Presidency of Madras. He then turned his attention to Hyderabad, which was another ally of the French,

---

[1] The scale of this book does not permit of the separate treatment of Ceylon. It passed from Dutch to British possession in 1802; in 1833 it received a constitution. Demands for reform in the 20th century, led to new constitutions in 1910 and in 1920-4. Ceylon became independent as a member of the Commonwealth in February 1948.

The British Empire in India

and whose Nizam (prince) had a highly trained force of 14,000 troops under a French officer named Raymond. (In the years of war to the death with France, intervention against France's allies in India was a simple measure of self-preservation on the part of the British.) The following year (1800) Oudh, wherein corruption and misrule were rampant, was forced by Wellesley to accept a 'subsidiary alliance'. But these successes left an even more dangerous enemy, the Maratha confederacy, to be dealt with.

The Maratha empire was founded by Sivaji in 1674 in the neighbourhood of Poona and extended at one time throughout central India from Nagpur in the east to Goa (Portuguese) in the west. For a century and a half the Marathas ravaged central and southern India, circulating round it in a kind of dust-storm of destruction. They avoided pitched battles, adopting guerilla tactics. Whereas other Hindu conquerors took pride in 'colonizing' the territory they conquered, constructing temples, roads, wells, and public works, the Marathas resorted merely to blackmail and loot. Their weakness, however, lay in their division among themselves, and they were eventually defeated 'in detail' under their several rival leaders. In the south, Colonel Wellesley (as already recorded) defeated one leader, Sindhia, at Assaye; in the north Lord Lake overran the Maratha territories in Hindustan; in 1803 the British entered Delhi and took under their protection the captive of the Marathas, the blind old Mogul emperor whom they found sitting under a tattered canopy. But although three great Maratha chiefs, Sindhia, Holkar, and the Raja of Nagpur, were forced into 'subsidiary alliances' (the other Maratha ruler, the Gaekwar of Baroda, wisely remained on the British side throughout) it was not until during the Governor-Generalship of Lord Hastings (1817) that the Marathas were finally disposed of. The Marathas' 'Peshwa' (their titular head) was banished to Bithur near Cawnpore on a generous pension and the whole of the Deccan was annexed (with the exception of one little kingdom of Satara) and became part of the Bombay Presidency; the state of Nagpur was formed into the Central Provinces.

These examples of British conquests early in the century bring out the great complexity of India as compared with China proper (the eighteen original provinces) which was, comparatively speaking,

71

of 'one piece', and emphasize that now, as for many years to come, the British were not confronting an 'Indian nation' or anything like one. Moreover, the enemies of the British were often the enemies of the Indian people as a whole, as, for example, the Pindaris, the Maratha freebooters who were rapidly making central India into a desert, and (later under Bentinck) the Thugs, a body of assassins who were dedicated to the service of the goddess of death and destruction, Kali, and who practised the ritual strangling of travellers whom they waylaid.

During the Governor-Generalship of Lord Hastings (1813–23) the Gurkhas were defeated and part of their territory of Nepal was annexed, and, when Hastings left, British supremacy over the native states was finally established and the whole peninsula was ruled by the British. The enemies that remained were on the frontiers—namely, the independent and aggressive kingdom that had been set up in Burma (*vide* Chapter 2), Afghanistan (to be the source of much trouble in the future), and the Punjab which under Ranjit Singh (1780–1839) had been unified and strengthened.

The extension of British rule brought British India into contact and conflict with political systems and alliances far away from India itself. For example, Afghanistan, regarded as an important buffer between Russia and British India, became for a time the centre of the storm. Here the Persians, instigated by the Russians, interfered, and the British, to protect their interests, had to intervene. In doing this they suffered a serious reverse, a British army being forced to retreat in mid-winter and being annihilated in the mountain passes. Another expedition had to be sent to avenge this disaster. Lord Ellenborough (Governor-General, 1842–4) conquered Sind, giving Britain command of the mouth of the Indus, where the great port of Karachi (in modern Pakistan) later arose. Ellenborough's successor, Lord Hardinge (Governor-General, 1844–8) found himself at war with the Sikhs who had crossed the Sutlej into British territory. Two wars were fought with the Sikhs, the first in 1845, the second in 1848–9. The Sikhs were the most formidable enemies the British had yet met in the subcontinent, and in the second war against them things were 'touch and go'. Had it not been for the British victory at Gujarat in 1849, it is quite possible that their empire in India

The British Empire in India

would either have shrunk vastly or have collapsed altogether. But an even greater trial was in store for the British, namely the Indian Mutiny of 1857.

The Indian Mutiny marks the division between the two periods of British rule in India, namely 1757–1857, 1857–1947; but before the events of 1857 are related, it is desirable to review the pre-mutiny record of the British in broad outline.

The Governor-Generalship which throws the strongest light on British pre-mutiny policy and achievement is that of Lord William Bentinck (Governor of Bengal, 1827–33; Governor-General, 1833–5). Bentinck had come under the influence of Jeremy Bentham, the apostle of Utilitarianism (whose motto was 'the greatest good of the greatest number') and on going to India Bentinck wrote to him, 'I shall govern in name, but it will be you who will govern in fact'.[1]

Bentinck soon came into collision with those who held that Britain should on no account interfere with Indian religion or religious practices. Things came to a head over the question of *Suttee*. *Suttee* was the ritual burning alive of Hindu widows on their husband's decease. In orthodox theory this practice was a voluntary action by the widow impatient for reunion with her god-husband, but in practice she was often compelled to sacrifice herself by relatives who wanted the prestige of a holy sacrifice in the family or one less mouth to feed. Sometimes the victim was led screaming to the funeral pyre. For the fifteen years previous to the suppression, recorded burnings in the Bengal Presidency had ranged from 500 to 850 a year. Governors-General had considered and shelved the problem for nearly thirty years: Bentinck acted. He made the practice illegal, with severe penalties, and the only reaction was a petition of protest by orthodox Hindus to the British Parliament.

Other Indian customs which Bentinck prohibited were child-sacrifice and infanticide.

Bentinck's period of rule was remarkable for a whole series of reforms, those of most permanent influence, perhaps, being in the field of education. He substituted English for Persian as the official language of government, and thus created a demand for education

[1] See Percival Spear, *India*, p. 256.

73

in English. The old school of 'Orientalists' opposed the change; Macaulay (stationed in India as a member of the Supreme Council, where he remained for four years) supported it. He poured scorn on Oriental languages and culture in general. Of Indian society, too, he had a poor opinion. 'To have found a great people sunk in the lowest depths of slavery and superstition, to have so ruled them as to have made them desirous and capable of all the privileges of citizens, would indeed be a title to a glory all our own', he declared on his return to England in a speech in the House of Commons. Macaulay's advocacy largely carried the day for the supporters of an English education against the Orientalists who favoured Persian or Sanskrit as the medium of instruction.

History in the long run may condemn, or applaud, Bentinck, Macaulay, and their generation, but whatever its final verdict it cannot be denied that they were at least sincere in their beliefs that 'Westernization' of their own special Victorian kind was best for the interests of India.

THE INDIAN MUTINY (1857)

The Indian Mutiny was not a 'Nationalist' rebellion, though it has sometimes been represented as such. India was still too divided by community and religion to think 'nationally'. Nor, on the other hand, was it a purely military mutiny, for it could not have spread as it did without a great degree of popular support.

There were in 1857 numerous groups in India with grievances against the government. One was those Indian princes who objected to the 'doctrine of lapse', introduced by Lord Dalhousie (Governor-General of India, 1848–56), whereby in default of a direct heir to a ruler who died, or an heir adopted with the Governor-General's approval, the state 'lapsed' to the British as the paramount power. There were also grievances arising from the claims to pensions of ex-sovereign families. But more influential than any disaffection among the princes as a cause of the Mutiny was the fear among both Hindus and Muslims that their religion was in danger. Bentinck's reforms (however humane and necessary) had cut at the very foundations of Indian tradition, and on this account it can be plausibly argued that he, more than anyone else, had sown the seeds of the Mutiny.

As is well known, the occasion of the actual outbreak was the 'greased cartridges' incident. These cartridges were supplied for the new Enfield rifle and had to be bitten before being placed in the rifle. The grease was said to contain the fat of cows (sacred to the Hindu) and pigs (impure to the Muslim) so that the two great religious elements in India were united for once in their grievances. The Hindu sepoys believed that the British were plotting to deprive them of their 'caste' (a necessary consequence of swallowing the fat of cows) while the Muslims believed that the aim was to alienate them from Islam—as a preliminary to converting them forcibly to Christianity. This was the spark which set off the explosion.

But no revolution can succeed without leadership. To whom could the mutineers look for leaders? The original mutineers at Meerut rose on 11 May 1857, shot their officers, marched to Delhi forty miles away, and compelled the aged Mogul Emperor Bahadur Shah (a pensioner of the British permitted to hold a 'shadow court') to become their leader. Shortly after, when the mutiny spread to Oudh, the Maratha leader Nana Sahib found himself in a like position. Thus it was that the mutineers aimed to revive two great rival empires—that of the Moguls and that of the Marathas, the first Muslim and the second Hindu. But neither faction could claim to stand for the great mass either of Indian Muslims or Indian Hindus.

The outcome of the mutiny was, considered in retrospect, a foregone conclusion. The British had only to hold out until adequate reinforcements became available. This they were able to do, and the mutiny was crushed. Yet the total strength of the East India Company's army in India in 1857 was only 238,000, of whom a mere 38,000 were Europeans. One factor which greatly helped the British in overcoming the mutiny was that the Sikhs remained neutral—among the sentiments that influenced them was a repugnance to the idea of a revived Mogul empire.

POST-MUTINY INDIA

Between the Mutiny and the end of the nineteenth century was a period of forty-three years, but the history of British India in those

years can be outlined in smaller space than can that of the previous
fifty-seven years, for the reason that it was mainly a time of peaceful
development, interrupted by no great wars, and peaceful development can be summarized in a few paragraphs without doing violence
to the facts.

The mutiny having been quelled, the concern of the British was
to see that it did not break out again, and that existing grievances
which had prepared the ground for the outbreak were removed.
To this end the entire government of British India was reorganized.
The East India Company, with its antiquated system of government, was abolished, and in 1858 an act of parliament was passed
enacting that in future India would be governed directly in the name
of the Crown, acting through a Secretary of State. On 1 November
the transfer to the Crown and the appointment of Lord Canning,
the then Governor-General, as the first Viceroy, was announced.
An amnesty was proclaimed for those concerned in the mutiny
except for those found guilty of murder, and it was declared there
should be no interference with religious beliefs, and that 'our subjects, of whatever race and creed should be impartially admitted to
office in our service, the duties of which they may be qualified by
their education, ability, and integrity to discharge'. The Bengal
army, which had been destroyed during the mutiny, was replaced
by a new force drawn chiefly from the martial races of northwest
India, though the other Presidency armies remained in existence
for some years to come.

The way was now open for progress and reform. The finances
of the country were reorganized, and new industries (e.g. indigo,
tea, and cotton) began to spring up. (The first cotton mill was
started in 1851—the germ, so to speak, of Indian industrialization.)
The universities of Calcutta, Madras, and Bombay had already been
opened in 1857, before the mutiny. Macaulay's plans for codifying
Indian law were completed; a rent act was passed to protect tenant
from landlord; the first step towards constitutional government was
taken by the introduction of the Indian Councils Act of 1861.
Public works on a large scale were undertaken, including irrigation
works and measures to prevent famine, the scourge of India (there
were famines in 1865, 1876, 1896, 1899, and 1943). These public

works will no doubt rank among the more lasting achievements of the British régime. Railways, roads, and canals were constructed on a large scale and these, as well as British law and education, remained in being after India and Pakistan had gained their independence.

One of the first acts of Lord Lytton when he was sent out as Viceroy by Disraeli in 1876 was to proclaim Queen Victoria as Empress of India (*Kaisar-i-Hind*). He also had instructions to deal with the Afghan question which was causing anxiety owing to further Russian advances in central Asia, but it was not until the invasion of Afghanistan by Lord Roberts that that country undertook to have no more dealings with foreign powers.

Under the Viceroyalty of a liberal peer, Lord Ripon, steps were taken to extend local government, but many educated Indians felt that the Indian Councils Act did not give them any real voice in the management of their own affairs. Then, in 1885, two retired members of the Indian Civil Service, Sir Allan Hume and Sir Henry Cotton, conceived the idea of forming an unofficial body, styling itself the Indian National Congress, 'to encourage sentiments of national unity'. This was to become the nucleus of the Indian Congress Party which was to bring India and Pakistan to independence and to remain the governing party in India for many years thereafter. Indian National Congress, however, remained very moderate in its aims until 1906 when the control of it was captured by Indian Nationalists with ambitions for speedy self-government.

But although the idea of independence for India had been born and was gaining ground among the Indian intelligentsia, the end of the century saw a Viceroy in office who had little sympathy with this notion. This was Lord Curzon (1899–1905). According to his convictions, there was no prospect that the Indians would be fit to govern themselves for many a year to come, and in the meantime the British must continue to accept the responsibility for good government imposed upon them by history. Curzon was imperiously-minded, and the reforms he instituted from above were exclusively in the interests of efficiency—not democracy. In many fields (taxation, land-tenancy, agriculture, cattle-breeding, university education, co-operative credit societies, famine-relief, preservation of ancient monuments, etc., etc.) he took the initiative with beneficial results, but without consulting popular opinion. One innovation he introduced, the partition of Bengal, was rescinded in 1911, but Bengal was once more partitioned when India and Pakistan became separate and independent states in 1947.

As the century closed, the British Raj in India was, to all appearances, likely to last indefinitely.

THE OPIUM WAR

Except for its short burst of naval enterprise in the fifteenth century (see p. 9) and its limited contacts with Roman Catholic missionaries, China remained aloof from the rest of the world until its seclusion was breached by Britain in the war of 1839–42. The 'Middle Kingdom' (as China called itself) was in Chinese theory the only civilized country 'under heaven' (*T'ien hsia*) and all those outside it were 'barbarians' (*i*). Thus China could have no dealings on an equality with other countries and all envoys from abroad were treated as tribute-bearers. With Russia alone was China in treaty relations (from 1689), but in this case a formula was found in receiving the Russian ambassador to 'save the face' of the Czar. Foreign trade was tolerated, but not encouraged, and from 1757 onwards was confined to the single port of Canton.

Complete isolation is good for no country in the long run, and although China had been ahead of the West in technology until the end of the Middle Ages, it had fallen behind in this respect by the time that contact with Europe, interrupted for over two hundred years, was resumed in the late Ming period. The Jesuits who came to China in the late sixteenth and early seventeenth centuries to convert the Chinese to Christianity were, for example, more proficient in mathematics than the Chinese, and were able to reform the Chinese calendar, foretell eclipses, etc. But the Catholic mission failed because the Jesuit policy of regarding Chinese ancestor-worship as a purely civil observance was rejected by the Vatican, and, moreover, the Emperor of China and the Pope differed as to the correct Chinese translation for the word 'God'. In 1724 the teaching of Christianity was forbidden altogether in China, a ban that was not to be fully lifted until 1858.

There had long been friction between the Chinese authorities at Canton and the foreign merchants, owing to their different ideas of law and justice, but the latter were for long prepared to put up with the humiliating conditions under which they lived because of the large profits of the trade (they were not allowed in the city of Canton, could not bring their wives to their 'factories', had to withdraw to Macao between the trading seasons, and could deal with the Chinese authorities only through the Chinese *Hong* (or monopoly) merchants). It was to be expected, however, that the Western nations, which were growing strong with their superior techniques and their industrialization, would not be willing indefinitely to submit to unequal treatment in their dealings with the Chinese.

Unfortunately, when the collision between China and Britain took place, it was on the issue of the illegal importation of opium. From 1834 onwards there had been a deadlock between the Chinese and the British over the question of the recognition of Britain on an equality with China, but in 1839 the seizure of the foreign stocks of opium as contraband by the Commissioner Lin Tse-Hsü, in a new drive to suppress the traffic in this drug, led to the outbreak of hostilities. The British attitude regarding the seizure of the opium cannot be plausibly defended, but it can be said in extenuation of this attitude that much more than the opium was at issue in the war and that was the claim of Britain to be treated on an equality with China. Had there been British diplomatic representation at Peking at the time it is likely that war could have been avoided.

As it happened, however, the war revealed the complete military inferiority of the Chinese. So long had they been immune from invasion that their strategy was little more than a ritual observance, their guns were inferior and outranged, their ships outsailed (quite apart from the fact that the British also used gun-boats propelled by steam). The Chinese were defeated in every action, but by delaying tactics in their negotiations with the enemy were able to postpone the outcome for over two years. But in 1842 they signed the Treaty of Nanking whereby China agreed to pay an indemnity to Britain and to open six ports in the South of China to foreign trade. Nevertheless, had there not been a weak alien dynasty (the Ch'ing, or Manchu, 1644–1912) on the throne which feared that the prolongation of the war might lead to its own collapse, it is improbable that a huge country like China, with a population of some 300 million, would have accepted a humiliating peace imposed by a force of foreign troops which never exceeded 9,000 men.

China had in the past several times been conquered by barbarian invaders, but the conquerors had speedily been absorbed into the Chinese civilization and had become 'more Chinese than the Chinese', but this defeat at the hands of the West opened up an entirely new chapter in Chinese history. The very existence of Chinese civilization was henceforth to be challenged by an alien one based on entirely different principles.

CHINA'S RESISTANCE TO CHANGE

Modern historical research suggests that it is wrong to assume that Chinese society had at any stage 'stagnated', since in fact it was constantly, though slowly and almost imperceptibly, undergoing change. Nevertheless, China's isolation for so long a time, uninfluenced by external forces, had led to its being completely self-contained and uninterested in what was happening elsewhere. The consequence was that its society had become very set in its ways. The Opium War made it clear without a shadow of doubt that whatever the virtues of the Chinese 'way of life', China was utterly antiquated in its weapons and its strategy, and therefore in no position to resist its enemies. Yet for nearly twenty years after the war no serious action was taken towards modernizing the country.

The Manchus, being barbarian in origin with no important culture of their own, had 'taken colour' from the people they had subdued, and were ultra-conservative in their outlook. Supported in this conservatism by the Chinese mandarins, their first reaction to defeat was to withdraw even further into isolation. No provision had been made in the Treaty of Nanking for stationing foreign envoys at the capital, which made this isolation easier to enforce. Moreover, the southern provinces, especially Kwangtung (of which Canton was the capital), did not co-operate in carrying out the terms of the Nanking Treaty and trouble with the foreigners ensued. At the same time, other Western Powers, beginning with the United States of America, brought pressure on China to sign treaties with them conceding the same privileges of trade and extraterritoriality that had been conceded under the Nanking and subsidiary treaties to Britain.

A feature of these early treaties was what became known as 'the most favoured nation' clause whereby China, in conceding new privileges to foreign countries thereafter, automatically made the same concessions to the countries whose treaties with China contained this clause. This meant that China was increasingly tied up with treaty obligations—which she was always trying to circumvent.

The reluctance of the Manchus to concede diplomatic equality to the foreigners, coupled with the obstructiveness of the southern provinces, led eventually to another war (1857–60) in which Britain and France were allies against China. China was again easily defeated, and signed new treaties (at Tientsin in 1858, and Peking, 1860) whereby new concessions were made—ports north of the Yangtze were opened to foreign trade and Britain and France were given the right to station envoys in Peking. By the same treaties, foreign missionaries were permitted to operate in the interior, and to own property, etc.—a privilege that was to have far-reaching effects. Other Powers later obtained similar treaties.

Meanwhile the Manchus were faced by a rebellion on a much greater scale than had hitherto threatened them, namely the Taiping Rebellion (1851–62). The rebels occupied a huge area of Southern and Central China, and it looked for a while as if the days of the Manchu dynasty were numbered. The original Taiping leader, Hung Hsiu-Chuan, claimed to base his new order of society on a Christianity of his own devising (in which he figured himself as the 'Younger Brother of Christ'), but in spite of this the Western Powers were not drawn to his support. For some years the British were officially neutral, but in the end supported the Manchus (notably through General Gordon's 'Ever-Victorious Army') and this undoubtedly influenced the final outcome. Nevertheless, it was the fact that the Chinese mandarins rallied to the Manchu cause under the banner of Confucianism that was the decisive factor in bringing about the defeat of the Taipings. As a consequence of the rebellion the Manchus found themselves less than ever in a position to resist foreign pressure and infiltration. The creation of the Chinese Maritime Customs, headed for many years by an Irishman, Sir Robert Hart, was a notable example of the management of Chinese affairs by foreigners, and, whatever the loss to Chinese sovereignty, it must be admitted that it was greatly to the advantage of efficiency and the Chinese revenues.

The new defeat at the hands of the foreigner induced the Chinese to adopt a certain number of modern innovations. These included the creation of a new sub-committee under the Grand Council to deal with foreign countries (the Tsungli Yamen), the starting of a Western-trained Manchu army armed with Russian guns, and the establishment of a government school at Peking for the training of interpreters, the Tung Wen Kuan (financed and indirectly controlled by the Imperial Maritime Customs). But these innovations were half-hearted, and aimed at adopting some of the apparent sources of Western strength while leaving Chinese society fundamentally unchanged. There was to be a further wave of reform, including the beginnings of industrialization, led by the great mandarins such as Li Hung-Chang (1823–1901). But when the 'modernization' of China was finally put to the test in 1894–5, during the war with Japan, it turned out to be a hollow sham.

COMMODORE PERRY REACHES JAPAN (1853)

While China, under the impact of the West, was retreating into its shell, another Far-Eastern country, Japan, was reacting very differently to the Western challenge.

Japan, as we have seen, retired behind its 'bamboo curtain' in the 1630s. It was not so much fear of foreign conquest that led the Tokugawa government to close the country but a fear that its own position in the state with relation to the 'feudal' and other elements might be undermined by the alliance of the latter with the foreigner. (The Shoguns, it should be explained, were the hereditary commanders-in-chief of Japan and had for centuries relegated the emperors to semi-divine seclusion at Kyoto, conducting the government themselves.)

But while physically secluded from outer influences, it must not be thought that Japan was altogether cut off from knowledge of the West. Through the Dutch settlement on the tiny artificial island of Deshima in Nagasaki Bay, the importation of works in Western languages (which in practice meant books written in Dutch) was allowed from 1716 onwards. The Japanese thus learnt at second— or third—hand of developments abroad. Towards the end of the eighteenth century foreign ships appeared in Japanese waters— but the foreigners were always rebuffed in their efforts to establish contacts with Japan. But the pressure of circumstances was to prove too powerful for the Shogunate to resist. It learnt (through Deshima) of the easy defeat of the Chinese in the Opium War, and therefore had previous warning of the strength of the forces they would have to meet if the Western Powers switched their attention to Japan. Nor was Japanese society in the same sluggish, almost static condition as that of China, and a movement away from feudalism towards capitalism had been taking place long before Japan's isolation was challenged.

With the increasing aggressiveness of the West, it seemed to be a matter of chance which of the Powers would be first to attempt to pierce Japan's curtain. The most likely was Russia or Britain. The Russian colonization of Siberia and the consequent pressure on China's northeastern front was proceeding apace (to culminate in the Russian occupation of the Amur basin in 1860), and in extension of their eastern drive, a Russian Admiral (Putyatin) was on his way to Japan with his fleet, empowered to sign a commercial treaty, only to find (in August 1853) that an American squadron had already appeared under Commodore Matthew Perry and had presented what amounted to an ultimatum to the Shogunate.

It was the development of American trade with Canton, the growth of the American whaling industry in the Pacific, the opening-up of California following the Gold Rush of 1849, and the progress of steam navigation that had prepared the way for Perry's mission. To secure coal supplies and the future good treatment of any American shipwrecked sailors were among Perry's aims, and the prospect of opening up trade with a closed country like Japan was probably less important since more incalculable in its advantages.

Perry's 'Black Ships', as they were known, four of them driven by steam, caused a tremendous sensation. Perry presented his demands, and then sailed away, returning six months later for an answer and in command of an even more powerful fleet. The Japanese hesitated. Quite obviously their naval and military resources were no match for those of the United States, and a blockade could easily starve the Shogunate capital of Yedo. So they decided to compromise while endeavouring to strengthen their defences.

The period that followed Perry's arrival was one of great tension and confusion in Japan. Whether or not the Shogunate would have survived had it not been for foreign intervention is the subject of debate, but it seems that internal developments were in any case preparing the way for a change. Economic forces were favouring the growth of a merchant capitalist class which was undermining the Shogunate administration (the *bakufu*). This may well be so, but the fact remains that the shock caused to the *Samurai* class (of professional warriors) by the advent of the foreigners was catastrophic, and this entailed a collapse of the military organization intended to resist the foreign onslaught.

THE MEIJI RESTORATION (1868–1912)

During this decisive decade the centre of political gravity shifted from the Shogunate capital, Yedo, to the ancient imperial capital, Kyoto. These years saw the abolition of feudalism, the indispensable prelude to modernization. The feudal lords 'restored' their territories to the emperor who now (1868) reassumed (or assumed for the first time in Japanese history, as Sir George Sansom believes) the full powers of government. The Shogunate was abolished. A tremendous programme of reform was thereupon inaugurated. A central, modernized system of taxation was established with a new system of coinage. Japan thereupon proceeded to copy in some degree the whole apparatus of Western civilization from banks, railways, lighthouses, telegraphs, printing, and newspapers down to cigars and cigarettes. The legal system was reformed with such effect that before the end of the century the Powers no longer had an excuse for retaining extraterritoriality. A measure of popular government was also introduced, and (in 1889) a constitution—which, however, retained the fullest administrative powers and a quasi-divine status for the emperor. A new army was created—at first on the model of the French army, but when France was defeated by Prussia in 1870 the model followed was that of the Prussian army (sentiment, we see, played no part in this revolution). The Japanese navy was simultaneously remodelled on the pattern of the British, the most powerful and up-to-date navy of the time. Japan was thus in a short space of years transformed into a modern state.

But one characteristic of the Meiji Restoration was outstanding and must by no means be overlooked, and that was that in copying the West the Japanese singled out only those things for imitation that they thought would strengthen their country, and aimed (with success) to keep their basic institutions essentially Japanese. This was what the Chinese had failed to do: their reforms were purely superficial.

In copying the West it was natural that the Japanese should choose those features of Western policy that were proving so eminently successful. One of those was 'Imperialism', the urge to expand in influence and territory. Japan, a small country, entered in its 'industrial revolution' in the last decade of the nineteenth century (some of the new industry, it must be admitted, however, was of a mushroom nature) and was looking for markets abroad. The obvious place to find them was Japan's huge neighbour, China. This quest for markets and territory required naval and military backing. It was here that there arose a conflict between the party in Japan which favoured an aggressive policy and the 'peaceful expansionists', but at the moments of decision the military party's counsels prevailed. Thus it was that Japan coveted Korea (a Chinese tributary) which resulted in the Sino-Japanese War of 1894–5.

THE SINO-JAPANESE WAR (1894–5), THE REFORM MOVEMENT
IN CHINA, AND THE BOXER UPRISING (1900)

China, as we have seen, failed to modernize itself, and when challenged by Japan, which had adapted itself to the new situation with amazing speed, was swiftly defeated. In 1895, by the Treaty of Shimonoseki, Japan not only seized Formosa and demanded a huge indemnity, but was now an Imperial Power on its own account and able to claim equality of opportunity with other Powers. And this meant in the first place an equality of opportunity to exploit the prostrate giant, its own one time teacher, China.

Up to 1895 the British had supported China as a bulwark against Russia, but the outcome of the Sino-Japanese War demonstrated in spectacular fashion that China was quite incapable of defending herself. During all those years, too, the traditional economy of China had been subject to undermining by foreign capitalist enterprise and was by the 1890s completely dislocated, and since the concentration of trade and economic power in the 'treaty ports' brought no compensating advantage to the inhabitants of the vast interior of China, this fact alone was enough to create a state of widespread discontent which prepared the way for civil commotion.

The complete defencelessness of China at this juncture resulted in a scramble among the foreign Powers for concessions of all sorts to exploit the resources of the country—its minerals, its forests, its river-traffic—and to lend it money. It seemed now that the empire under the effete Manchu dynasty, might break into pieces at any moment, and by carving up the country into 'spheres of influence' the Powers were preparing the way for its political partition. Germany obtained a foothold at Kiaochow, France at Kwangchowwan, and even Britain, which had striven to prevent further inroads on Chinese territory, felt compelled to secure a lease of Weihaiwei to offset Russia's occupation of Port Arthur.

What could the Chinese do to save their ancient country from break-up and partition? The Japanese had succeeded in modernizing themselves to meet the Western challenge with great success. Why had the Chinese failed to do so? The answers were many and various—the far greater size of China, its greater conservatism, and (perhaps more important than all) the fact that there was a decadent Manchu dynasty on the throne, weakened still further by the Taiping and other great rebellions and the encroachment of the foreigner. The measures to industrialize China and to strengthen its armed forces taken by the more progressive mandarins had proved quite inadequate for the purpose. Could anything effective still be done before it was too late?

Certain of the Chinese intellectuals thought that the answer was Yes. Outstanding among them were K'ang Yu-Wei, and his lieutenant, Liang Ch'i-Ch'ao. Both of them were scholars educated under the old classical system of education, but they were nevertheless men of vision. Their belief was that China could be radically reformed within the framework of the existing Chinese dynasty, the Ch'ing. K'ang Yu-Wei obtained the ear of the young Kuang Hsü emperor, Tsai-t'ien, and persuaded him to initiate a programme of far-reaching reform. In the summer and early autumn of 1898 in what are known as 'The Hundred Days of Reform', the emperor issued a series of startling decrees, abolishing the old examination system, reforming the army, establishing a university at Peking, on modern lines, and introducing a score of innovations copied from the West. Most of those reforms remained on paper, however, for the Empress Dowager Tz'u Hsi, the real ruler of China, became alarmed, since she learnt that the reformers intended to remove her as the great obstacle to progress. Relying on the support of the armed forces, she staged a *coup d'état* in September when Yuan Shih-K'ai betrayed the emperor's plans to her. The emperor was imprisoned in the Imperial palace, and K'ang and Liang fled abroad. Those reformers who could not escape, or who refused to do so, were executed, and most of the reform decrees were rescinded by Tz'u Hsi. In the end the only creation of the 'Hundred Days' which survived the reaction that now set in was the University of Peking (as it does to this day under very different auspices). The ambitious move had failed.

Meanwhile, an anti-Manchu revolutionary had staged an unsuccessful rebellion in Canton (1895). This was Sun Yat-Sen, destined to be the leader of revolutionary China in later years—but the time was yet not ripe for his success.

There now ensued a movement of a very different kind from the 'Hundred Days', culminating in a widespread rebellion, namely the Boxer Uprising.

The Boxers were a secret society, connected with the White

Lotus, which first came to official notice in the eighteenth century. The White Lotus and its affiliated societies had always been associated with rebellion. Another associated society, the Great Sword, had been active in stirring up resistance to the Germans in Shantung when they occupied Kiaochow in 1898. The Boxers first re-emerged, after many decades of quiescence, in Shantung in May 1898. They worshipped the gods (both Taoist and Buddhist) of the popular novels and plays and practised ritual 'boxing' which was connected with the Taoist cult of longevity—and hence of 'invulnerability'. They exploited the prevailing discontent arising from famine and economic distress and dislike of foreigners (especially missionaries) and soon gained a large following among the peasantry. To begin with, they were 'anti-dynastic' (i.e. aiming to dethrone the Manchus), but having suffered a reverse at the hands of Government troops, they were won over to the side of the Manchus.

Alarmed by the growing menace of the Boxers, the foreign ministers in Peking called up their legation guards from Tientsin. The Boxers entered Peking (June 1900) and when the foreigners reduced the Taku forts to secure the retreat of a foreign relief force, a state of war was declared by the Chinese Court. For eight weeks the legations were besieged, but were then relieved by a much larger force of the eight associated Powers (Britain, France, Russia, Germany, Japan, Austria-Hungary, Italy, and the United States). The Empress Dowager and her court fled from Peking into the interior of China the day that the legations were relieved. The uprising thereupon collapsed.

The Powers now imposed a humiliating peace on China, condemning it to pay a large indemnity (£67 million) under the terms of the Boxer Protocol (1901). The signing of the Protocol marked the lowest ebb of China's fortunes in its long history.

Since the Boxers represented a widespread popular movement extending to all parts of the country, they are regarded by the present-day Chinese (notably the Communists) as the virtual founders of Chinese Nationalism. Hitherto China's policy had been dictated by dynastic or provincial interests; henceforth a really national movement was to develop aimed at getting rid of the alien Manchus and restoring China to its position as a great united country. Moreover, the Powers gave up the idea of partitioning China.

THE INFLUENCE OF EVENTS IN INDIA AND CHINA AND JAPAN ON SOUTHEAST ASIA

To what extent did these happenings inside the two great territorial blocs to the west and east of Southeast Asia influence affairs in this intermediate region in the nineteenth century?

The answer must be—in no very spectacular fashion, but nevertheless in some appreciable ways.

Although the Straits Settlements were under India until 1867, the Indian government paid little attention to them. They were principally interested in them as places to which to send their convicts. The effects of the Indian Mutiny did not extend to the Straits Settlements, which remained remote and quiet. The Malay States, too, were concerned with India mainly in respect of the South Indian (Tamil) labourers who were brought in in considerable numbers from the late nineteenth century onwards to work on the sugar, coffee, and (later) the rubber estates. There was also a small colony of Madrasi Muslim, Tamil, and other Indian traders in the towns. But the Indians in Malaya were not yet 'politically-minded'.

Chinese immigration into Southeast Asia had continued to be on a limited scale for the greater part of the century, but it increased with the opening-up of the tin-mines in the Malay Peninsula and Indonesia and was (in the twentieth century) to amount to a flood. The Overseas Chinese, who came almost exclusively from Kwangtung and Fukien, kept up their contacts with their families at home, but did not yet import their Nationalism—for it did not yet exist. Striking evidence of this is afforded by the fact that when Lord Elgin called at Singapore in 1857, on his way to conduct war against China, he was entertained to dinner by the Singapore Chinese merchants. About the same time, the Chinese Secret Societies in Southeast Asia were reinforced by Taiping rebels who were in flight from China, and the same rebellion caused the exodus of rebellious elements into Tongking where they took part in local uprisings (see p. 66).

Altogether, India and China, which had so greatly influenced Southeast Asia in the first millennium or so of its history, made comparatively little impact on the region from 1800 to 1900. This emphatically was a 'European century' in Southeast Asia. As for modern Japan, it had scarcely yet appeared on the scene.

5

THE COLONIAL RÉGIME AT ITS ZENITH, 1900-39

TIN AND RUBBER IN MALAYA

Political maps have their uses, but they can sometimes be highly misleading. For example, a political map of Southeast Asia in 1900 would not differ very greatly from a political map of the same region in 1940. For the most part, the same areas would be labelled 'British Malaya', 'Dutch East Indies', 'French Indochina', etc., in both maps. But the colouring or shading would be uniform over every area, suggesting that they were administered or developed to the same extent in 1900 as in 1940. This, of course, would be completely misleading. All these colonial countries had undergone the most intensive economic development in the intervening forty years, and the population had vastly increased. It is true that even at the end of the colonial period the region still offered almost unlimited scope for further development, could support a much larger population than it then did, and that pockets of it still remained unadministered, or even unexplored—but this fact does not detract from the achievement during this phase. The wealth of the region had been enormously increased and it now possessed the means for further expansion. But these developments would not figure in a purely political map.

A case in point is Malaya. The Malay States had a total population of well below half a million in 1850; in 1931 it was some four millions (in 1957 the Federation's population was 6,277,000; that of Singapore 1,446,000). It is obvious that it would have been impossible to maintain such a greatly increased population without a corresponding exploitation of the country's resources. Moreover, the standard of living for the majority was much higher in 1931 than it was in 1850. And, without greatly increased revenues, it would have been impossible for the governments to have paid for the social services that were built up in the period—notably for health, education, welfare and housing. Indeed, most of Southeast Asia passed through a phase of development not dissimilar from that through which Western countries had passed during the earlier stages of the Industrial Revolution. The Malay States can be taken as an example, though the circumstances helping the change were more favourable than elsewhere.

After the crisis of the short war of 1875 peace was restored in the Malay States, and while the successive British Residents were working out the 'Resident System' in close association with the Malay rulers and paying the greatest respect to Malay opinion, they were simultaneously reorganizing the collection of the revenues and endeavouring to increase them. As regards agriculture, rice and coconuts were the basic crops, and continued to be so, but the aim of the administration was to diversify the crops and to move forward from a purely 'subsistence' agriculture (whereby the people merely grew enough food to live on) to the growing of 'cash-crops' (whereby money became available for development and for improving the standard of living). To feed the growing population great new rice fields were opened up, and new cash-crops were experimented with. The Chinese were successful sugar-growers, for example, and in Perak the government introduced the cultivation of the pepper-vine and thus created a new industry. In this same state, Sir Hugh Low started government plantations and gardens, and large sums were spent on the introduction and cultivation of Arabian coffee, cinchona (for quinine), tea, and (most significantly as will in a moment be seen) rubber. However, the great days of rubber still lay in the future, and the main source of revenue for the first decades of British protection was tin.

The mining of gold and other metals in the Malay Peninsula had been carried on from time immemorial, but tin became in the eighteenth and nineteenth centuries by far the most important of the metals, and in the twentieth century accounted for some 90 per cent of all the mining in Malaya. But up to the middle of the nineteenth century the industry was still carried on on a comparatively small scale. It was the influx of Chinese miners with improved techniques and backed by Chinese capital from the Straits Settlements which first enlarged its scope (though at the same time it caused political complications—as has been seen). The Malay chiefs granted mining concessions to the Chinese, and in addition to drawing rents and royalties from the tin-mines, were sometimes in partnership with the Chinese miners.

The Malay method was *lampan* mining, using a stream of water to wash away the earth from the tin-ore, but the Chinese introduced the open-cast *lombong* method, whereby a large hole was dug, the tin-bearing soil was carried to the surface in baskets and was washed in a trough of running water to separate the ore from the earth. The 'tailings' (refuse from mining) were sometimes washed a second time by women and children, using wooden pans. In solving the problems of flooding and of a controlled water-supply the Chinese miners showed great ingenuity, but they were not slow in adopting the greatly improved methods which were now coming in from Europe (the by-products of the same Scientific Revolution whose importance has already been stressed). One of these was the steam-engine and centrifugal pump imported by the famous Capitan China Yap Ah Loy who had seen the specimens put on show by Sir Hugh Low.

By 1904 Malaya was producing about 50,000 tons of tin annually, more than half the world's output. But the further expansion of the industry under the conditions of world competition which was yearly increasing needed more modern methods and much greater capital which only the West could supply. European capital was slow in entering the tin industry in Malaya, and had practically withdrawn when a short boom (1882–4) came to an end, and did not return on any scale until the beginning of the twentieth century. At this time the bulk of the tin-mines were Chinese-owned, and up to 1912 the Chinese still produced some 80 per cent of Malaya's tin, but the introduction of the tin-dredge completely changed the situation and revolutionized the industry. The first tin-dredge was imported in 1912. These dredges could operate in swampy land and could profitably exploit land too poor in ore to be profitably worked by the older methods. But a tin-dredge was extremely costly and involved a capital outlay beyond the resources of Malayan Chinese tin companies. Thus it was that the Europeans more and more increased their share in the industry, and in spite of some losses to Chinese enterprise during the 'Emergency' (1948–60), it still represented about 60 per cent of the total in the 1960s.

The effect of this development was early reflected in a rapid increase in the revenues of the Malay States. In 1876 the total combined revenue of the three states of Perak, Selangor, and Sungei Ujong was M$ 561,000; in 1888 it was $3,658,000. In 1897, the revenue of the Federated Malay States (Perak, Selangor, Negri Sembilan, and Pahang) was $8,297,000; in the peak year of 1927 it was $105,404,000; in 1901 the revenue of the Straits Settlements was $7,042,000; in 1937 it was $37,848,000. The great increase was largely due to the export duties on a new product—*rubber*.[1] The cultivation of rubber was destined to turn Malaya into one of the best-off countries in the Far East, with a *per capita* income higher than any other country in the region except Japan.

The story has often been told of the expedition of Sir Henry Wickham to Brazil (1876) when he obtained some 70,000 rubber seeds. From Kew, where those seeds germinated in the hot-houses, seedlings were sent to British tropical colonies, including Ceylon. From Ceylon twenty-two plants reached Singapore in 1877—some were planted in the Botanical Gardens in Singapore; others were planted in Sir Hugh Low's garden at Kuala Kangsar. Such were the origins of the great rubber industry in Malaya and beyond.

Yet by 1897 (twenty years after the arrival of the first rubber seedlings) only 345 acres were under rubber and in 1905 only 200 tons of rubber were produced in Malaya. However, by 1910, stimulated by the rapid development of the motor-car with its need for tyres, a rubber boom was at its height. Rubber had first become profitable in 1906, but henceforth the industry went ahead, checked only by a minor world slump in 1921, and a much greater one from 1930–2. By 1937, under a restriction scheme, Malaya had some 3,302,170 acres under rubber, 2,026,348 being estates of over 100 acres each (both European and Asian owned), and over 1,275,822 being Asian smallholdings. The net export of rubber from Malaya

[1] The Malayan dollar was stabilized in 1904 at the exchange rate of 2/4d. (sterling).

in 1937 was 681,638 tons, accounting for 47·8 per cent of the exports (1930) and making the largest contribution to the Malayan revenues.

The disadvantage of having, so to speak, 'all one's eggs in two baskets' became ominously clear in the time of world trade depressions, when the price of rubber and tin dropped to extremely low levels. Attempts, therefore, were constantly being made to diversify Malaya's economy, especially in agricultural production, and as well as coconuts (which had always been grown, and which accounted for some 600,000 acres in 1938), African oil palms, pineapples, vegetables, fruit, tapioca, sago, sugar, tea, areca nut, cloves, chillies, etc., were grown in increasing quantities.

The history of Malaya in those years is (as Winstedt points out) 'mainly statistical'.

PROGRESS IN TRANSPORT, PUBLIC WORKS, HYGIENE, AND EDUCATION

With these greatly enlarged revenues it was possible for the Malayan governments to proceed with development on a considerable scale.

The primary requirement in the interests of industry was a modern system of communications. In 1874 the only internal means of communication (as has been mentioned earlier) were the rivers and local jungle-paths. In the first place the new communications were largely to facilitate the mining of tin. The pattern of communications included, by the turn of the century, cart-roads, railways, ports, and coastal steamship services. By 1906, the Federated Malay States had approximately 1,600 miles of metalled cart-roads and 270 miles of unmetalled roads. After the First World War the system was greatly extended, largely with tarred roads, to meet the requirements of motor vehicles. By 1937 the length of roads in the Federated Malay States alone was 4,558 miles, of which 2,939 were metalled, and of these 2,183 were surfaced with bitumen. The early railway lines were short ones running from tin areas to the west coast (that from Taiping to Port Weld was opened in 1885; from Kuala Lumpur to Bukit Kuda (1886), and later to Port Swettenham (1899)). The main trunk line in the west from north to south linking Johore Bahru and Penang was finished in 1909; in 1918 the northern end was joined to the Siamese railway. Another line, the east coast railway through Pahang and Kelantan, was not completed until 1931.

The extension of these communications necessitated, of course, the building of many bridges, and the growth of the towns entailed the erection of public buildings, drainage systems, sewage farms, and the like. The care of public health, moreover, presented an ever-increasing problem. It was in connexion with the latter that Malaya (in common with Burma and the Dutch, French, and American colonies) achieved the most striking and beneficial results.

The establishment of Town Sanitary Boards was a very important step towards the improvement of urban health and hygiene. Hospitals were built all over the country, and in 1900 an Institute of Medical Research was established at Kuala Lumpur to investigate tropical diseases both in men and animals. But the most widely known measures taken were those for the control of malaria—the 'bugbear of the tropics'. Sir Ronald Ross had discovered in 1897–8 that the disease was conveyed by the female anopheles mosquito, and this discovery was first of all put to practical use in Malaya. By systematic drainage and the oiling of streams (to create a film on the surface to prevent the *larvae* (young) of the mosquito from coming to the surface to breathe), the death rate from malaria was vastly reduced. But these preventive measures were very expensive, and had it not been for the revenues from rubber and tin, Malaya could not have afforded them. During their occupation of Malaya (1941–5), the Japanese discontinued these anti-malarial measures with the result that malignant malaria (the variety that was so often fatal) immediately resumed its ravages and many thousands died.

As regards education, this was in the early days left to individuals or groups, including religious missionaries. The latter were early in the field and opened schools soon after British rule or protection had been established. They afterwards received grants-in-aid from the government, but were mainly supported by voluntary donations. Government schools came later. Their beginnings were modest, but by the 1930s a very extensive educational system had been built up.

In the Malay States the emphasis was naturally on the Malay

language and in the Malay schools there were no fees and attendance was compulsory for all Malay boys between the ages of seven and fourteen who lived within one and a half miles of a school (there were about 1,500 of these in the Malay States alone by 1939). A Malay College was established at Kuala Kangser in 1905 mainly for the training of the sons of princely Malay families for a career in the Malayan Civil Service.

Since English was the administrative language of Malaya, there was in consequence a considerable demand for education in it, and it was the medium for all secondary and higher education. The King Edward VII College of Medicine was established in Singapore in 1910, and this was combined with Raffles College to form the University of Malaya after the liberation of the country from the Japanese. Technical and vocational education were also provided for on a considerable scale.

Although many thousands of Chinese in Malaya attended the English schools, there was not room in them for all Chinese of school age, and in any case the rise of Chinese Nationalism had created a demand for education in the Chinese language. The original Chinese schools were all 'Old Style' (teaching the classical 'Four Books'), but after the Revolution of 1911 the medium of instruction was *Kuo Yü* (a form of Mandarin). Chinese schools sprang up everywhere, and while they were reluctant in the early years to apply for government grants-in-aid (since to do so limited their independence) most of them applied for them during and after the great slump of 1930–2. The Chinese schools, most of whose teachers came from China, became the centres of the spread of Chinese Nationalism and also, to a smaller extent, of Chinese Communism and this brought some of them into conflict with the local authorities.

Indian vernacular schools were few in number in Malaya until 1912 when the Labour Code first obliged rubber and other estates of over 100 acres to maintain schools for the children of the workers, who were mostly Southern Indians. But Indian vernacular education remained on a low level of efficiency until well in the 1920s.

These facts are selected to indicate the progress made in Malaya between the beginnings of British protection and the Japanese invasion of 1941–2. The history of Malaya in these years is indeed to be found mostly in the annual reports of the Residents and Advisers in the Malay States and of the Colonial Secretary in the Straits Settlements. The purely political events in the period were few and can be briefly enumerated. In 1909, a Federal Council was created in the Federated Malay States (FMS), including representation of the non-Malayan communities. In the same year the four northern Malay States (Kedah, Perlis, Kelantan, and Trengganu) were transferred from the suzerainty of Siam to that of Great Britain, and treaties with the Rulers were entered into on the same lines as those concluded with the other Malay States. It was hoped that the unfederated States would join the Federation, but since this for several reasons did not take place, a policy of decentralization was introduced in 1935 whereby a large measure of sovereignty was restored to the individual Federated Malay States.

In this chapter special attention is given to the material progress in Malaya in the Colonial Period, but what happened in Malaya also happened in varying degrees in the other Colonial territories of Southeast Asia, and this must be kept in mind when progress in Burma and the history of Dutch, French, and American colonies or protectorates comes to be summarized. The Colonial policies differed in some important respects, but the metropolitan powers were united in their aim of stimulating 'development', which meant exploiting the natural resources of their territories and creating new wealth. All of them were heirs of the Scientific Revolution.

A 'PLURAL SOCIETY' ARISES IN SOUTHEAST ASIA

One effect of the European régime in Southeast Asia was the creation of what has become known as a 'Plural Society' in the European dependencies. This meant a society composed of two or more racial communities living side by side but without inter-marrying to any extent, with differing standards of life, and without a common culture. This was particularly the case in Malaya, and to a lesser extent in Siam, Indonesia, and French Indochina. The 'Plural Society' also existed in a measure in Burma (where large-scale Indian immigration had taken place), and with respect to the Filipinos and the small Chinese minority in the Philippines.

A 'Plural Society' arises in Southeast Asia

The direct cause of the 'Plural Society' was immigration on a large scale to meet the demands for labour and to man the services created by the economic opening-up of the Southeast Asian countries. Hitherto the volume of immigration had been small, but with its increase to a flood (as in the case of Chinese immigration into Malaya and Siam), the new arrivals more and more formed communities separate from the indigenous peoples. This development has been made the subject of criticism of the Colonial Period, and it undoubtedly created an obstacle to the growth of nationalities in the region, but whether or not it was a disadvantage in the long run for these countries or otherwise is a matter for debate.

In the case of Malaya, the Chinese had for centuries been coming down from China and had formed small communities in many centres. The earlier immigrants were exclusively males, and their ambition was to make a fortune and to return to China, but, needless to say, the majority did not manage to do this and remained where they were. The Muslim religion was an obstacle to their obtaining Malay wives, and many married women from non-Muslim races, including Balinese slaves. (In the Buddhist countries, such as Burma, Siam, and Vietnam, the barrier of religion did not exist, and through intermarriage the Chinese immigrants were usually absorbed into the local community within two or three generations.) But with the establishment of European power, ensuring peaceful conditions for trade and labour, the numbers of Chinese immigrants greatly increased. In Malaya (including Singapore), in 1911, the Chinese numbered 917,000 in a total population of 2,673,000 (34 per cent); in 1931, 1,709,000 in a total of 4,385,000 (39 per cent); in 1941, 2,379,000 in a total of 5,511,000 (43 per cent); in 1960, 3,783,000 in a total of 8,543,000 (44 per cent).

The Chinese provided most of the labour for the tin-mines, and also accounted for the greater number of retailers and artisans in the towns and cities. They were mainly urban, and did not cultivate rice, except to a very limited extent in the Straits Settlements (the best rice-land in the Malay States, in any case, being reserved for the Malays from 1913 onwards). Only in the time of the great slump of 1930–2 did they move to the countryside in any numbers to grow food (during the Japanese occupation, they did so for the like purpose, on a greater scale, forming a community of some half a million 'squatters').

The Chinese artisans and workmen were able to command higher wages than the Malays, and the latter resented the economic encroachment of the immigrants. Nevertheless, without the Chinese Malaya would not have been able to expand economically as it did, and the Malays benefited indirectly from the increase of wealth of the country, though not in proportion to their numbers. But, under British protection, the Malays were secured in possession of their rice-lands, their princes retained their privileges under the treaties, and from their aristocracy were appointed about a sixth of the Malayan Civil Service (a small body totalling about 240, of whom the remaining five-sixths were British officials).

The majority of the Indians in Malaya were employed on the rubber estates. Their labour was recruited in south India, first through agents and the indenture system, later, after indentured labour had been abolished in 1910, through a system of assisted passages. Although an Indian Government Commission (the Sastri Commission) reported favourably on the treatment of Indian labour in Malaya, further immigration of unskilled Indian labour was banned for political reasons by the Indian government shortly before the Second World War. There was also a much smaller community of South Indian merchants and a few thousand Punjabis. The Indians in Malaya numbered 267,000 in 1911, 624,000 in 1931, 744,000 in 1941, and 911,000 (with Pakistanis) in 1960.

In spite of the existence of a 'Plural Society' and the latent Malay resentment of Chinese economic encroachment, the relations between the communities before the Japanese occupation was harmonious under the firm but gentle government of the British.

The position of the Chinese in Siam between the two world wars was much less favourable than it was in Malaya. Their exact numbers are a matter for conjecture, but there were probably over a million Chinese in a total population of 14·5 million in 1937. Traditionally, the Chinese immigrants had been specially absorbed into the local (Buddhist) community, but with the increase in their numbers in the twentieth century with the arrival of newcomers accompanied by their womenfolk a barrier grew up between them and the Chinese which was emphasized by the growth of Nationalist sentiment. Moreover, the Chinese, as elsewhere in Southeast Asia, had acquired the lion's share in the local retail and rice trade and a monopoly of certain occupations. Their largest concentration was in and around Bangkok, though they were to be found in every Siamese province.

Friction between the Chinese and the Siamese authorities had occurred as early as 1910, but from the late 1920s onwards there was a determined attempt by the Chinese to circumvent the Siamese laws regarding schools, accompanied by an equal determination on the part of the Government to enforce these laws. The object of the immigrants was to use Chinese mainly or solely as the medium of instruction while the Siamese government wanted to ensure that all persons born in, and living in Siam, should be able to speak Siamese fluently. At the same time the Siamese government passed a series of laws intended to restrict the Chinese share of certain trades and occupations and to encourage Siamese citizens to engage in them. In the 1930s large head-taxes were imposed on Chinese, and their immigration was severely restricted.

In Burma, where the Chinese community numbered only about 300,000, they constituted no 'problem'. This was not, however, the case in Indochina. In this country similar resentments on economic grounds were to the fore respecting the Chinese minority (about 800,000 in a total of 24 million) as existed with regard to their fellow Chinese in Siam. Neither by the French rulers nor the people of Indochina generally can the Chinese immigrants be said to have been made welcome. Phrases such as 'the Chinese stranglehold', 'the Chinese cyst', and 'the Chinese excrescence' were heard on every side. The Chinese for their part had their grievances. Not only did the restrictions on trade hamper their merchants, but they claimed that taxes were seven times as heavy for a Chinese coolie as for an Annamese. Chinese employed in agriculture were comparatively few (they grew pepper and mulberries with the skill the cultivation of these plants called for), but in trade they were well to the front, controlling the bulk of the rice business; the fish trade (especially in Cambodia) was largely in their hands, and they had much the largest share of the boat-traffic on the rivers.

Passing southwards to Indonesia, we shall find that the situation of the Chinese in this inter-war period had much in common with that of their brethren elsewhere in the region, but with some important modifications. The Dutch had for over two centuries used the Chinese as middle-men between themselves and the native Indonesians. That is to say that they used them for the purpose of tax-collection. Up to the end of the nineteenth century the Chinese bought the opium 'farms' (the monopoly of the sale of opium) and the right to run the pawnshops, but measures taken by the Dutch in 1900 to restrict the use of opium and to transfer the monopoly of pawning to the Government, as well as establishing agricultural credit-banks to rescue the Indonesian farmers from Chinese and other usurers, deprived them of this role of 'middleman' to a great extent. But the stigma attaching to their traditional function lingered on. In Indonesia, the middle-class man, *par excellence*, was the Chinese. He enjoyed appreciation for his industry, frugality, and reliability, but on the other hand he was reproached for lacking interest in the country in which he lived and for having an undue interest in the country from which he originated. The Indonesian Chinese (numbering less than 2 million in a total population of some 70 million in 1939) were distributed over a very wide area, being most numerous in the towns. The Dutch applied to them a special code of law administered in special courts.

The expression 'Plural Society' has real meaning only when it is applied to a society with a very large minority or minorities. In the Malay Peninsula, the Chinese were only a few hundred thousand less numerous than the Malays; if Singapore were added, then they were slightly in an overall majority for the whole of Malaya. For this reason Malaya can be identified as a true 'Plural Society'. In Siam the Chinese also bore a fairly large proportional relationship to the Siamese. But in Indochina and Indonesia they represented only a small fraction of the total population, and since their economic influence was out of all proportion to their numbers, the existence of these minorities with different loyalties and with different ways of life to those of the indigenous peoples was to become more and more of a problem as Southeast Asian Nationalism began to grow.

DUTCH COLONIAL POLICY

Up to the 1890s, the Dutch had deliberately refrained from extending their administration to their vast island empire outside Java, but then the fear of foreign intervention and other factors convinced them that they could no longer delay establishing effective authority throughout the whole archipelago. This undertaking was virtually completed by Governor-General van Heutsz (1904–9). Van Heutsz at last brought to an end the long and bitter war with the Achinese. But he was also active in more peaceful spheres, and it was he who laid the basis of a popular educational system for Indonesia.

Java meanwhile remained the focus of Dutch attention. The Dutch exchequer (as we have seen in Chapter 3) had benefited enormously from the Culture System, and it continued to profit after this system was virtually ended by the Agrarian Law of 1870 which opened the way for private enterprise to succeed State exploitation. But a change of attitude towards the colonies was in the last decade of the century taking place in Holland. This happening can be described as nothing less than qualms of conscience leading to a 'change of heart'.

The new feeling, which was widespread in Dutch governing circles, was voiced by Dr Abraham Kuyper, who became Prime Minister in 1901. He had long before written a pamphlet, *Ons Program*, in which he had argued that the Dutch government must adopt a policy of moral responsibility for native welfare, and this idea he incorporated in the 'Speech from the Throne' that year. The speech declared, 'as a Christian power, the Netherlands is obligated in the East Indian Archipelago to imbue the whole conduct of the government with the consciousness that the Netherlands has a moral duty to fulfil with respect to the people of these regions.' The policy thus announced became known as the 'Ethical Policy'. As an earnest of the new spirit, a loan of 40 million guilders advanced by the Netherlands treasury to the East Indian (Indonesian) government was cancelled so that the funds might be released for the improvement of economic conditions in Java and Madura.

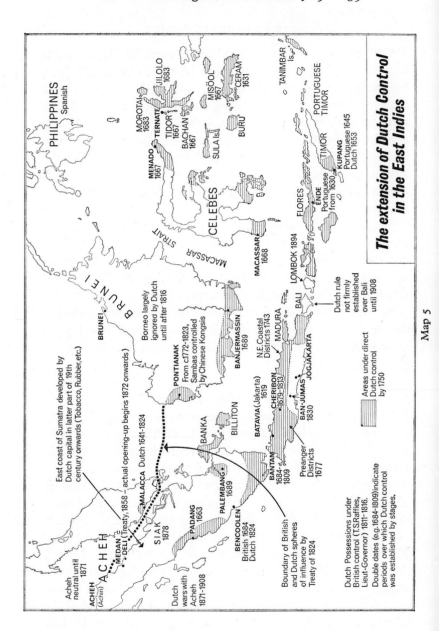

The extension of Dutch Control in the East Indies

Map 5

Dutch Colonial Policy

The reforms now contemplated centred on a programme of 'decentralization'. This envisaged the delegation of powers from The Hague to Batavia, from the Governor-General to departments and local officers, and from European to Indonesian officers. (In the meantime, the Socialists, who had for the first time entered the Dutch parliament, were loudly proclaiming the doctrine of 'Government of the Indies for the Indies'—with the ultimate aim of self-government.) This decentralization also entailed the establishment of autonomous organs managing their own affairs in co-operation with the government. In practice, however, the Decentralization Law of 1903 and the decrees of 1904–5 creating local councils composed of Indonesians, Europeans, and Chinese fell far short of the scheme which the Governor-General had submitted to the Dutch government as far back as 1867. In fact, up to the outbreak of the First World War, which cut off Batavia's communications with The Hague, the Governor-General remained completely under the control of the home government.

In the meantime the officials who were charged with implementing the 'Ethical Policy' were utilizing the village (*desa*) as the pivot for the improvement of native welfare. A regulation was passed in 1906 which provided for a village government, comprising the headmen and village officers, and measures were taken to improve agricultural production and the veterinary services, to establish village schools, to provide credit, and to improve health (the Dutch doctors and health officers were among the best in Southeast Asia). But although an elaborate village administration was built up, there was such excessive interference at every stage from the authorities above that the local self-government became largely nominal, and the general effect was to turn the villages against Dutch rule. J. S. Furnivall (a Burma civil servant who was also a close student of the Netherlands East Indies) described the Dutch method as being in three stages—'Let me help you; Let me show you how to do it: *Let me do it for you.*' It was, in fact, a case of excessive paternalism.

But Dutch plans for the improvement of Indonesia now began to be impeded and cut across by the beginnings of Indonesian Nationalism—a development, however, which must be reserved for a later chapter. The inauguration, too, of the *Volksraad*, or Parliament, by the Dutch can best be considered in this connexion.

SIAM'S GRADUAL TRANSFORMATION: THE REVOLUTION OF 1932

King Chulalongkorn, whose services to his country have received notice in a previous chapter, had thirty-four sons and forty-three daughters. The sons were sent to English public schools, universities, and technical colleges, and quite a number of them showed exceptional ability. Others received training in the British, German, Russian, and Danish armies, and in the British navy. They all played a part in the modernization of their country.

Siam's move to modernize itself was, as has already been seen, prompted by a desire to secure acceptance on an equality with other nations. Law reform prepared the way for the removal of extraterritoriality, and one by one the Powers relinquished their privileges. The Anglo-French convention of 1896 had 'neutralized' central Siam, but in 1907, by a convention with France, Siam returned to the French protectorate of Cambodia the province of Battambang conquered in 1811, and in compensation received back from France the maritime province of Krat and the district of Dansai, which had been ceded in 1904. This convention modified the extraterritorial rights enjoyed by France in Siam, but the first Power to renounce these rights altogether was Britain, which, by the Treaty of Bangkok of 1909, yielded its consular jurisdiction over British subjects living in Siam. By this same treaty the sovereignty over the four northern Malay States was transferred from Siam to Great Britain (the last Power to yield its extraterritorial rights in Siam was the United States which, in search for some compensating advantage, delayed giving up its extraterritorial rights until 1921).

Chulalongkorn died in 1910 and was succeeded by his son Vajiravudh (Rama VI). Rama VI (as we will call him) was educated at Cambridge and also served for a time with the British army. He was a lover of the arts and of the theatre, and an accomplished writer in the Thai language (he contributed a series of articles to a Thai newspaper under the pseudonym of Asavabahu (Pegasus), attacking the Chinese as the 'Jews of Asia'). He relied on favourites for advice rather than on elder statesmen, and the appointment of members of his clique to sinecures and the unparalleled corruption that ensued resulted in widespread discontent and two attempts were made to dethrone him. During his reign, in 1917, Siam entered the First World War on the side of the Allies and sent a small expedition force to Europe, but part of the Siamese army was pro-German and anti-French and hatched a military plot to dethrone the king.

Under Rama VI there were few important administrative reforms, but his social reforms, directed to bring Siam in line with Western nations, were to have long-term consequences. One of these was a law enforcing monogamy, and another was the edict of 1916 ordering all Siamese to adopt surnames. Rama VI also introduced the Gregorian Calendar, started compulsory elementary education (1921), made vaccination compulsory, founded Chulalongkorn University (1917), and instituted the Red Cross Society. He started a public-school on the lines of Oundle (in England) under the famous head-master Sanderson, and through his influence Siamese women adopted European fashions and hair-styles.

Rama VI died in 1925 and, having no son, he was succeeded by his younger brother, Prajadhipok, the seventy-sixth child of Chulalongkorn and his thirty-fourth (and last) son. Rama VII, the new king, was faced by the need for economy since his late brother's extravagance had played havoc with the country's finances. He therefore dismissed many of his brother's favourites and cut down the Royal Corps of Pages from 3,000 to 300. These measures, coupled with a boom in trade, however, enabled the Treasury to balance the budget without resorting to foreign loans or increased taxation. Many developments took place in his reign (including the building of Dom Muang airport, the improvement of public health, and the foundation of a Royal Institute of Literature and a National Library and Museum). Then came the great world slump (1929–32) whose effects began to be felt in the Far East in 1930.

The world slump hit Siam less hard than it did some other countries in Southeast Asia since she was rice-producing (with a large surplus) and could therefore feed herself and had no large export industries and there was thus no mass unemployment. Nevertheless the slump caused Siam to get into great financial difficulties. Failing foreign loans (which were not available in the existing international situation), the government had to resort to unpopular economies including the cutting of salaries which caused particular hardship to the junior official class. The discontent of this class was already great since the monopolizing of all the key positions by the very numerous princes of the royal house stopped promotion. Also hostile to the government was a group of army officers, also hit by salary cuts and hostile to princely influence. These disaffected elements combined and by a *coup d'état* brought about the Siamese Revolution of 1932.

This crisis has been termed a 'middle-class revolution' since the population as a whole were merely onlookers. The leader of the revolution was Luang Pradist (Pridi) Manudharm, a Paris-trained lawyer. He drafted a constitution and with military help took over control of Bangkok on 24 June 1932. No blood was shed. The king was retained, but lost all his prerogatives except the right of pardon. The new government was a party dictatorship. Pridi and his lieutenants did not take over the actual government, but chose P'ya Manopakorn as President of the Executive Council to appease conservative opinion. This arrangement was not a success, and the conservatives managed to draft a constitution in which the royal powers were still considerable, and the restrictions placed on princes of the royal family were also relaxed. The conservatives thereupon proceeded to get rid of Pridi by declaring him 'Communistic' and he was forced into exile. The following year he returned to Siam, a popular figure, but his views were too socialistic for the majority of the ruling faction. The keynotes of the time were anti-Communism and Nationalism, and Phibun (or Pibul), representing the army interests, conducted a campaign against Pridi.

In 1935 Rama VII abdicated. He was unwilling to accept the restrictions placed on his sovereignty. He was succeeded by his nephew, Prince Ananda Mahidol, a ten-year-old boy at school in Switzerland, and a Regency Council was appointed to act during his minority.

The ensuing régime represented an uneasy alliance between

Phibun, as head of the government, and Pridi as Minister of Finance. The accent was on Nationalism, and a drive was made to diminish the influence of the Chinese minority in Siam. Much heavier taxation was levied on foreigners in general, Chinese immigration was greatly restricted, and a number of occupations, previously monopolized by Chinese, were now reserved for Siamese nationals.

In June 1939 the official name of the country was changed from Siam to Thailand.

BRITISH POLICY IN BURMA

One consequence of attaching Burma to the Indian empire was for the latter to regard it as a mere appendage to itself. The early Chief Commissioners, Sir Arthur Phayre and Sir Albert Fytche, had an expert knowledge of the Burmese language, religion, and customs, but after 1871 the office of Commissioner, and thereafter of Lieutenant-Governor (1897) was held by officials trained in India and looking forward to return there on promotion.

In Chapter 3 we have already seen the ill effects of the adoption of the 'village' system on the Indian model; another effect of the 'Indian' connexion which has been adversely commented on by historians was the negative attitude adopted towards Burmese religion. The Queen's Declaration of 1858 at the close of the Indian Mutiny had expressly declared that the government would abstain from interference in Indian religion (which was interpreted to include a refusal to give official recognition to any one religion at the expense of the others), and, since Burma was part of India, it seemed logical to extend the undertaking to that country. Now Buddhism was not only the religion of the people but under the kings had been the state religion, but the British nevertheless deprived it of State support. The consequence was a decay in monastic discipline which resulted in the rise of an ignorant, disorderly class of monks who preached sedition and created unrest. Moreover, the monasteries had in the old days undertaken the education of the people, and their decay left a vacuum which was only partly filled by the substitution of lay schools. To this undermining of traditional Burmese society has been ascribed much of the unrest and instability which characterized Burmese history for the next half century.

The Montagu-Chelmsford Report, upon which the Government of India Act of 1919 was based, recommended that Burma's case should be reserved for special consideration. The alternative proposals for Burma, however, aroused a storm of protest. As D. G. E. Hall remarks, 'Burmese national sentiment was worked up to a fever pitch, boycotts were organized, and a vociferous demand for Home Rule went up'. The British Parliament, therefore, decided to extend to Burma the 'Dyarchy' system that the Government of India Act had introduced into the Indian provinces.

The 'Dyarchy' system was one in which the control of certain matters of government were transferred to a Legislative Council consisting of 103 members, 79 of whom were elected by democratic franchise, while to the Governor and his Executive Council were reserved certain other departments. The transferred matters included education, public health, forests, and excise, while the reserved subjects were defence, law and order, finance, and revenue. The franchise qualification was surprisingly liberal—it extended to all householders over eighteen without sex disqualification.

In 1928, the Simon Commission reported in favour of the separation of Burma from India. The matter, however, was left to the confirmation of a general election, and after a complete reversal of position on the part of the Anti-Separation League, the Legislative Council approved separation and the Government of India Act of 1935 provided for the separation of the two countries to take effect on 1 April 1937.

It cannot be claimed that the measures adopted for the government of Burma were successful in creating a contented, unified country, but this was because Burmese Nationalism had manifested itself at an early date and was working to nullify the efforts of the British in this direction. Compared with the opportunities afforded them by the situation in Malaya to maintain a harmonious political atmosphere, the British in Burma were far less fortunate. At the same time, history will probably decide that the British régime in Burma performed an essential function in assisting the evolution of the country. 'Dyarchy', for example, gave the Burmese a real opportunity to learn the rudiments of self-government. As for the creation of social services, the record of the British in Burma was parallel to that in their other dependencies, although the money at their disposal for the purpose was much less per head in the other territories than it was in Malaya. There were many notable improvements in the period, not only in education and public health, but in the 'Burmaization' of the public services. The admission of Burmese into the Civil Service meant that when Burma eventually obtained its independence, it had a nucleus of highly-trained officials which was able to keep the country on an even keel in spite of a long series of internal convulsions.

THE FRENCH IN INDOCHINA

A merely political map of Indochina would give a particularly inexact picture of the territory. Indochina was often pictured as an Annamese (or Vietnamese) farm-labourer balancing a long pole on his shoulder with a sack of rice hanging from it at each end—the bags of rice representing the rice-growing deltas of the Red River of Tongking in the north and of the Mekong in Cochin-China in the south. The connecting pole stood for the strip of coastal plain in between. The deltas were densely populated and the coastal strip supported many inhabitants, but a few miles inland there was a vast expanse of jungle and swamp—highly malarious in spite of the efforts of the French to extend their control of the disease to these areas. Further inland still were the mountains and high plateaus, sparsely populated. The total population was great and growing (from 15 million in 1910, to 23 million in 1940), but the standard of living was very low. Usury added to the miseries of the people, for moneylenders (native Vietnamese, Southern Indians (*chettiars*), and (especially) Chinese) obtained extortionate rates of interest from them in spite of French efforts to establish agricultural banks and co-operatives.

The French idea of the relation of the Colonies to France involved a highly protectionist policy. The slow tempo of industrialization in Indochina was largely due to the tariffs imposed by France to benefit its own industries, especially textiles, iron and steel, and machinery. The great slump of 1929-32, however, restricted the demand of Indochina's neighbours, and forced the metropolitan country to buy more goods from the colony. In 1935, for the first time, France bought from Indochina more than it sold to it. In particular a publicity campaign made Indochinese rice popular with French housewives. From 1933 to 1937 France imported an average of 647,000 tons of rice, or 41 per cent of the total exports; even 150,000 tons of coal (anthracite) found their way to France around the Cape of Good Hope. But the imperial character of the trade relations between France and its colony presented grave dangers to the Indochinese economy. In retaliation, Far Eastern countries set up high tariffs against Indochinese goods, and Indochinese tariffs prevented the competition of cheaper foreign consumer goods, especially Japanese, and restricted the demand for manufactured articles. Moreover, the policy cramped the growth of Indochinese industrialization.

'Measured in terms of production and trade, of road and rail mileage, even of sanitation and education, the progress', says Charles A. Micaud, 'was obvious.' Indochina was exporting 700,000 tons of rice in 1900, almost 2,000,000 tons in 1937; about 200 tons of rubber, corn, and coal in 1900, and in 1939, 78,000 tons of rubber, 1,500,000 tons of coal, and 546,000 tons of corn. Thirty-six thousand kilometres of roads, of which 18,000 were paved, and 3,000 kilometres of railways were built. A modern irrigation scheme was added to the ancient one to protect and enrich the deltas.

In 1939, half a million children in Indochina attended elementary schools; 10 per cent of those went on to higher elementary schools and 1 per cent to secondary schools. In these institutions the principal medium of instruction was French. The University of Hanoi had 631 students in 1937, most of them Vietnamese. There were 450 medical institutions, and labour conditions had been greatly improved by labour inspectors administering the labour codes, establishing better labour conditions and shorter hours of work.

But (as was also urged against the British and the Dutch in their possessions) critics of the French régime (especially the Vietnamese Nationalists who were by now becoming very vocal) condemned the

The French in Indochina

abnormally low wages of agricultural and industrial workers—about one-third of that of the Moroccan labourer and one-thirteenth of the French worker. This was undoubtedly a well-based charge, and the answer given by the French (as by the British and Dutch) that wages paid in their colonies were nevertheless much higher than in most other parts of Asia, is not at all convincing. The development of trade unionism was necessary to remedy—or at least reduce—the inequality. Strikes, however, were successful in raising wage-rates in the later Colonial period. Nor had the French eliminated unscrupulous exploitation, and indirect taxes, forming 70 per cent of the federal budget, weighed heavily on the people. Indochina (said both the Vietnamese Nationalists and the French Socialists) was being exploited by a handful of French colonialists for the direct advantage of France and not for the good of the Vietnamese.

The strongest indictment of French rule in Indochina, however, was that it frustrated the ambitions of the able Vietnamese—the *élite*. They were given no encouragement, since all the responsible posts were closed to them. To teach colonial peoples to become independent was no part of French policy, for was not Indochina (like the other French colonies) 'part of France'? Self-government for a part of the *République une et indivisible* (the 'Republic one and indivisible') would have been a contradiction in terms. So the French argued, and their colonial administration was in keeping with this theory—a highly centralized system on the Napoleonic pattern directed from Paris.

AMERICA REPLACES SPAIN IN THE PHILIPPINES

The *Maine*, the United States warship, was blown up in Havana harbour on 15 February 1898. It was this incident which started the Spanish-American War. When the Americans decided to carry the war to the Philippines, they naturally looked for any allies they could find among the Filipinos and against the Spanish. The obvious possibilities were the revolutionaries who were then in exile in Hong Kong and Singapore, and those who agreed to come were shipped back to the Philippines to resume the struggle. One of them was Aguinaldo, whom Commodore Dewey returned to the Philippines on 19 May 1898 and he at once announced the renewal of hostilities against Spain. The revolutionaries thereupon set up a republican government at Malolos, some forty miles north of Manila. But when Spain collapsed and the United States took over, the revolutionaries found themselves, not masters of their own country, but in revolt against a new and vigorous 'colonialist' power. It was not, however, until 19 April 1901 that the insurrection was ended and Aguinaldo took the oath of allegiance to the United States.

In January 1899, President McKinley (who was assassinated in America in 1901) appointed a commission under William H. Taft (later to be President himself) to investigate conditions in the Philippines and to provide for a civil government to take over from the military government. What were the Americans going to do with the Philippines now that they had got them? President McKinley says, 'I went down on my knees and prayed Almighty God for light and guidance more than one night'. The answer that he received was (1) that the Americans could not give the Philippines back to Spain—that would be immoral, (2) that they could not turn them over to France or Germany, 'America's rivals in the Orient'—that would be bad business and discreditable, (3) that they could not leave them to themselves—they were unfit for self-government, and (4) 'there was nothing left for us to do', McKinley concluded, 'but to take them all, and to educate the Filipinos, and uplift and civilize and Christianize them, and by God's grace do the very best we could by them, as our fellow men for whom Christ also died.'

And this was what the Americans tried to do for the next forty years (though the Spanish Catholics would claim that they had at least 'Christianized' the Filipinos some three centuries previously). Early United States government was a benevolent paternalism. They began by cleaning up the plague-ridden islands. Conditions at the time were not overdrawn by Dr Heiser who described Manila as 'a crowded slum, where the wretched dwellers crept through human excrement under one another's houses to reach their own.' Throughout the islands, save for the antiquated and polluted Spanish water system, there was not a reservoir, not a pipeline, and not an artesian well. Plague was in every alley, the morgue was filled with victims of cholera, smallpox, or tuberculosis, and the Philippines had the highest infant mortality rate anywhere in the world.[1]

The American record in hygiene, public works, and education in the Philippines is remarkable by any standards. Schoolteachers were brought in by the boat-load from the United States to work side by side with public health officials, with the result that the Philippines is the one Asian country where English is generally—and well—spoken.

Self-government, however, was not truly on the way until the establishment of the legislative assembly in 1907. Henceforth the Philippine Nationalist Party, the *Nacionalistas*, were in control. Their leader was Manuel Quezon. Under the Republican Presidencies in the United States (those of Theodore Roosevelt and Taft) there was no undue haste to grant independence to the Philippines, but when the Democrat Woodrow Wilson was elected to the Presidency in 1912 the Nacionalistas instinctively felt that they were in for better times. In 1916 President Wilson approved the Jones Bill, which provided for widening autonomy in the Philippines and pledged the United States 'to recognize their independence as soon as a stable government can be established therein'. (The United States was thus the first Power explicitly to declare the independence of a colony as an aim in the foreseeable future.) During the First World War, however, independence became an academic issue and was shelved in favour of the more urgent business of fighting Germany. After the return of America to Republicanism there was a reaction in the United States against the idea of early Philippine independence and General Wood was sent to the islands to 're-impose the executive authority of the United States'.

The story of how the Philippines did eventually obtain its independence belongs to a later chapter and for this it must be reserved. What is called for at this point is a brief appraisal of America's record in the Philippines on the social and economic side.

[1] Quoted by Claude A. Buss in Mills and associates, *The New World of Southeast Asia*, Minneapolis, 1949, p. 31.

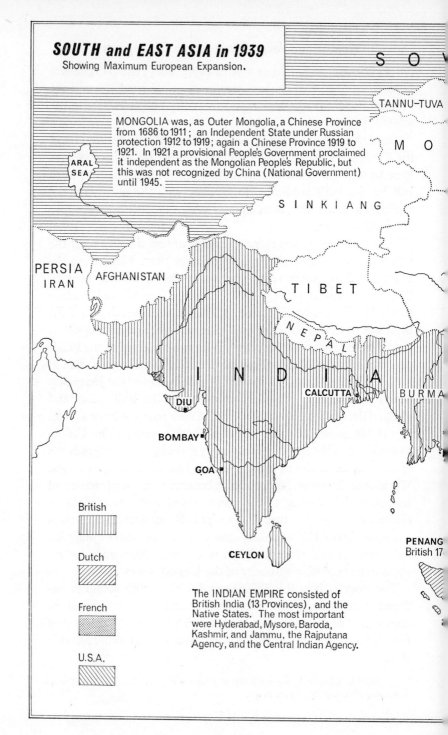

SOUTH and EAST ASIA in 1939
Showing Maximum European Expansion.

S O V

TANNU–TUVA

MONGOLIA was, as Outer Mongolia, a Chinese Province from 1686 to 1911 ; an Independent State under Russian protection 1912 to 1919; again a Chinese Province 1919 to 1921. In 1921 a provisional People's Government proclaimed it independent as the Mongolian People's Republic, but this was not recognized by China (National Government) until 1945.

M O

ARAL SEA

S I N K I A N G

PERSIA
IRAN

AFGHANISTAN

T I B E T

N E P A L

I N D I A

CALCUTTA

BURMA

DIU

BOMBAY

GOA

CEYLON

PENANG
British 17

British

Dutch

French

U.S.A.

The INDIAN EMPIRE consisted of British India (13 Provinces), and the Native States. The most important were Hyderabad, Mysore, Baroda, Kashmir, and Jammu, the Rajputana Agency, and the Central Indian Agency.

Map

ET UNION

LAKE
BAIKAL

OLIA

MANCHUKUO
(MANCHURIA)

SAKHALIN
Japanese

VLADIVOSTOK

PEKING
(Peiping)

CHINA

KOREA

Japanese
1910

JAPAN

HANKOW

SHANGHAI

RYUKYU
ISLANDS
Japanese

= Areas of
China under
Japanese
Military Occupation
1937–

CANTON

MACAO
HONG
KONG
British
1842

FORMOSA
(Taiwan)

AM
ailand)

FRENCH
INDO-
CHINA

SAIGON

PHILIPPINES
U.S.A. 1898

NORTH
BORNEO

LABUAN Br.

BRUNEI

SARAWAK

SINGAPORE
1819

BRITISH MALAYA consisted
of the Straits Settlements –
Singapore, Penang with
Province Wellesley, Malacca,
(all British territory), and the
Protected Malay States.

Perak, Selangor, Negri Sem–
bilan, and Pahang were the
Federated Malay States, and
Kedah, Perlis, Kelantan,
Trengganu, and Johore were
the Unfederated Malay States.

TIMOR Portuguese

The Americans had inherited the semi-feudal system of big land-lords from the Spanish régime. This they did little to change, in spite of the compulsory acquisition of extensive lands belonging to the Church, and the social inequalities remained after the Japanese occupation and after independence. On the economic side the fault was the development of trade in the direction of the United States and the increasing dependence of the Philippines upon it. (Some 80 per cent of the trade was with America—mostly in raw materials.) Free trade with the United States encouraged the 'money-crop' system, brought profits to the landlords and the *compradors* (the Filipino business agents), but lesser benefits to the masses. Rice was imported although it could have been produced locally. Industries for the production of consumer goods were not established. The economic situation deteriorated more and more as the date of independence grew nearer—for complete 'independence' of the United States would obviously mean the economic ruin of the Philippines.

THE COLONIAL PERIOD IN PERSPECTIVE

Each new régime finds it necessary to blacken its predecessor. Therefore to expect that the Colonial Period will be seen in true historical perspective in the present age of Nationalism and 'Anti-colonialism' is to ask too much. Nevertheless, the student of history who lives in the contemporary world is called upon to make this attempt. If he approaches the matter fairly and objectively, with a full knowledge of the facts, he may arrive at the conclusion that the Colonial Period was an essential phase in the evolution of modern Southeast Asia.

6

THE RISE OF NATIONALISM IN EAST AND SOUTH ASIA, 1900–31

'Nationalism', a development of modern times, is the desire of a politically compact people, speaking the same language and sharing the same historical traditions and social customs or creed, to be united as a sovereign nation. The beginnings of the idea can be traced back a considerable way. Japan reacted to foreign pressures by consolidating its nationhood, and the revolt of the Filipinos against the Spanish régime from 1896 onwards can be regarded as the beginnings of Philippine Nationalism. But the country whose Nationalism stimulated the growth of Nationalism in Southeast Asia in opposition to it was China.

The Boxer uprising of 1900 first manifested popular resentment of foreign encroachment on a nation-wide scale. The uprising was suppressed and the Boxers were dispersed, but the Powers henceforth realized that the partition of China was impracticable in face of the awakened national feeling. The Manchu Court returned from its flight into the interior, and with foreign support the dynasty lingered on for a few more years. In an effort to conciliate Chinese opinion, the Manchus introduced a constitution (largely modelled on that of Japan) but this was intended to keep power firmly in Manchu hands while paying lip-service to democracy. The Chinese revolutionaries meanwhile, whose leaders were mostly living abroad in exile, organized a series of revolts, which, however, were all fairly easily suppressed.

The Manchu plan was to build up a huge army to hold back the forces of Chinese Nationalism, for which support was yearly growing among the Chinese people, and for this purpose large loans were obtained from the foreign banking interests. These loans, which were ostensibly intended for civil as well as military purposes, were secured increasingly on the railways which were now being greatly extended. The consequence was that in addition to the huge Boxer indemnity, secured on the Imperial Maritime Customs, the Salt Gabelle, and the *likin* (internal customs), China was saddled with a great additional debt, and the Manchus were virtually the creatures of the foreign Powers. Nevertheless, a National Assembly was created followed by provincial legislatures and these gave some opportunity for the expression of popular opinion.

While this was happening, the real power lay with the armed forces. During the Boxer Uprising, Yuan Shih-K'ai, the mandarin who had made a reputation for himself when representing China in Korea, managed to keep his modern-trained troops out of the fighting, preserving them as a kind of 'private army', and by corruption and intrigue he made himself the most powerful man in China. But it was some years before the opportunity came for him to further his secret personal ambitions.

China in the first years of the twentieth century was the victim of the ambitions of the foreign Powers. Although they no longer aimed at partition, they were still engaged in deadly rivalry among themselves to exploit China's resources. Foremost among the rivals at this juncture were Russia and Japan, and their rivalry concentrated on the three eastern provinces of China known to the West as Manchuria. Already the Russians controlled the railway running across Manchuria to join their Trans-Siberian line, which they used as a basis of the further extension of their influence. Their method to begin with was one of 'peaceful penetration', but the military party in Russia now obtained the upper hand. In the course of the Boxer Uprising of 1900 the Russians sent large military forces into Manchuria and soon gave evidence of a determination to turn it into a Russian protectorate. When peace was signed with the Boxer Protocol, the Russians made excuses for not withdrawing their forces from Manchuria. On the contrary they began to increase their activities throughout the entire region.

These measures alarmed Japan. They were afraid that Russian ambitions would not only exclude them from Manchuria but would deny them a place in the exploitation of Korea. Already a Russian company was claiming special timber rights along the Yalu River (the boundary between Manchuria and Korea). If Japan was to challenge Russia it was necessary for it to secure an alliance with some European Power to offset the possibility that Russia would be joined in a war by one or more of the European Powers (Russia and France had already signed a treaty to secure common action in Europe). Britain was the one Power that offered itself as a possible ally, since it was diplomatically isolated and needed support to resist Russia's ambitions. On 30 January 1902 the first Anglo-Japanese Alliance was signed in London by Count Hayashi, the Japanese Ambassador to Britain, and Lord Lansdowne, the British Secretary of State for Foreign Affairs. It gave an assurance guaranteeing Japan against the danger of having to face a European coalition, and, thus secured, Japan felt itself free to bring its quarrel with Russia to a head.

THE RUSSO-JAPANESE WAR (1904–5) AND ITS EFFECTS

In June 1903, after a year and a half of intensive military preparation, the Japanese requested Russia to give a date for its withdrawal of its troops from Manchuria. The Russians do not seem to have believed that Japan really meant to go to war, and conducted negotiations with Japan for eight months without giving a definite answer to the crucial question of the withdrawal. The Russian fleet in the Far East was not concentrated for action (most of the ships were at Port Arthur, but several were icebound at Vladivostok and two were lying at the Korean port of Chemulpo). On 6 February 1904 the Japanese ambassador at St Petersburg suddenly broke off negotiations and left the Russian capital. Two days later the Japanese fleet went into action, crippling the Russian fleet at Port Arthur. For the rest of the war Japan had control of the sea.

Russia had far greater military and economic resources than Japan, and Japan's best hope for victory lay in crushing the Russian armies before any reinforcements could be sent from Europe. So the Japanese generals constantly assumed the offensive. Korea was soon overrun and on 2 January 1905, after a desperate siege, Port Arthur surrendered. Then, in March, the main forces of the two

Powers met in full battle at Mukden, and the Russian army was defeated—but not crushed. Meanwhile, the Russian European fleet had been sent many thousand miles to the Far East to regain control of the sea, only to be annihilated by the Japanese at the great naval battle of Tsushima. Nevertheless, Russia might have continued the war had not civil disorders and the threat of revolution forced the Czar to accept the mediation of President Theodore Roosevelt. In August 1905 the Russians and Japanese signed the Treaty of Portsmouth, New Hampshire.

By the Treaty of Portsmouth, Russia abandoned all rights to interfere in Korea (which was annexed by Japan in 1910), surrendered the southern half of Sakhalin Island, and agreed to cede to Japan the lease of Port Arthur and the Liaotung peninsula. The Russian government also agreed to surrender two-thirds of the Chinese Eastern Railway between Port Arthur and Harbin.

But more important than the treaty itself was the far-reaching effect of Japan's victory on the peoples of the Far East. For the first time in history, an Asian nation had met a modern Western Power in war and defeated it. Japan itself was henceforth one of the Powers. The moral to be drawn was that any Asian people, providing that they were industrialized and in possession of modern arms, could hope to challenge the domination of the West. The old widespread superstition that the West was invincible, being supported (so it seemed) by some supernatural agency, had been disposed of for ever. The news (as Lord Curzon put it) 'reverberated through the whispering-galleries of the East'.

From the Russo-Japanese War henceforth, Nationalism was to be transformed from a vague sentiment into a policy of action.

THE CHINESE REVOLUTION OF 1911

While the Manchus were desperately attempting to hold up the collapsing of their dynasty, the revolutionary movement gathered momentum. It was directed mainly by Chinese revolutionaries in exile in Japan, the Treaty Ports, or Southeast Asia. The Hsing Chung Hui (Society for the Revival of China), the Kung Fu Hui (Restoration League) and the Hua Hsing Hui (China Revival

League) were founded in succession. Meanwhile the attempted Russian Revolution of 1905 (resulting in the creation of a parliament (the Duma) for the first time) had impressed the Chinese middle class of the necessity of a revolution if China were to be rescued from its servile dependence on the good will of foreigners.

The opposition to the Manchus abroad centred on Sun Yat-Sen. In the same year as the battle of Tsushima (1905) he arrived in Japan from Europe and was warmly welcomed by his fellow revolutionaries who had taken refuge there. Since the anti-Manchu activities were scattered, the three societies above-mentioned were amalgamated to form the Tung Meng Hui (Revolutionary League) with Sun as president. The programme of the Tung Meng Hui was: 'Drive out the Manchus; restore China; establish a republic; and equalize land ownership'. The new League established its own newspaper, the *Min Pao* (People's Herald).

In the first issue of *Min Pao*, Sun Yat-Sen proclaimed the Three Principles of the People (*San Min Chu I*)—the Principle of Nationalism, the Principle of Democracy, and the Principle of the People's Livelihood. These three principles compressed Sun's solution of China's problems. The Three Principles were to be expanded and amended in later years, but they were adopted as the basis of Nationalist China when it became established (after 1927) by the Kuomintang under Chiang Kai-Shek.

During the next five years, famines in China added to the general discontent and favoured the planning of rebellions. In 1906 a rising took place in Hunan and Kiangsi. Among the rebels were six thousand miners from the Anyuan Colliery of Pinghsiang. The Tung Meng Hui took part in the rising under the slogan, 'Establish a republic and equalize land ownership', but the rising failed owing to the lack of unified leadership. In the two years 1907 and 1908 Dr Sun personally organized six armed uprisings in Kwangtung, and other uprisings took place at Anking, Anhwei. In 1907 Hsu Hsi-Lin, a returned student, Superintendent of the Police Academy at Anking, stabbed En Ming, Governor of Anhwei, when the latter was attending the terminal opening of the academy. Hsu then mobilized the students to rise but his small force was soon vanquished by Manchu troops. A year later, a revolutionary officer in the New Army (recruited by the Manchu government and equipped with modern weapons), Hsiu Ch'eng-Chi, launched a second rising by organizing a mutiny of the artillery and cavalry battalions on the outskirts of the city. But again the attempt at revolution failed. The same thing happened to a number of other risings.

The same year that the Manchu government promulgated a nine-year programme of constitutional reform (1908), the Emperor and the Empress Dowager, Tz'u Hsi, died within twenty-four hours of one another (since the death of Tz'u Hsi would have restored the Kuang Hsü emperor to power, it was suspected that Yuan Shi-K'ai might have had a hand in the latter's sudden death, before that of the Empress Dowager, for he would have no doubt remembered to settle old scores with Yuan, who had betrayed him at the *coup d'état* of 1898. But no proof of Yuan's complicity has yet been produced). The dead emperor was succeeded by his three-year-old nephew Pu Yi,[1] under the reign title of Hsuan Tung. The real power was in the hands of Pu Yi's father, Tsai Feng, the Regent.

The revolutionary movement was now expanding with gathering speed, and following agitations in the provinces, the government was forced to announce that the period for the preparation of a constitutional government was being shortened and that a parliament would be set up sooner than it had originally intended. But when a cabinet was formed in 1910 all the key posts were filled by Manchu nobles and officials. Tsai Feng was commander-in-chief of the army, and his two brothers secretary of the navy and chief of staff respectively. It was clear that Manchu 'democracy' was only make-believe.

But what, we may ask, had become of the 1898 reformers who believed in the possibility of the reform of China within the framework of the Manchu empire? After the *coup d'état*, K'ang Yu-Wei and Liang Ch'i-Ch'ao had fled to Japan where they continued to advocate a constitutional monarchy. *Min Pao*, the Tung Meng Hui organ, on the other hand, propagated the ideas of democratic revolu-

---

[1] Pu Yi abdicated in 1912, was restored for a short time in 1917, became the Emperor of Manchukuo (a Japanese puppet) in 1932, was imprisoned by the Communists, and was in the early 1960s still alive—a penitent Communist. An astonishing career!

tion, and a bitter controversy was carried on between the two factions in the Chinese press overseas for many years.

In the spring of 1911 one more abortive rising organized by the Tung Meng Hui took place in Canton. On 27 April Hsuan Hsing and his followers, who formed the vanguard of the rising, attempted to storm the yamen (palace) of the Viceroy, but owing to repeated changing of the orders only four of the ten sections came into action and the rising again failed. Those who fell included the Seventy-Two Martyrs celebrated in the history of the Chinese Nationalists.

The successful revolution of 1911 was preceded a month or two before by a movement against the Manchu attempt to 'nationalize' (i.e. appropriate) the railways in Szechwan in order to provide security for the further foreign loans they were attempting to raise to pay for their armed forces. Then on the night of 10 October 1911 (the 'Double Tenth'), under the direction of the revolutionary leaders, the New Army rose at Wuchang. They occupied the arsenal and powder magazines and attacked the yamen of the Viceroy. The Manchu officials fled in confusion and the city fell into the hands of the revolutionaries. Next day the revolutionaries set up a military government under Li Yuan-Hung, a brigade commander of the New Army. The victory at Wuchang gave an impetus to the revolutionary movement all over the country. Workers, peasants, and ex-soldiers flocked to join the revolutionary army and within a few weeks most of the provinces declared their independence of the central government (a prelude to the division of China for many years to come).

In this crisis the Manchu Regent appealed to the one man who could possibly help them. This was Yuan Shih-K'ai, then living in nominal retirement, 'disgraced' because his power had threatened the throne. Yuan affected to hesitate, but when he did decide to intervene it was in the interests of his personal ambitions and not of bolstering up the tottering Manchus. He accepted the premiership, but he relied for the success of his secret plans on the support of those troops who were loyal to him and of those military officers who were under an obligation to him or whose services he had bought.

In the meantime two revolutionary blocs had been formed, one in Wuchang and one in Shanghai. They vied with one another for leadership. After discussion it was decided to hold a convention at Wuchang to set up a provisional government. But when Wuchang came under the bombardment of troops still loyal to the Manchu emperor, the convention moved to Hankow, and when Nanking fell to the revolutionaries it was transferred there.

In late December Dr Sun Yat-Sen arrived in Shanghai from Europe (where he had been attempting to secure financial and other support for the Revolution). He was thereupon elected Provisional President of the Republic of China which was declared to have come into being on 1 January 1912.

When the provisional government was formed, the 'constitutionalists' (who favoured a régime not greatly different from the one that had been displaced) seized some key posts in it. A provisional constitution was thereupon drafted, modelled on those of the Western democracies.

But the Chinese Conservatives, who wanted to be rid of the Manchus but not to see a real revolution take place, cast in their lot with Yuan Shih-K'ai on account of his formidable military strength. The foreign Powers, who did not want to lose the advantages they had gained or the money they had lent to China, also favoured the 'Strong Man' of China, and advanced him loans to tide him over his financial difficulties. Yuan thereupon forced the Manchu emperor to abdicate (February 1912). Sun Yat-Sen, fearing the partition of the country, decided to give up his provisional presidency to Yuan, provided that he would break off relations with the Manchus and that he would whole-heartedly support the Republic and observe the provisional constitution. This Yuan promised to do, and Yuan succeeded Sun as Provisional President of the Republic. Thus overnight Yuan Shih-K'ai exchanged his imperial premiership for a revolutionary presidency.

Following the formation of Yuan's government, the 'Opposition' (so to speak), who wished to restrict Yuan's power, formed three parties in succession—the Tung Yi Tang (Unification Party), Kung Ho Tang (Republican Party) and Min Chu Tang (Democratic Party). In August 1912 the Tung Meng Hui was reorganized to form the Kuomintang (KMT). This was the party to be closely associated with the fortunes of the Chinese Republic for many years to come. Yuan, as a counter-move, brought over and merged the Unification, Republican and Democratic Parties into the Chin Pu Tang (Progressive Party)—a party of his own, as rival to the Kuomintang.

Yuan Shih-K'ai had now succeeded the Manchus as a dependent of the foreign Powers. The history of the next few years in China is to be sought largely in the loan negotiations. In 1913, Britain, France, Germany, Russia, and Japan organized the Five Power Consortium, and Yuan, in return for loans, placed China's finances under the control of this Consortium. Yuan's object was to expand the military forces under his command and to crush the revolutionary opposition which was strong in the southern provinces. Every move he took was backed by intrigue, bribery, and (when expedient) murder.

Sun Yat-Sen before long realized that Yuan's promise to 'support the Republic' had been purely a matter of tactics and that he had no intention of honouring it. Sun therefore determined to organize a campaign to secure Yuan's resignation. Yuan, however, having the support of the constitutional monarchists and of the foreign Powers, was in a strong position. In June 1913 he recalled the Governors of Kiangsi, Anhwei, and Kwangtung who were supporters of the Kuomintang, and when Li Lieh-Chun, Governor of Kiangsi, refused to give up his post and called upon the whole country to rise against Yuan, the latter brought his 'punitive army' into action and Li Lieh-Chun suffered a disastrous defeat. As a result, the governors of several provinces, who had declared their independence in support of Li, submitted to Yuan Shih-K'ai. This campaign against Yuan was known as the 'Second Revolution'—but it was a revolution in reverse.

The military opposition to Yuan had now been removed, and his ambitions increased. The constitution, however, was still a fetter to his power, and this he decided to circumvent or, if necessary, to violate it. On 6 October 1913 he brought pressure on Parliament to elect him President, and arranged for several thousand hired ruffians, under the name of the 'Citizens' Society', to surround the parliament house and to allow no member to leave until he had been elected. The Powers, however, duly recognized Yuan as President. When the Kuomintang members of parliament continued their opposition, Yuan dismissed them from the assembly. In May 1914 he promulgated his 'Constitutional Compact', abrogating the provisional constitution, and the Revolution of 1911 can be said at this point to have come to an abortive end.

By the Constitutional Compact, the President's term of office was extended indefinitely, and he was given the power to nominate his successor. In fact, the Compact gave the President the dictatorial powers of an emperor—and an emperor in fact Yuan secretly decided to be.

To begin with, events moved in his favour. In August 1914 war broke out in Europe. Japan seized the opportunity to take possession of the German settlement of Tsingtao and the German-owned Kiaochow-Tsinan Railway. Yuan made no protest, since to further his plans he needed Japanese support. But in January 1915 Japan presented the notorious Twenty-One Demands which would have the effect of reducing China to a Japanese colony. The demands included the transfer of all German rights in China to Japan, recognition of Japan's privileges in Liaoning, Kirin, and eastern Inner Mongolia, the joint operation with China of collieries and steel works in Chinese territory, the employment of Japanese advisers and the joint administration of the police forces in the principal Chinese cities, placing China's arsenals under joint operation, and many other privileges relating to ports, finance, and mining. After some protest and negotiation, Yuan accepted the main Japanese demands on the grounds that China had not the military strength to resist Japan.

Yuan now went forward with his monarchial plans, relying on the fact that Britain, France and Russia were fully occupied with the war in Europe. He worshipped heaven at the Temple of Heaven in Peking (which only an emperor had the right to do), chose a title for his reign (*Hung Hsien*), and got his American adviser (Frank J. Goodnow) to write articles declaring that a monarchy was better suited to Chinese conditions than a republic. But neither Japan (which wanted China as a colony) nor the mass of the Chinese people were willing to see the empire restored in the person of Yuan Shih-

K'ai. There were risings in many places in China, and in this dangerous situation the European Powers withdrew their support for Yuan's ascension of the 'Dragon Throne'. Yuan thereupon resumed his presidency, but died of frustration and nervous exhaustion shortly afterwards (6 June 1916).

From this time onwards for many years China was divided under the local leaders, the 'War Lords'—one clique associated with the Allies another with Japan. In 1917 the Peking government (encouraged by Japan) declared war on Germany. In October 1917 the Communist revolution took place in Russia. When the war in Europe ended, and the Versailles Conference assembled to settle the peace terms, the Chinese delegation demanded that the 'Twenty-One' demands between Japan and Yuan Shih-K'ai should be annulled—but this demand was refused. Thereupon there was a great surge of popular indignation in China, and the students in Peking staged an agitation which became known as the 'May 4th Movement', and from this moment the Chinese Communists date the beginnings of the long process which ended in the establishment of the People's China in 1949.

REFORMS IN INDIA AND THE RISE OF THE CONGRESS PARTY

Since in this book the history of South and East Asia is viewed primarily as it would appear to an informed onlooker situated in Southeast Asia at the present day, it is now incumbent on us to pass westwards to take account of what was happening simultaneously in the Indian Sub-continent.

In Chapter 5 mention has been made of the state of India at the time when British power there was at its height; the emphasis in this chapter will be on the growth of nationalism and the beginnings of the movement towards independence.

The outbreak of the World War 1914–18 formed the dividing line in India between the new and the old worlds. Before the war, new ideas such as Nationalism and new movements such as that of the Indian National Congress were already in being, but in 1914, the British Raj in India was firmly established and to all appearances it seemed that it would endure indefinitely. After the war, the change was so great that Europeans who had been absent from India for only a year or two on war service were bewildered by the transformation that met their eyes.

Yet the post-war attitude of mind was in many respects only an intensification of a process that had begun before the war, and from the time of the Morley-Minto reforms which were embodied in the Council's Act of 1909 it is generally true to say that the history of the Indian Subcontinent is a history of political conflict between the nationalist politicians, notably the party called the Indian National Congress, and the British government.

When the war broke out, India, as the dependency of Britain, was at once drawn into it. The Lahore and Meerut divisions were hurried to France to help hold the line until the new armies were ready to take the field. They were then withdrawn and sent to Mesopotamia. Indian troops assisted in the defence of the Suez Canal and fought in General Allenby's victorious campaign in Palestine, and also in Gallipoli and East Africa. Over 500,000 Indians served on the various fronts and suffered 96,000 casualties. Indian representatives signed the Treaty of Versailles on behalf of their country.

But the drawing of India into the war on the side of Britain without the expressed consent of the Indian people through the machinery of democracy stimulated the growth of nationalist feeling. Thereupon, in response to insistent demands on the part of the Indian Nationalist Congress and other political parties, the British cabinet issued a statement in the following terms:

The policy of his Majesty's government, with which the Government of India are in complete accord, is that of the increasing association of Indians in every branch of the administration and the gradual development of self-governing institutions with a view to the progressive realization of responsible government in India as an integral part of the British Empire.

The Secretary of State for India, Edwin Montagu, then visited India, and in consultation with the Viceroy, Lord Chelmsford (1916–21), drew up a report which was embodied in the Government of India Bill, 1919. These Montagu–Chelmsford reforms provided for the setting up of a two-chamber legislature with greatly enlarged powers, though the executive remained under the control of the Viceroy-in-Council who was responsible to the Secretary of State for India and the British Parliament. The legislatures were to have 70 per cent elected members and the franchise was extended to about 30 per cent of the total population.

In the provinces a novel experiment known as 'dyarchy', or double rule, was introduced, whereby certain portfolios such as public works, forests, excise, and education were transferred to ministers responsible to the legislature, but others such as law and order and defence were reserved to the Governor and his executive counsellors (the extension of 'dyarchy' to Burma has already been referred to, see p. 110). A Chamber of Princes (the Rulers of States not within directly ruled 'British India') designed to give them the opportunity of discussing matters of common interest and presided over by the Viceroy was set up at Delhi.

Following on the First World War was a period of great unrest in India. There were a number of successive incidents which gave rise to grievances. One was a judicial report recommending that terrorist crimes should be tried without a jury, another was the offence given to Muslim sentiment by the severe terms of peace imposed on Turkey, then Habibullah Khan, the Amir of Afghanistan, invaded British territory and created much trouble among the border tribesmen, and in Malabar the Moplahs, an Arab-Muslim community, rose and committed horrible atrocities upon the Hindu peasants. But more serious than any of these incidents for its effect on Anglo-Indian relations was that at Amritsar in the Punjab in April 1919, when General Dyer fired on a crowd which had assembled in defiance of orders and 372 persons were killed and many injured. (Mr Nehru afterwards dated his change of mind from co-operation with the British to revolution against them to this incident.)

Lord Reading, who was Viceroy from 1921 to 1926, managed to improve the situation and to restore a certain amount of order, but after his departure M. K. Gandhi ('Mahatma' Gandhi) now came prominently onto the scene as an irreconcilable revolutionary. He obtained control of the Indian National Congress which in 1929 declared its aim to be complete independence (*swaraj*) which was to be attained by the boycott of foreign goods and by civil disobedience.

The next phase is characterized by the attempt of Lord Irwin (afterwards Lord Halifax), who succeeded Lord Reading as Viceroy, to collaborate with Congress. In the meantime, British members of Parliament were getting anxious at the trend of events and the government appointed a commission under Lord Simon to take evidence on the spot as to the working of the Montagu–Chelmsford reforms. The Commission, though boycotted by the Indian Congress on the grounds that it contained no Indian members, was able to fulfil its task of enquiry and produced a mass of valuable evidence for the information of the British Parliament and the guidance of the administration in India.

The next step taken by the British government was to convene a round-table conference in London of Indian politicians of all parties to meet members of the British government in London. Through the influence of Lord Irwin, Gandhi attended the second session of this conference, but the conference failed to come to an agreement on the subject of the Minority Communities (representation of the 'untouchables' etc.). Gandhi declared that he would resist to the death any attempt to 'vivisect Hinduism'. Whilst the conference was in progress there had been a political truce between Congress and the Indian government, but this had broken down by the time that Gandhi returned to India. Gandhi thereupon resumed his policy of 'non-cooperation', defied the law (as in organizing illegal salt-making—salt being a government monopoly), and was imprisoned with some of his followers. Shortly after this he swore to 'fast to the death' when it was proposed to institute separate electorates for the depressed classes. But the terms of the decision regarding electorates having been modified, Gandhi was released from imprisonment.

The above is an outline of events in India up to the end of the 1920s. It will be apparent that a spirit of Indian Nationalism had come into being and all the time was growing stronger. But at the same time the divisions between the peoples of the Sub-continent, and particularly the gulf which separated Hindus and Muslims, had been made even more obvious during the struggle between Congress and the ruling Power. How could the breaches be healed so that India might proceed towards self-government with some hope of unity when it was attained? Lord Birkenhead taunted the Indians with being unable to agree on constructive proposals. This taunt provoked such indignation among the Indian politicians that it was possible for them to assemble an all-parties conference which set up a committee to draft an agreed constitution. The Chairman of the Committee was Pandit Nehru. The report it made was an able document. It accepted Dominion Status instead of complete independence outside the British Commonwealth, and it ruled out separate communal electorates. The first provision was a compromise in order to carry the Liberals and the Minorities along with Congress, and the second was a device for keeping Hindus of all shades together—even at the price of offending the Muslims. In consequence, the Muslim leader, Jinnah, left the conference, and the Muslims remained aloof from the anti-government movement which followed the presentation of the report. But even in the Congress there was nearly an open split over the report, though Gandhi managed to affect a characteristic compromise. The Nehru Report with its goal of Dominion Status was accepted for one year, with the proviso that if Dominion Status was not granted by the end of 1929 resort should be had to mass disobedience.

Could Indian Nationalism, then, hope to be a united Nationalism? There were, on the eve of the 1930s, still many Hindus at least who thought it might, but the portents were in favour of the development of two separate Nationalisms in the Sub-continent—the Hindu and the Muslim.

THE REVIVAL OF THE KUOMINTANG AND THE REUNIFICATION OF CHINA

Nationalism has been described as an *anti* movement, namely one that comes into being *against* something. In South and East Asia it came into being, first against the Colonial Powers, and secondly as one Nationalism resisting the pressures of other Nationalisms. Conditions were favourable to its growth in India since the pressure tending to unite Indians (and Hindus and Muslims were united in their demand for self government) was a single, unified one, namely that of the British Raj. In China, Nationalism arose against a number of 'Colonialisms' represented by several foreign Powers, and was therefore not as single-minded in its aim. Groups of Powers were able to divide it into cliques (corresponding to their own groupings) after the fall of Yuan Shih-K'ai and also to exploit the traditional jealousy between North and South China.

After Yuan's death, Li Yuan-Hung, who after leading the revolutionary army in 1911 had been elected Vice-President, succeeded him in the presidency. But he had none of Yuan's strength of purpose and did not attempt to copy his imperial ambitions, and the country began to break up into provinces or groups of provinces. In 1917 there was an abortive attempt by an old Manchu general, Chang Hsun, to restore Pu Yi to the throne, and thereafter the control of affairs at Peking fell into the hands of a group of northern generals and politicians known as the Anfu clique, who were in the pay of the Japanese and who mortgaged resources and rights in Manchuria and Mongolia in return for a series of loans. Nevertheless, this corrupt clique, whose authority was confined to a small part of the country, was recognized as the legal government of China by the Powers and was given the surplus of the national revenue-collecting agencies such as the Customs and the Salt Gabelle (after payment of loan interests and the Boxer Indemnity) controlled by foreign officials. For the rest of the country, the *tuchuns* (military governors, or 'warlords', only nominally responsible to Peking) followed their own devices and ruined the countryside in their constant 'wars of rice bowls', and by their alliances and intrigues to seize power in Peking. One of these *tuchuns* was Chang Tso-Lin, the dictator of Manchuria, who became the agent of the Japanese and who ruled the three eastern provinces with an iron hand in their interest (and his own).

Whilst China was in a state of political confusion, Chinese Nationalism, under the influence of the rise of capitalism, especially in the Treaty Ports, was being shaped by the political and economic theories then current in either the 'middle-class' or Socialist West. The Nationalist leaders, broadly speaking, advocated the promotion of democracy and science, and denounced feudal aristocracy, feudal rites and morals as well as Confucian ethics. Intellectuals such as Hu Shih and Lu Hsun advocated a new literature and a new style of writing. They were 'progressive' and 'revolutionary', but still accepting the framework of a bourgeois-capitalist state of society. But a movement that was to have spectacular consequences in the years to come was already in being—namely the beginnings of Chinese Communism.

When the Communist Revolution took place in Russia in October 1917, its effects were felt in China—but only, to begin with, among a small group of intellectuals. After the 4th May Movement of 1919 there had been general unrest and a series of strikes directed mainly against Western capitalist enterprise, but so far uncoordinated. Then in May 1920 the first Communist group was formed in Shanghai by Chen Tu-Hsiu and others, and the following year, with the assistance of the Communist International, the First National Congress of the Chinese Communist Party was held in Shanghai (1 July 1921). Among the delegates from various places was Mao Tse-Tung, representing the Party organizations in Hunan.

Meanwhile, Sun Yat-Sen, the 'Father of the Chinese Revolution', had for many years since the collapse of the Kuomintang in 1913 been living mostly overseas or in the Treaty Ports. But in 1921, while the northern warlords were locked in internecine strife, he established himself in Canton as Emergency President of the Republic, relying on the support of the local warlord Chen Chiung-Ming. He then began to prepare for a Northern Expedition to reunite China in the name of the Kuomintang and of the Revolution. But later, Chen Chiung-Ming (bought over, it seems, by the Chihli warlords with foreign connivance) staged a *coup* which compelled Sun to fly from Canton.

Hitherto Sun Yat-Sen had looked to the West for sympathy and assistance, but after his ousting by Chen Chiung-Ming and the refusal of the Powers to allow his Canton government a share of the customs revenues locally collected, he turned in another direction for help—namely to the Soviet Union and the Communists. This was the beginning of the Kuomintang-Communist co-operation which was to last until Chiang Kai-Shek's purge of the left wing of the KMT in April 1927.

When, by a counter-coup against Chen Chiung-Ming, Sun was able to return to Canton (1923), he included a number of Communists in his government. Russian advisers arrived in Canton from Moscow. In January 1924 Sun convened the First National Congress of the KMT. Among the Communists who attended it were Mao Tse-Tung and Li Ta-Chao. The Congress accepted an anti-imperialist, anti-feudal policy, and endorsed Sun's principle of 'the land to the tiller', and the KMT agreed to accept Communists as members in their individual capacity. The Congress also adopted a manifesto in which Sun re-enunciated his Three Principles of the People.

Sun Yat-Sen died in Peking in March 1925. On his death-bed he signed his will, which was to feature largely in KMT propaganda. He was succeeded as leader of the Kuomintang, however, by a personality very different from himself, namely Chiang Kai-Shek, the head of the Military Academy at Whampoa near Canton which Sun had established with Soviet help. Chiang had strong affiliations with the Chinese banker-merchants of the Treaty Ports (the 'Comprador class', as the Communists call it) and was very much on the right wing of the Kuomingtang. Chiang realized that before long there would have to be a 'show-down' between the right wing leadership and the Communist left wing of the Party.

This 'show-down' took place when the long-delayed Northern Expedition eventually got under way. Anti-foreign feeling in China was now so strong, and resentment against the warlords so great, that a Nationalist party such as the Kuomintang was assured of wide-spread popular support when it adopted a slogan of anti-foreignism. The Northern Expeditionary Army met with little or no resistance in the southern and central provinces. The question threatening its success was whether it was to be the instrument of a 'National-bourgeois' reunification of China or a Communist revolution. Chiang Kai-Shek thereupon decided upon a sudden move to crush the Communists within his party. On 12 April 1927, in Shanghai, Chiang ordered a purge of all Communists inside or outside the party, and massacred all those he could lay hands on.

Following this action on the part of Chiang, there appeared two rival governments—the left-wing government with Wuhan as its capital, and Chiang Kai-Shek's counter-revolutionary government seated in Nanking. Under pressure from Chiang (with foreign support), the Wuhan government crumbled, and the Communist 'hard core' became refugees, holding out in the mountains or wherever they could find a refuge for years to come. The future, for the next few years, belong to Chiang and the Kuomintang. Chiang gained the ascendancy against the Wuhan government, won over the northern warlords by negotiation with them, and advancing to Peking (whose name he changed to Peiping) he was able to give a greater unity to China than it had possessed since the abdication of the last emperor of the Manchus. But one great obstacle to the achievement of a strong, united China remained—namely the ambitions of Japan.

THE GROWTH OF JAPANESE IMPERIALISM

Japan had had things pretty well its own way whilst the Western Powers were preoccupied with the First World War, but when it was over the latter were free to turn their attention to the Far East. While the war was still on, Japan had decided to save China's face by dropping the more extreme of the Twenty-One Demands. But, under duress, China had been forced to sign two treaties, conceding the transfer to Japan of German interests in Shantung and giving new privileges to Japan both in south Manchuria and the eastern part of Inner Mongolia (as above related). Those concessions amounted to the bulk of four out of the five groups that comprised the original Japanese demands. It was the fifth group of demands that was the most objectionable; and this was dropped.

At the Versailles peace conference (1919) the Twenty-One Demands (or what remained of them) came under attack from the Chinese delegation. But when Japan was confronted by the demand that it should yield its succession to the rights of Germans in Shantung, it threatened to withdraw from the Conference rather than agree. With great reluctance President Wilson gave way to the Japanese since (for one thing) it was revealed that Britain and France, in a secret agreement, had undertaken to support Japan's claims to Shantung. But the benefits of this particular diplomatic victory over Shantung were offset by an anti-Japanese trade boycott in China. Less tangible, but in the long run perhaps more serious, was the hardening of popular anti-Japanese sentiment in the United States.

Two years later, in 1921, the famous Washington Conference took place. There was a Naval Treaty fixing a ratio of 5:5:3 between the capital ship tonnage of Great Britain, the United States, and Japan respectively. In point of fact, the naval settlement was very much to Japan's advantage for it meant not only that no first-class naval base would be built by Britain or America in Hong Kong or the Philippines, but that Japan obtained a measure of security that it could not have achieved in an unrestricted naval building race with the United States.

Yet an even more important consequence of the Washington Conference, certainly from the angle of Japan's prestige, was that it saw the end of the Anglo-Japanese Alliance, one of the recognized bases of Japanese foreign policy. It had been one of the prime objects of American policy since Versailles to see that this alliance did not continue. But Great Britain's decision not to renew the Alliance—'however politely swathed in face-saving references to the League Covenant and the new Four-Power Treaty', says Richard Storry, 'inflicted a wound received in sorrow and re-membered in wrath.'

On 1 September 1923 occurred one of the greatest disasters in Japanese history—the earthquake in the Tokyo–Yokohama area. Well over half Tokyo, already the third largest city in the world, was completely destroyed, and comparable ruin befell numerous towns in the area. The death roll amounted to about a hundred thousand. But the Japanese set about the rebuilding of the two shattered cities with characteristic courage, and within three or four years there was little sign that either Tokyo or Yokohama had ever suffered calamity.

In the 1920s it seemed that, putting behind them the blunder of the Twenty-One Demands, the Japanese were moving (quite firmly this time) into an era of real, if still modified, Liberalism. The trend was encouraged by Saionji, one of the earliest *Genro*, or 'elder statesmen', who lived on into the 1930s to warn his countrymen of the dangerous course they had then embarked upon. Reactionary Conservatism, however, was strong in the House of Peers and the Privy Council, and particularly in the army. 'Big Business' (represented by the huge Mitsubishi concern in particular) was, on the other hand, all in favour of reduced armaments. Relations with China had been smoothed over, and a diplomatic settlement was reached with Russia on the questions of Sakhalin and of the fisheries. The only issue which caused real concern was the American legislation, passed by Congress in 1924, prohibiting 'oriental', including Japanese, immigration into the United States. On the whole when a new emperor ascended the throne on 25 December 1926 under the reign title of *Showa*, meaning 'enlightened peace', it seemed as if the portents conveyed by the title would be justified. But clouds were beginning to gather on the horizon.

China, having been divided under the 'warlords' since the death of Yuan Shih-K'ai, was now showing signs of reunification under Chiang Kai-Shek. In 1927 his military forces, in their northward advance, gained control of the Yangtze Valley, and he and his government made no secret of the aims to secure the abolition of extraterritoriality and to re-establish control over the whole of the territory of the late Chinese empire, including the Chinese Eastern Railway and the Japanese zone in Manchuria. To begin with, it looked as if the new liberal spirit of its government might lead Japan to acquiesce in Chiang's plans, but as it happened, the rising tide of militant Nationalism in China produced an ultra-Nationalist reaction in the Japanese army.

During the years 1927–30 extreme political and economic ideas were fermenting in the Japanese army, favoured by a slump in Japanese trade. One symptom of the strong undercurrent of reaction was the formation of a secret society of junior officers to plan a *coup d'état*. It was not, however, for some years that things came to a head—a period marked by a tougher policy towards China by the Tanaka Cabinet then in power than had been pursued by any previous Japanese government—and when they did it was not only the young hot-heads who were concerned, but Japanese generals and other senior officers. On 18 September 1931 the Japanese

Kwantung[1] Army set about the seizure of the city of Mukden, the curtain-raiser of the occupation of all Manchuria. The Kwantung Army, it seemed, had acted on its own responsibility—with the apparent connivance of the Army General Staff. Whatever the facts, the Cabinet was powerless to act and the situation was now out of control. From now onwards Japanese Imperialism (which had grown out of Japanese Nationalism) was committed to a career of expansion which would be brought to a definite end only with the Japanese defeat in the Pacific War in 1945. In the meantime, however, a prolonged period of struggle was to ensue.

[1] It is important to distinguish Kwantung (in northern China) from Kwangtung (a province of southern China), since they are frequently misprinted for one another.

7

NATIONALISM EXTENDS TO SOUTHEAST ASIA, 1908-39

SAREKAT ISLAM AND NATIONALISM IN JAVA

On the whole, Nationalism arose in Southeast Asia somewhat later than it did in China and Japan or in the Indian Subcontinent, though there were sentiments already existing in these countries which only needed encouragement to turn them into full-fledged Nationalist movements. It was events such as the Filipino revolt against Spain, the outcome of the Russo-Japanese War, and the Chinese Revolution of 1911 which provided this encouragement. An essential quality of Nationalism, it seems, is that it can develop only in response to a challenge, and this challenge was to be found in Southeast Asia in the intensified action of the European Colonial Powers in opening up their territories and consolidating them.

The Nationalist Movement began to manifest itself in Indonesia —or rather in Java—somewhat earlier than in the other countries, and for this reason it will be appropriate to consider it first.

It is notable that the Movement first arose during the period when the Dutch were putting their 'Ethical Policy' into practice. As a means for improving the agricultural production, education, and health of the people, the Dutch (as has been seen in Chapter 5) attempted to teach them how to manage their own affairs, using the *desa* (village) as the unit. But in doing it, they tended to treat the villagers like children and this aroused widespread resentment. Therefore, when a purely native movement arose, it was natural that the Indonesians should support it as a means of establishing their self-respect.

The first Nationalist Society to be formed was Budi Utomo ('Glorious Endeavour') (1908), with the aim of organizing schools on a national basis, taking its inspiration from the Indian poet

Rabindranath Tagore and (to a lesser extent) from Mahatma Gandhi. But three years later, it was followed by another association of a very different character. This was Sarekat Dagang Islam (Islamic Traders' Association), the offshoot of an Islamic revival among Sumatrans and Javanese intended to offset a renewed drive for converts on the part of the Christian missionaries. But its first action was directed, not against the Dutch, but to protect Javanese traders in *batik* (painted sarongs, etc.) against the sharp practices of the Chinese traders in exploiting the industry. From this beginning the Society extended its programme to encouraging mutual economic support, and to promoting the intellectual and material well-being of Indonesians and 'the true religion of Islam'. At its first congress, held in 1913, at the instance of its leader, Tjokro, it passed a series of resolutions in favour of national advancement 'in ways that do not conflict with Government or the Law'. At its first nation-wide congress, held in 1916, 80 local societies, with a combined membership of 360,000, were represented and passed a resolution demanding self-government on the basis of union with the Netherlands.

In the meantime a political movement which had for its object, not co-operation with the Dutch Authorities but their replacement by Indonesians, had come to the surface. In December 1912, Ki Hadjar Dewantoro, Dr Douwes Dekker, and Dr Mangunkusomo founded the Indische Partij at Bandung. Its objectives were set out in a newspaper article by Dekker (an 'Indo', or Dutch-Eurasian journalist) in which he claimed that Indonesia belonged to the *blijvers* (natives) who had been born in Indonesia, whatever their racial origin. In consequence of their open opposition to Dutch Authority, the three men were exiled, but their place was taken by three Dutch Socialist officials, one of whom was Sneevliet, who was destined to meet his death in front of a Gestapo firing squad in Holland in 1942.

In face of these developments, the Dutch tried to win over the Nationalists to a policy of an advance towards self-government by constitutional means by creating a 'parliament', the Volksraad. In 1916 the Netherlands Parliament passed an act bringing it into being, but it was not until 1918 that it held its first meeting. Half of its members were elected by local and city councils, and half were appointed by the Governor-General. But, it was in no sense a representative body, for it had a European majority and in any case its powers were limited to the offering of advice to the government. Later on (1925) the number of its members was raised from 48 to 61 and it was given an elective majority, but the Indonesians still had only 30 seats and the powers of the assembly were very slight. The Dutch, right up to the Japanese occupation, were unwilling to effect any real transfer of power.

In the years following the First World War, however, there were many thousands of Indonesians who still hoped to secure their aims by constitutional methods. On the other hand, the revolutionaries had been stimulated to direct action by the success of the Russian Revolution of 1917. These developments led to a split in Sarekat Islam when it held its Congress at Surabaya in 1921. A Communist section of the movement had already broken away to form the Perserikatan Komunist di India (Indonesian Communist Party) affiliated to the Third International. But the Marxist challenge to Sarekat Islam was taken up by the Muslims, whose leader, Haji Agus Salim, declared that the Prophet had expounded historical materialism twelve hundred years before Marx was born. In the subsequent voting the Muslims carried the day and the PKI members were excluded from the Society.

In 1922 Sarekat Islam established relations with the Indian National Congress and adopted a policy of non-co-operation with the Dutch. In the years 1923–6 there was a series of attempted risings, accompanied by strikes. Through Singapore, the PKI established contact with the Chinese Communist Party. In 1926, the Communists tried to start a revolution in West Java and Sumatra, having received vague promises of support from the USSR. But the Dutch immediately took strong and resolute action with the result that the revolutionary movement collapsed and some 1,300 members of the PKI were arrested and imprisoned in New Guinea. Sarekat Islam was left as the main organ of Indonesian Nationalism, though by this time many other political parties had come into existence—some being offshoots of parties in Holland, while others represented Chinese or other communal interests.

Dutch policy, like British Conservative policy in Ireland in the 1890s, was to 'kill home rule by kindness', that is to say to improve conditions for the people to such an extent that the Nationalists were deprived of their main weapon against them. When the great slump of 1929–32 hit Indonesia in the early thirties, the authorities took energetic measures to encourage native industry, and when the revival of trade and industry began, there were improved relations between the Dutch and the Indonesians leading to greater co-operation between them. Nevertheless, the struggle for independence was continued with unabated determination.

In face of this trend, the Dutch made no attempt to copy British policy in India and Burma which was designed to meet parallel movements. On the contrary, fearing to stimulate subversive action against themselves, they showed the greatest reluctance to increase the facilities for secondary and higher education. What they did do in this direction was too little and too slow for the Nationalists who attempted to fill the gap by setting up 'wild' schools on their own, literally by the thousand. These schools were mostly highly inefficient, and all they managed to do was to spread disaffection without providing much in the way of education.

In 1936 the Volksraad passed a resolution calling upon the government of the Netherlands to convene a conference to devise methods to bring self-government into effect and to fix a time-limit for it. But nothing was done, and it was not until July 1941, when Queen Wilhelmina and her Government were refugees in London and the Japanese were in occupation of the whole of Indonesia, that the Dutch decided to accede to the Volksraad's demands.

BURMESE NATIONALISM AND THE BRITISH

Nationalism, when it spread through Southeast Asia, did not follow a single consistent pattern; it took different shapes in the several countries according to local conditions and varying with the policies pursued by the metropolitan Power. There was indeed a broad similarity in the course it followed in Indonesia and French Indochina because the policy of both of the Dutch and the French was

to slow down rather than accelerate the transition to self-government. In Burma, on the other hand, the official policy of the British
government was to facilitate the process. Attention has already been
given to developments in Burma under the 'dyarchy' system, so
that for the purpose of this chapter it remains only to show how
Burmese Nationalism developed within the constitutional framework provided by the reforms of the 1920s.

Whatever the demerits of the 'dyarchy' system, it did at least
provide an outlet for popular opinion in the early years of the growth
of Burmese Nationalism. In consequence, there were in the twenties
and early thirties none of the rebellions and few of the acts of violence
which were general in Indonesia and Indochina in the same period.
It was not until the late thirties that the Nationalist movement
veered round fully to revolution as a means of achieving full independence. Until this change took place, the history of the movement is to be traced mainly in events within the legislature and in
conflicts in the field of education.

Right from the start of the 'dyarchy' constitution, the Opposition
in the new legislature was nearly always stronger in voting power
than the government and was solidly Nationalist. The dominant
party was the People's Party led by U Ba Pe, and often referred to
as the 'Twenty-One Party' from the number of those who signed
its first programme. There was a smaller Independent Party, led
by Sir J. A. Maung Gyi, which gave its support to the government.
And there was a third party of extreme Nationalists under U Chit
Haing which boycotted the Legislative Council.

U Ba Pe and his party were moderates, who were anxious to use
the Legislative Council to compel the government by constitutional
means to adopt the reforms they thought were required. These
included better education to fit Burmese for self-government, rapid
Burmaization of the public services, the promotion of indigenous
economic development, the curtailment of foreign exploitation, and
the provision of more money for 'nation-building' departments
and for agricultural credit. But in spite of some notable progress,
especially in the spheres of education and public health, the system
did not really work. The electorate were apathetic and the Burmese
leadership was rendered ineffectual through personal rivalries. As

J. S. Furnivall summed up on the experiment, 'The condition of the cultivators deteriorated, racial tension became more acute, crime increased, and disaffection spread.'

It must be remembered, too, that in addition to the 'reserved' powers of the Governor-in-Council, the Governor in person exercised complete control over the so-called Excluded Areas—the Shan States, the Karenni, and the Kachin and Chin tracts—which lay outside the jurisdiction of the legislature. (These were all included later in the Union of Burma.)

The fault lay in the fact that the framing of 'nation-building' reforms was undertaken by the Nationalist members of the Council, whereas the means of financing them remained in the hands of the British, for Finance was one of the 'reserved subjects' under the constitution. Thus the Nationalists were not limited in shaping their demands by any sense of financial responsibility: it was the function of the executive to find the money. The Finance Department, on the other hand, felt compelled to refuse to finance many of the reforms on the grounds of financial stringency. It was thus impossible to work out a nicely-adjusted long-term policy, involving the co-operation of the government and the electorate. Burmese Nationalism was therefore trying to learn to govern the country in a lop-sided way—with liberty to voice its demands, yet with no responsibility to ensure that the demands were within the capacity of the country's resources. Burma was artificially tied to India, and faced by increasing Indian immigration and economic competition, the Burmese feared that one day their country might become the vassal state of the Indian Commonwealth when it achieved its independence. It is not surprising in the circumstances that the Burmese chose separation from India when the opportunity arose at the Round Table Conference called after the report of the Simon Commission (see p. 110).

The fact that Burma was politically part of India made it well-nigh impossible to control Indian immigration into Burma. In particular, the Indian moneylenders (*Chettiars*) gained control of a great part of the rice-land, and when, during the depression of 1929–32, they called in their loans and foreclosed mortgages on more than two and a quarter million acres of paddy land in the

Irrawaddy delta, many thousands of dispossessed Burmese cultivators were left without employment.

The period 1937–41 marked the rise of two important Burmese political figures—Dr Ba Maw, founder of the *Sinyetha* (Poor Man's) party, and U Saw, leader of the *Myochit* (Patriotic) party.

Ba Maw, a European-educated Burmese, was first elected to the Legislative Council in 1932 as an anti-Separationist, and in 1936, although his party made a poor showing at the elections, the new parliament was so divided by factional rivalries that he was able, by clever manipulation in alliance with non-Burmese elements in the house, to make himself Burma's first Prime Minister in 1937. But Ba Maw was under constant attack from his political enemies, who unseated him in late 1938. During the Japanese occupation, Ba Maw became the head of the Japanese puppet régime.

U Saw, Ba Maw's rival, was a very different personality. Unlike him, he had received only an elementary school education and obtained support from quite another stratum of the Burmese population. He edited a newspaper, *The Sun*, which was openly anti-British and pro-Japanese. On a special mission to London in 1941, U Saw failed to obtain an unqualified pledge from Mr Churchill of post-war dominion status for Burma. Later he was imprisoned in Ethiopia and was not able to return to Burma until 1946. Then, in 1947, he hired ruffians to assassinate the Prime Minister, Aung San, and was arrested, tried, and executed.

By the time that the Second World War broke out in Europe in 1939, the left-wing Nationalists were actively planning revolution. Prominent among them was a youthful Burmese group known as the Thakins ('thakin' was the Burmese equivalent of the Indian 'sahib', applied to Europeans, and the revolutionaries addressed one another by this title to suggest that it was they and not the British who should be the masters of Burma). The Thakins accepted Buddhism as an integral part of Burmese culture, but their leaders did not repudiate Western learning and technology. They were ready for collaboration with the Japanese when they invaded Burma, and in 1941 about thirty of them accepted the invitation of the Japanese to proceed to Formosa where they received training in their collaborationist role.

VIETNAMESE NATIONALISM AND THE FRENCH

Something has been seen above of the way in which Nationalism in Southeast Asia developed in opposition to Dutch and British policies in Indonesia and Burma, and the question may now be asked as to how it became shaped in reaction from the highly cultural 'Colonialism' of the French in Indochina.

The failure of the French to lead the countries of Indochina towards self-government was similar in essentials to the Dutch failure in Indonesia, and arose from the same causes. Neither the French nor the Dutch realised the necessity of preparing peacefully to hand over power to the local populations until it was too late. The British in Burma, on the other hand, did at least give the people some experience in self-government, and the eventual granting of independence was smoothly effected. Moreover, by admitting Burmese in to the Civil Service, they bequeathed to independent Burma a corps of able administrators who helped to keep the country united through a troubled period.

The French policy shut off the Vietnamese intellectuals—the *élite*—from the administrative posts, and thus threw them into the lap of the revolutionaries. When a belated attempt was made in 1938 to introduce reforms to remedy this, the latter were too few to satisfy the intellectuals, and too late to stay the floodtide of disaffection. 'Despite sporadic application of Liberal and even Socialist theories to Indochina', says Virginia Thompson, 'the general administrative trend had been towards a divide-and-rule policy as the best means of hampering the growth of Annamite nationalism. Eleventh-hour gestures of liberalism, inspired by the fear of a European war, were all too tardy and too inadequate to counter the results of half a century of cultivation of enmity and distrust among the native intellectuals and the failure to give the masses any real cause to rise to the defence of a government that had never awakened their loyalty by extensively improving their standard of living.' And this is not an unfair summing up.

The early Nationalist associations in Indochina put forward a moderate programme. It was only when lack of any marked success in promoting their aims had discredited them with the bulk of their followers that the more leftist associations robbed them of popular support. Belonging to the category of moderates was the Tong-kingese Party of the Pham Quynh and the Constitutional Party of the Bui Quang Chieu. Their failure led to the rise of parties which concentrated on direct action. In 1927 the New Annam Revolutionary Association (Tan Viet Cach Menh Dang) was established, drawing its support from the Nationalist-minded lower middle classes and the Communists. It organized a series of strikes, in consequence of which it was subjected to severe repression by the government, and in 1929 was dissolved. The Communist elements of the old Cach Menh Dang then joined the New Annam Revolutionary Youth Association (Viet Nam Cach Menh Thanh Nien Hoi) to form the Indochinese Communist Party under Nguyen Ai-Quoc (later to be known as Ho Chi Minh). In 1931, two years after its foundation, the Communist Party claimed 1,500 members and some 100,000 peasant adherents.

The Viet Nam Quoc Dan Dong, founded about 1927 in Tong-king, was modelled on the Chinese Kuomintang (Quoc Dan Dong is the Vietnamese equivalent of Kuomintang—literally 'National People's Party')—but was equivalent only to the extreme left wing of the latter, and ignored Chiang's purge of 1927. It followed a revolutionary line, and in February 1929, after making an unsuccessful attempt on the life of Pasquier, the Governor-General of Indochina, it succeeded in murdering Bazin, head of the Labour Recruiting Bureau. But in the next stages of its revolutionary programme, which included the engineering of a mutiny at Yenbay and throwing bombs at the Commissariat at Hanoi, it failed entirely when it tried to set up a government of its own. Thousands of its supporters, together with many Yunnanese who had joined them, were executed and the French convict settlements were filled to overflowing. When the Second World War broke out, the French were still to all appearances firmly in the saddle in Indochina.

THE FILIPINOS PRESS FOR INDEPENDENCE

Account has been taken in Chapter 5 of the differing American attitudes towards Philippine independence of the successive Republican and Democratic administrations—the former tending to delay and the latter to expedite the process. But private interests often cut across political loyalties in the United States, and the great depression of 1929–32 advanced the cause of Philippine Nationalism inside America.

Hitherto the Filipinos had clamoured for *political* independence, while secretly they feared that it might bring *economic* independence as well—and this would have spelled ruin to the Islands. The average share of the United States in Philippine trade amounted to nearly 80 per cent, but once independence came it was logical to assume that the tariff walls of America would automatically go up against imports from the Philippines. This very argument was the one which (ironically enough) during the slump gave a great boost to the popularity of the Philippine Nationalist movement in certain quarters in the United States. So long as the Philippines could export their products to the USA on a free-trade basis (as had been the case—almost unnoticed—since 1909) they were a menace to the livelihood of Americans now that there was world trade depression. Thus it was that groups of farmers, patriotic societies, and labour unions joined in a campaign to secure independence for the Philippines at the earliest possible moment.

A commission headed by Sergio Osmena and Manuel Roxas arrived in Washington from the Philippines in December 1932 to give their moral support to the passage in the Hare-Hawes-Cutting Bill which provided for independence after a transitional period of ten years, a quota limitation on Philippine imports into the United States, a gradual application of the American tariff, and an annual immigration quota in the United States of 50 Filipinos. President Hoover vetoed the bill on the ground that by it America repudiated its responsibilities, and because the Philippines, left alone, would only doubtfully be able to maintain its independence, but his veto was overriden and repudiated in the islands.

Before the decision could be changed, it was necessary for a change to take place in the United States administration. This was achieved when Franklin Roosevelt became President (1932). Manuel Quezon himself went to the United States to help draft a new bill. This bill became the Tydings–McDuffiie Act, which was approved by the President on 24 March 1934. It provided for a ten-year transitional period during which the United States was to remain the supreme authority, after which the Philippines would be given outright independence. In view of the Philippine economic dependence on the United States, the act established a system of quotas to cushion the shocks of readjustment. Thereupon the Filipinos met in a constitutional convention to draw up a fundamental law for the eventual Republic and for the Commonwealth that was to be created in the meantime. The constitution decided upon closely following the American model. In 1935 Quezon was elected first President of the Commonwealth.

The Philippine people were filled with gratitude to the American people. President Quezon voiced a generally-shared sentiment when he said: 'When that starry flag finally comes down from Santiago [a local cape] in 1946, it will find somewhere in its folds the grateful hearts of a people—a new and vibrant republic facing with optimistic hope its rising dawn.' But before the starry flag *did* come down (according to promise, in 1946) there was to supervene a period of great misery and tribulation for the Philippines—the three-and-a-half years of Japanese occupation (December 1941– June 1945).

THE IMPACT OF THE KUOMINTANG ON THE OVERSEAS CHINESE

It has been logical and convenient to consider the rise in Indonesian, Burmese, and French Nationalism primarily in terms of opposition to the Colonial Power. In the case of Malaya and Siam, however, such a procedure is not a valid one. A true 'Malayan' Nationalism was not yet in being, and what existed so far was only an incipient 'Malay' Nationalism as an expression of fear of the large Chinese minority in Malaya: in Siam, where there was no Colonial Power, Nationalism was daily growing in response again to the Siamese fear of their large Chinese minority. The presence of the Overseas Chinese was also a factor in the development of Indonesian, Vietnamese, and Filipino Nationalism, but on a much smaller scale, and was subordinate to the Dutch, French, and American factor in promoting it.

The Chinese in Southeast Asia were almost exclusively drawn

from the Southeast maritime provinces of Kwangtung and Fukien, and (in a minor degree) from the interior province of Kwangsi. Up to the twentieth century, the Chinese immigrants had been comparatively few in number and constituted only a small proportion of the total population, but with the flood of immigration following on the opening-up of Southeast Asia by the Western Colonial Powers, they began to form sizeable minorities in several of the Southeast Asian countries (by 1948, in the entire region they would number about 8,500,000 in a total population of 160,000,000).

When the Chinese began to arrive in Southeast Asia in considerable numbers, bringing their womenfolk with them, they began to create a 'problem'. The Chinese Revolution of 1911 produced in the long run a great change in the attitude of the Overseas Chinese. From being conscious only of their family, clan, or tribe they became aware that they belonged to the great Chinese Nation—divided politically for the time being though it might be. The Chinese Nationalist Party (the KMT) derived great support from the Chinese of Southeast Asia, and their nationality law (following the First Principle, Nationality, of the Three Principles of Sun Yat-Sen, incorporated later into the Nationalist Government Constitution), claiming *all* Chinese, irrespective of any other national status they might possess (e.g. of British subjects if born in the Straits Settlements) as nationals of China according to the *jus sanguinis* ('the law of the blood', or nationality from male parentage, as distinguished from the *jus soli*, or 'law of the soil', or nationality from place of birth) was the source of much friction with the local governments with whose laws it conflicted. Chinese Communism, too, was making itself felt in Southeast Asia as a subversive influence. All this was on top of the economic power of the Overseas Chinese, which was out of all proportion to their numbers. It was in opposition to the Overseas Chinese that (as has already been insisted upon) Malay and Siamese Nationalism began to emerge. The former, however, was much the slower in developing.

MALAYA

Before the Second World War Malay Nationalism had scarcely come into being. There was, however, a negative state of fear and resentment of Chinese economic pressure which provided a favourable soil in which national feeling could germinate—indeed had already germinated. The Malay *rayats* (peasants) did not share proportionately in the growing wealth of the country, and in a vaguely restive and discontented state they looked abroad and saw the growing National movement in Indonesia. This had a religious as well as an economic basis, but the Mohammedanism of the Malays was of too tolerant a character to act as a driving force. But from the beginning of the twentieth century the increasing prosperity of the Malay aristocracy under British rule had enabled them to send their sons to Cairo, Beirut, or Mecca for education, and here they came under the influence of Pan-Islamism. When they returned to Malaya they communicated their new ideas to their fellow Malays and formed literary associations and debating societies which, however, did not grow into political parties. The Malays before 1939 were on the whole content to leave the protection of their interests to the British.

The Chinese, for their part, were satisfied with the favoured economic position that they enjoyed under British rule, but resented their treatment as aliens—as they were regarded even when their families had been in Malaya for generations. They took pride from the fact that under the Kuomintang China was once more unified, and the *towkays* (heads of businesses) were pleased that Chiang Kai-Shek was taking a firm (not to say a violent) line with the Communists.

This incessant banging of the Chinese Nationalist drum, however, on the part of the Nanking Government upset not only the colonial governments of Southeast Asia, but also the Malays and Indonesians and the independent Asian Government of Siam. By treating all Chinese resident in Southeast Asia as Chinese citizens, the Nanking Government virtually created an *imperium in imperio* (a 'government within a government') in all the countries with Chinese minorities. The Nanking Government consuls in these countries issued all Chinese, irrespective of whether they possessed another nationality or not, with Chinese passports, and they sent to Malaya, etc., educational missions which laid down the policy for local Chinese schools.

Until 1932 there was no restriction of Chinese immigration into Malaya, and the influx was regulated by supply and demand alone. The number of Chinese in Malaya (including Singapore) increased from 917,000 in a total of 2,673,000 in 1911 to 2,379,000 in a total of 5,511,000 in 1941, in which year they were the largest single community for the first time, although the Malays (including other Malaysians from Indonesia) were still in a majority of a few hundred thousand on the mainland.

In 1930 the Kuomintang was not registered as a society by the Malayan governments, and was therefore illegal (the Societies Registration Law had been passed in the 1880s to enable the authorities to deal with the scourge of the Secret Societies). The Malayan governments were reluctant to remove the ban, but the British Foreign Office urged that now the Nationalist (KMT) government had been recognized by Britain it was no longer logical or reasonable to refuse recognition of the party in Malaya. Discussions took place in China between Sir Miles Lampson, the British Minister, and Mr Wang Cheng-Ting, the Chinese Government Representative, whereby a compromise was reached. The Malayan governments were to take steps to amend the local legislation, making it clear that the Kuomintang was not, as such, an illegal society in Malaya, and that there was no objection to any Chinese in Malaya being a member of the KMT in China, and that there would be no interference with the KMT members so long as their activities were not inimical to the interests of the local governments and provided no attempts were made to re-establish control over local branches of the organization.

The latter condition, however, was not observed, and the Kuomintang continued to operate almost openly, and to circulate lists of 'Humiliation Days' on which the sins of 'Imperialism' against China were to be celebrated. Moreover, from 1937 onwards the Chinese government was at war with Japan, and the activities of the local Chinese (either under KMT or Communist instigation) in boycotting Japanese goods or in entering shops and tarring those goods suspected of being Japanese was an embarrassment to the Malayan governments since Britain was then at peace with Japan.

The Malayan Communist Party had been in existence from the

early 1920s, but its activities came to the surface only from 1934 onwards when it ordered strikes, sabotage in the Singapore Naval Base, transport boycotts, demonstrations against increased taxation, etc. But until after the outbreak of war with Germany in 1939, the deliberately subversive activities of the Communists caused much less trouble to the authorities than did the obstructive nationalism of the Kuomintang.

Following the *coup d'état* in China in 1936, when Chiang Kai-Shek was kidnapped by Marshal Chang Hsueh-Liang, a National Salvation Movement against Japan was inaugurated in which both the Nationalists and the Communists participated. But although there was a re-naming of local Communist organizations in keeping with the new understanding, the alliance between the two parties was an uneasy one and each continued to work entirely on its own.

If, up to the outbreak of the war with Japan, no Malay political organizations had come into being to offset the pressures of the Chinese it was not because there was no disposition on the part of the Malays to resist these pressures. The fact was, however, that the British through their strict observation of the treaties of protection with the Malay States identified themselves with the Malays as the 'people of the country' and the Malays as a whole felt that they could rely on the British to keep Chinese political encroachment within bounds. Nevertheless there were many Malays who felt that the British were too lenient in dealing with the Chinese economically and otherwise, and this prepared the way for Malay collaboration with the Japanese when they invaded Malaya.

SIAM (THAILAND)

The Chinese immigrants into Siam were readily assimilated until greatly increased immigration and the introduction of Chinese women turned them into a self-sufficient minority. We have already seen (p. 107) how King Rama VI had characterized the Chinese as the 'Jews of the East', and their practical monopoly of trade and industry (including the rice trade) increased their unpopularity. Thus it was to be expected that the measures adopted after the Revolution of 1932 to enhance Thai Nationalism would be directed against the Chinese. The claims of the Nanking government with respect to the Overseas Chinese in addition aroused great resentment among the Siamese.

The policy of the post-revolutionary Thai government was on the one hand to encourage the Siamese to engage in trade and commerce, and on the other to exercise discrimination against the Chinese. From 1936 onwards the government entered increasingly into business on its own account—it first established paper-mills, a sugar factory at Lampang, a silk factory at Nagara Rajasima, a tobacco factory at Bangkok, an oil refinery at Klong Toi, a cannery at Pak Chang, a textile-mill, and a soya-bean oil distillery, and was planning to engage in the manufacture of cigarettes, leather, and cement, to build rice-mills and a tin-smelter, and to operate tin-mines and co-operative stores. The government followed this up by a new taxation system obviously directed mainly against the Chinese. By the new code of taxation passed by the National Assembly on 29 March 1940 the burden was to be borne by the merchant class, which was, of course, largely Chinese.

In addition to those measures, a new amendment to the Aliens' Registration Act was passed, whereby all aliens were required to pay a yearly registration fee not exceeding 10 baht (M$15) in addition to the original immigration fees.

'As law followed law, dislodging foreign business men from the fields of commercial enterprise which they had held, in some cases for centuries', says Landon, 'the natural tendency among the Chinese was to seek Thai citizenship in larger numbers than previously.' This, however, was a development not entirely welcome to the Siamese, and they met it by raising bars to such naturalization.

The Chinese complaint was that not only were they, a helpless minority, discriminated against with a breath-taking series of regulations and decrees, but also that they were not allowed a decent interval in which to adapt themselves to the new situation.

In reply, it seemed, to Kuomintang Nationalism, the Premier, Pibul (Phibun) Songkram, in 1939 proclaimed the principles of *Ratha Niyom*, which was rather like a mixture of the First Principle, Nationality, of Sun Yat-Sen, with the New Life Movement which had been inaugurated by Chiang Kai-Shek in China. As the fervour for nationalism grew and highly-placed Siamese vied with one another in showing their enthusiasm for *Ratha Niyom*, agitation against the Chinese increased, reinforced by active government measures. By the middle of August more than thirty Chinese schools and ten of the eleven Chinese newspapers had been closed, hundreds were being arrested in the 'probes' of Chinese secret societies, and raids on Chinese schools, newspaper offices, and houses were becoming a daily occurrence; several prominent Chinese were in gaol for remitting money to China, and the entire Chinese community was in an uproar.

On the eve of the war with Japan in 1941 the active indigenous Nationalisms in Southeast Asia were the Burmese, the Vietnamese, the Thai, the Indonesian, and the Philippine. In Malaya, 'Malayan' Nationalism had not yet germinated, though the ground was favourable to the growth of a 'Malay' Nationalism, whose seeds had already been sown. The one great external Nationalism, which was stimulating the growth of the indigenous ones, was the Chinese. Indian Nationalism had appeared to date only in a moderate and undemonstrative way in support of the Indian Congress among the million and a half Indians distributed through Southeast Asia, and in such a form as caused no hostile reactions from the neighbouring communities or the local governments. In the British Borneo territories, Nationalism had not yet come into being as they were still in a very early stage of political development. The whole region, however, was about to come under the temporary domination of another Asian Nationalism which had now assumed the character of an Imperialism—namely that of Japan.

8

SOUTH AND EAST ASIA IN THE 1930s

In the three preceding chapters, an account was given, first of the Colonial System at its zenith, and then of the Nationalism that eventually took its place. But had it not been for the Pacific War, it is probable that the Colonial Powers would have remained in control of most of Southeast Asia—if not of South Asia—for many years to come. So in order to gauge more accurately the complex forces at work, we must survey the region as it was in the 1930s in greater detail.

An ordinary visitor to South and East Asia in the 1930s might well have remained unaware that anything out of the way was happening. The countries under Colonial rule were all outwardly peaceful, their governments seemed to be in complete control of the situation, and trade and industry (except for the short interruption of the 1930–2 slump) were developing fast. A visitor to the Indian Subcontinent, however, or to China, could not have failed to detect an atmosphere of civil ferment in which revolution seemed only just round the corner.

The last three stages in the Indian Subcontinent's move towards independence were (a) the return of the Labour government to power in Britain in May 1929, leading to the Act of 1935, (b) the events from 1935 to the Second World War, and (c) the subsequent happenings until the British withdrawal in 1947.

The Labour Prime Minister, Ramsay Macdonald, and many members of his party, were known to be friendly to Indian Nationalism, but there were, in the House of Commons, besides the Conservative Opposition, some sixty Liberal members led by Lloyd George who were more cautious. The Viceroy of India, Lord Irwin,

Mass Disobedience in India

was himself a Conservative, but he had realized early that the National movement was real and growing and that repression was not the real answer to the problem. On the Indian Nationalist side, the leader was Mahatma Gandhi. Hitherto those who opposed him (especially the 'die-hards' in British politics) had been disposed to 'write him off' as either a harmless eccentric or as an irresponsible demagogue. But Lord Irwin, at least, knew him as a man of strong personal magnetism with an insight into Indian sentiment. Irwin himself was a zealous Christian (an Anglican), and the two men who now set together to find a solution for the deadlock represented Christendom and Hindustan in their essence.

Lord Irwin's terms of reference were contained in a declaration of the British Labour government that 'the natural issue of India's constitutional progress is Dominion Status'. A Round Table Conference (already referred to, see p. 132) was then called between the British government and representatives of Indian opinion. Gandhi and the right wing of Congress at first agreed to Dominion Status as their aim, but the Indian public had been worked into a state of emotion by long agitation, and the left wing of Congress, led by the young Nehru, was able to insist on conditions that the British government could not accept. One of these was that the constitution for the new Dominion should at once be drawn up by the Conference. The position of the British Labour government, with its dependence on the Liberals, was weak and the declaration itself had already been severely attacked inside the Conservative Party (Winston Churchill had defected from Mr Baldwin's leadership on this issue). Gandhi had to make a decision, and he chose to break with the British government rather than with his own left wing. In the absence of a further British gesture, the Lahore Congress, in December 1929, opted for mass disobedience.

The Congress aim, as previously, was so to paralyse the working of the government as to compel it to concede the Congress demands —but these demands (strangely enough) were also the declared aims of the government! The only difference between the government and Congress turned on the question—'How, and how soon?' Mounting economic discontent, which presaged the onset of the great depression, favoured the civil disobedience movement. Gandhi then announced his defiance of the salt laws on the ground that the salt tax was iniquitous, and he himself walked to the sea at Dandi and solemnly made salt on the seashore. The response was so general and the popular enthusiasm so tumultuous that the government could not fail to attempt to restore order. On 5 May 1930 Gandhi was taken into 'protective custody', and by the end of June some 60,000 Congress supporters were in prison—mostly for symbolic defiance of the law.

Gandhi had won the first round, but there were important elements in India that he did not represent—notably the Liberals and the Muslims. Lord Irwin's counter-move to mass disobedience was to secure the participation of Liberals, Muslims, and the Indian Princes in the Conference. Gandhi thereupon entered into negotiations with the Viceroy and they declared a truce. Civil disobedience was to end, and political prisoners were to be released.

The truce was a failure, and for this world opinion (in the 1960s) seemed inclined to blame both sides. Yet it cannot be denied that Congress had alienated Muslim opinion in the course of its manoeuvres and thus made a united independent India impossible of achievement. Civil disobedience was revived in 1932–3, and Samuel Hoare (Secretary of State for India) and Lord Willingdon (Viceroy) seemed to think that Congress could be permanently broken by stern repression. The Congress claim to be the voice of all India was untenable in 1930, and even more so in 1932, but the attempts to break Congress resulted, not in its collapse, but only in renewed bitterness which made the final settlement after the Second World War even more difficult.

Nevertheless, the Government of India Act of 1935 was passed from strength—not from weakness. Britain was now emerging from the great trade depression and had weathered the most serious challenge to its authority since the Mutiny. The Act was thoroughly thought out and represented a draft constitution for an Indian Dominion. Dyarchy was abolished in the provinces but was now adopted for the central government. There were separate constituencies for Muslims and other communities, and there were reserved seats for the 'Untouchables' and for other special interests. A novel feature of the Constitution was the introduction of the federal principle, with the establishment of full responsible government in the provinces and dyarchy at the centre.

One of the weaknesses of the Constitution was that there was no recognition that India contained separate cultures as well as regions and communities, and that the Muslims and Sikhs (for example) regarded certain sections of their communal life as sacred and would accept no dictation from outside authority. In any case, it was un-realistic for Congress to regard the Muslims as 'just a minority', even though the Hindus were more than twice as numerous. Gandhi maintained that Congress represented all Indians, and that there was therefore no need for Muslim parties. The result was that the Muslims henceforth stood aside from Congress and the Indian Subcontinent was thus doomed to partition.

The conclusion of the Second World War virtually marked the end of the British Raj in India. On the eve of its outbreak one may enquire what, in retrospect, the Raj had meant to India. Outstand-ing was the British establishment of law and order. The Moguls, too, had made law and order their primary object, though with much less regard for impartial justice, and with less completeness and success. But more important even than order was introduction (through education) of the concept of the rights of the individual and of the responsibilities of individuals to all other men. These ideas cut right across the age-old institution of caste and were revolutionary to the orthodox Hindu Society of the nineteenth century. Nationalism, too, which provided the driving force, was an innovation imported from the modern West.

CHIANG KAI-SHEK AND THE ASCENDANCY OF THE KUOMINTANG

We are sitting, so to speak, in an observation car—the weight of a curved pendulum pivoted on Northern Siberia which swings from west to east and east to west across Asia in alternation. Now, once more, we swing from India, passing over Southeast Asia, which is to all appearances tranquil, to the troubled China of the 1930s.

In our account of the rise of Nationalism in China (see p. 136), we have already referred to the Northern Expedition under Chiang

Kai-Shek, intended to reunite the country, and to his collision with the Communists in the course of carrying it out. We must now proceed to consider this dramatic 'show-down' more closely.

The military reunification of China was accomplished in two stages. The first, in 1926, had brought the Nationalist armies to Hankow after only two months of campaigning, for nearly everywhere they received a warm welcome from the people. The second stage was delayed by further dissentions inside the Kuomintang, and it was not until June 1928 that the army entered Peking. For this entry, the ground had had to be prepared by secret 'deals' with the northern warlords. Chiang's forces were now in control of most of China, but, under the surface, the country was still split up into factions. To appreciate the reason for this we must travel back a few months. In the advance towards the Yangtze, the KMT propaganda corps, manned by Communists and trained by Russians, had called upon the peasants to rise against the landlords. Meanwhile, in the cities, the Communists, working through the labour-unions, were hitting at the capitalists by strikes and riots.

In April 1927 Chiang had to make a decision. His army was now besieging Shanghai in its northern advance. Should he allow the left wing of his party to gain the upper hand and expropriate the property of the great Shanghai capitalists, or should he throw in his lot with the latter? He was influenced in his decision not only by his personal inclinations and his alliance by marriage with the Soong banking family, but by the need of money to pay his troops. He therefore came to an understanding with the Shanghai financiers, and the city fell without a struggle. On 12 April Chiang ordered the liquidation of all the workers' pickets in Chapei, Woosung, Pootung, and Nanshih, and any other Communists or Communist-supporters who were within reach. The KMT–MCP alliance had met a violent end.

The left-controlled Hankow government now dismissed Chiang from his supreme command, but, with the support of the Kuomintang right wing, he thereupon set up a rival government at Nanking. The final split, however, came much further to the left when both right wing and moderate KMT members combined against the extreme left wing. (The KMT leader, Wang Ching-Wei, attempted to effect a compromise between the two sides, but failed.) The Communists were at this point identified with Russia, and the non-Communist members of the Kuomintang were convinced that Russia intended to replace their party by the Chinese Communist Party and through it to manipulate China's policies at home and abroad in its own interest. For this reason, Chiang was able to close the ranks of the Kuomintang against the Communists, both Russian and Chinese. Borodin, the Russian adviser, and his staff, had to escape from the country, and diplomatic relations with the USSR, which had been opened in 1924, were now broken off.

Chiang now resumed his march to the north, but having reached Peking in the summer of 1928 (as before mentioned) he could go no further, for the Japanese made clear their determination to prevent his forces from occupying Manchuria. The Kuomintang leaders thereupon returned to Nanking, taking with them the embalmed body of Sun Yat-Sen for interment in a vast mausoleum which was being built near the Kuomintang capital for its reception. They thereupon set to work on a new constitution. Not only was this based on Dr Sun's 'Three Principles', but the organic law, passed in 1928, established a government on a pattern he had devised. But the government was closely interlocked with the Party, and the key administrative posts were reserved for Chiang himself and his adherents. Henceforth the Four Big Families of Chiang Kai-Shek, T. V. Soong, H. H. Kung, and the Ch'en brothers (Ch'en Kuo-Fu and Ch'en Li-Fu) were to be the power behind the régime. Between them they controlled, directly or indirectly, all the banking institutions of the country; they supervised the Kuomintang treasury, floated government bonds, and controlled the note issue.

While Chiang was organizing his government, the Communist leaders, who had survived his April purge, were endeavouring to find retreats out of reach of his armies. One group of them under Ho Lung, Yeh T'ing, and Chu Teh had withdrawn into the mountains of Kiangsi, and it was here that the Communists created their first experimental Socialist state and applied their theories of land reform. From here they organized an armed revolt in 1927, marching south to Nanchang, and aiming to occupy Canton. But (as the

Communist historians put it) 'lack of co-operation with the peasant movement deprived them of mass support', and they lost the major part of their strength as a result of the reverses sustained in eastern Kwangtung. Of the forces remaining, one contingent joined the peasant movement in Haifeng and Lufeng, and the rest moved to Southern Hunan under Chu Teh. 'To save the Revolution', the Communist Party called for armed uprisings in various places during the harvest and from the autumn of that year to the spring of the next a series of revolts and risings developed throughout the countryside. One which took place in the autumn between Hunan and northern Kiangi was led by Mao Tse-Tung.

Against the Communists, Chiang conducted a series of campaigns ('encircling movements') until the pressure upon them became so strong that in October 1934 they abandoned their Kiangsi and other bases and undertook an adventurous journey *en masse* through western China, via Kweichow, by various routes, skirting the outward edge of Tibet and Turkistan, and eventually in a year reaching Shensi. This was in October 1935 and their arrival here concluded the 'Long March' of several thousand miles, involving large-scale fighting, heavy losses, and marked by great sacrifices and heroism.

But for many years to come the Communists were to be on the defensive, struggling to survive against heavy odds, while the Nationalist (KMT) government was in effective control of a large part of China, recognized by the Powers, and working out its economic programme within the structure of foreign capitalism. But the Nanking government was, nevertheless, all the time threatened both by other internal and by external enemies. The internal enemies were first of all Feng Yu-Hsiang (the 'Christian General') who wished to control Shantung as soon as the Japanese evacuated it in accordance with the agreement they had made, and then the Kwangsi faction which made war on Nanking—but Chiang's alertness destroyed the Kwangsi forces. In the North, dissatisfaction with the government was aggravated by famine, while in Manchuria trouble was developing with Russia over the Chinese Eastern Railway. A state of war existed for some months until the Chinese accepted a restoration of the *status quo*. Inside the Kuomintang, too, there was friction. Wang Ching-Wei, the left wing advocate of reform, was expelled from the Party in 1930. Meanwhile the party dictatorship inaugurated the period of 'tutelage' during which (according to Sun Yat-Sen's ideas) the people were to be taught by the Kuomintang how to govern themselves—but the period of tutelage was destined to last right up to the moment of the Communist triumph in 1949.

But the external enemy that was to prove the undoing of the Kuomintang government and its hopes of establishing the new China on the principles of Sun Yat-Sen, was Japan. The trends in Japan which were to result in its extension of its territorial ambitions to China proper (as distinguished from the Three Eastern Provinces) are outlined in the next subsection. On 18 September 1931 Japanese forces launched a surprise attack on the Chinese army stationed at Shenyang (Mukden). The Chinese troops offered no effective resistance and the Japanese followed up their occupation of this city by capturing all of Liaoning, Kirin, and Heilungkiang, and by the end of 1932 the whole of Manchuria was in their hands. Later in the same year the province of Jehol, the part of Inner Mongolia abutting on Manchuria, was also overrun by the Japanese, who then turned on Peking.

Popular reaction in China to the Japanese aggression was vigorous. A total boycott of Japanese goods was effected, proving so ruinous to Japanese industry that in 1932 a 'punitive' expedition was sent to Shanghai using the international settlement as a 'neutral' landing-place (a striking demonstration, if one were needed, of the weakness of China under the 'treaty-port' system). The Chinese troops around Shanghai resisted with stubborn bravery, but were eventually overcome by superior forces. The Japanese, having administered their 'lesson', then withdrew. There was also widespread civil resistance to the Japanese in other parts of China—but this was not backed up by the Chinese army.

Whether Chiang Kai-Shek had sufficient resources to resist the Japanese is a matter for debate, but the fact remains that he decided to come to terms with them. By the so-called Tangku truce with Japan it was agreed that an area of some 5,000 square miles south of the Great Wall should be demilitarized and that the Chinese government should take active steps to suppress the boycott and other anti-Japanese activities. The Nationalist government, it was clear, was much more intent on crushing Communist opposition than in resisting foreign encroachments on Chinese sovereignty.

For the next four years this 'appeasement' policy was continued, but it was becoming increasingly clear that the Japanese were not content with their gains. Manchuria they had turned into a puppet state ('Manchukuo'), setting up the ex-emperor of Manchu China, Pu Yi, as its 'Emperor', but they now aimed at a complete economic mastery of the five north-eastern provinces, control over China's foreign policy, and the establishment of a military grip on the entire country. In face of this the Chinese people began to clamour for stronger action, and Cantonese troops were sent to the north to demonstrate. In December 1936 Chiang Kai-Shek, while on a tour of inspection, was kidnapped at Sian and held prisoner by Marshal Chang Hsueh-Liang. While imprisoned in a temple in the mountains of Shensi, he was visited by Communist leaders and forced to agree to co-operate with them against the Japanese. Although this enforced truce between the Kuomintang and the Communists was to prove an uneasy one, it continued, at least in name, for the whole period of the coming Japanese war, and it marked the end of Japan's hopes of getting what it wanted by diplomacy and intimidation. The stage was thus set for the final appeal to force in 1937.

Sino-Japanese hostilities reopened in July 1937 with a clash between Chinese and Japanese troops stationed near Peking (in virtue of the Boxer Protocol). The campaign that followed gave Japan the possession of large blocks of Chinese territory which it occupied, with relatively little changes, until the end of the war. In 1938 the Japanese occupied Nanking and Chiang and his government retreated further up the Yangtze to Chungking, which became their capital and remained out of the enemy's reach until the Japanese surrender allowed them to return to Nanking (1945).

Meanwhile, China had in 1931 invoked the intervention of the League of Nations—with, however, negligible results. The League, on receiving the Lytton Report on Manchuria, decided that 'no collective or co-ordinated action could be taken against Japan as the necessary elements of co-operation were not assured'.

Chiang Kai-Shek and the Kuomintang

Defenders of the Kuomintang régime maintain that had it not been for the Japanese invasion it would probably have consolidated most of the country and industrialized it. No one can, of course, say for certain whether or not this is true, but there was a period of ten years (1927–37) before the Japanese invasion proper during which the Nationalists could fairly be expected to give some proof of their capacity to do this. What then was their actual record?

In 1913 China had some 5,400 miles of railways; in 1931, 8,950; in 1926, it had only a few miles of motor roads; in 1937, about 50,000 miles of them. In 1913, there were 1,200,000 cotton spindles; in 1936, 5,585,066. In 1949, the year of the final disappearance of the Nationalist government from the mainland, China, with an output of 158,000 tons of steel ranked twenty-sixth among the 35 countries producing more than 10,000 tons annually (in 1960 the People's government claimed to have produced 18·45 million tons as compared with Britain's 24 million tons).

So much may serve as an index of industrial achievement. How can we measure national progress in terms of the Three Principles of Sun Yat-Sen—Nationalism, Democracy, and Economics? The Kuomintang government in 1926 occupied the British Settlement in Hankow and were allowed to retain it. 'Nationalism' had made further inroads on special foreign privileges in China before 1941, but when China became an 'ally' of America and Britain, final agreements were reached, and on January 11 1943 treaties were signed whereby the two Western Powers renounced all their remaining privileges. Among other anomalies, the foreign administration of the customs was abolished. These can be counted as Kuomintang achievements towards the restoration of China's full sovereignty.

As regards the exploitation of Chinese 'Nationalism' overseas, the results of this in Southeast Asian countries have already been stressed in Chapter 7.

But in terms of 'Democracy' and 'People's Livelihood' the progress was very little indeed. The government remained a party dictatorship until the end, the standard of living of the majority of Chinese remained extremely low, and the land problem was still unsolved when the Communists took over.

167

JAPAN TAKES THE PLUNGE

Having observed something of the effects of Japan's aggression against China, the reader may well enquire what had been happening inside Japan itself to result in such a policy.

In the weeks following the Mukden incident of September 1931, while the Japanese army in the field boldly extended the scope of its operations, the Japanese representatives at the League of Nations, and in London, Washington and other capitals declared that the measures were only temporary and would soon cease. Indeed, on 30 September, in response to a resolution by the Council of the League, the Japanese promised to withdraw their troops to the South Manchurian Railway zone. But instead of withdrawing, the Japanese troops continued to fan out through Manchuria. 'What was happening', says Richard Storry, 'was a breakdown in co-ordination between the civil and military wings of the Japanese structure of state power.'

While the Wakatsuki government was striving to establish its authority and to recover control of the army, its hands were tied by the state of mind of the Japanese people. When the Japanese troops went forward without any apparent opposition, a wave of nationalist enthusiasm swept through the country. For any Japanese publicly to say that what their troops were doing was wrong or unwise seemed treasonable. Successful aggression goes to the head of any people. As the gunnery officer of the German battleship *Derfflinger* (at the battle of Jutland with Britain in 1916) expressed it, 'When we found that we weren't being fired at by the enemy, the pure joy of battle rose within us.' World disapproval merely cemented Japanese patriotic feeling.

Supported, so it seemed, by the sentiment of the mass of the Japanese people, the ambitions of the militarists knew no bounds. Another officers' plot in Tokyo, hatched in October 1932, envisaged the annihilation of the whole Japanese Cabinet by air bombardment and their replacement by a military junta (or council of state). But while the plot fizzled out, the Premier was unable to re-establish civilian authority, and in December he resigned.

Wakatsuki was followed by Inukai, a man of seventy-five, who

Japan takes the Plunge

tried to open negotiations with the Chinese. Japanese military action continued in force in China, meanwhile, and 'Manchukuo' was established under Pu Yi the puppet (as already related), but when the League of Nations Commission, under Lord Lytton, arrived, the Japanese actually hoped to persuade it that Manchukuo had been established by the will of the 'Manchurian people'. (The population of the Three Eastern Provinces was nearly all Chinese—largely by fairly recent immigration from south of the Great Wall.) But the ultra-nationalist fanatics who were bent on gaining full control of the machinery of the Japanese government, were oblivious of world opinion, and sought to further their aims by assassinating all those who stood in their way. A series of violent outrages culminated in the murder of the aged Premier by a gang of nine young officers and army cadets who invaded his official residence on 15 May 1932. Inukai met them with composure and suggested that they should talk things over before using their weapons. But they shot him down in cold blood.

For the next thirteen years, right up to the end of the Pacific War, there were to be no more party cabinets in Japan. The army refused to supply a minister of war to a government headed by a party leader, and the Minister of War, the most important member of the Cabinet, had by common consent to be a soldier. Nor was the state of public sentiment favourable to party government. Although the murder of Inukai, and of other public men carried out by another group of assassins, the 'League of Blood', disturbed the people of Tokyo, there was a widespread sympathy for the murderers when they stood their trial, for they were regarded as unselfish patriots. Moreover, the social democratic movement was now split between those who supported the patriotic 'national socialism' of the Kwantung Army (the core of overseas aggression) and those who remained faithful to the aims of international socialism. The Kwantung Army was hostile to capitalism as represented by the great mercantile firms of Japan, such as the Mitsui and the Mitsubishi (the *zaibatsu* that were to become so familiar to Malayans during the Japanese occupation), and had declared that it would exploit the wealth of Manchukuo on its own for the advantage of the Japanese people—later extending this system to Japan itself.

Action in Japan was meanwhile taken against anyone suspected of Marxism, often in the typically Japanese form of assassination.

The one remaining safeguard against Japan's committing itself to a course of fanatical militarism was the continued influence of the *genro*, or 'Elder Statesmen', whose function it was to check the excesses of the hot-headed patriots. Indeed, Admiral Saito, the 'Elder Statesman' who succeeded Inukai as Premier, declared that 'Everything will be all right so long as we old men are here to put on the brakes.'

Meanwhile the Japanese army was itself split, and the internal history of Japan during the years 1932–6 is virtually that of the struggle between two factions, the *Koda-ha*, or 'Imperial Way School', and the *Tosei-ha*, or 'Control School'. The former insisted that Japan's great enemy was Soviet Russia with which there would soon be war, while the latter maintained that the Japanese should remain on friendly terms with Russia while expanding into China. For the first two years the *Koda-ha* was the dominant faction, but was thereafter replaced by the *Tosei-ha*. The transfer of power was marked by the usual violence and bloodshed, which culminated in the *coup* of 26 February 1936 when two infantry regiments of the First Division mutinied, together with some sympathizers from the Guards Division. They simultaneously invaded the homes of the Prime Minister and other public men. The Prime Minister, Admiral Okada, escaped death by being mistaken for his brother-in-law, but two former Premiers, Saito and Takahashi, as well as the Inspector-General of Military Training, were killed. The Emperor himself, however, now intervened, telling the Minister of War that this was a mutiny that must be crushed within an hour, and though this time-limit was exceeded by four days, this was duly done. The mutiny finally discredited the *Koda-ha*, which was believed to be behind the whole affair.

Meanwhile, Japan had been diplomatically isolated (as isolated as it had been in 1895 when the Triple Intervention of Russia, France, and Germany had compelled it to evacuate Port Arthur). Those countries that supported the League of Nations regarded Japan as an outlaw, in the same category as Fascist Italy and the new Nazi Germany. It was indeed to these countries that Japan now looked for an understanding, and the Anti-Comintern Pact was signed with Hitler's Germany in December 1936. The Japanese motive in signing the Pact was to secure Japan's north-west flank preparatory to a further advance into China.

In August 1937, fighting began in Shanghai, but the war that ensued, both here and in the north, was an undeclared one. China appealed to the League of Nations, which duly condemned Japan for having violated the Nine-Power Washington Treaty and the Kellogg Pact of 1920, but the League's action to check Japan was as unavailing as it had been after the Manchurian Incident in 1931. The Japanese advanced up the Yangtze Valley, and in December captured Nanking. Here they were guilty of atrocities against the Chinese on a great scale, but although these shocked the world, they were not reported in the Japanese press.

But although the Japanese soldiers, elated with victory, would no doubt have joyfully obeyed orders to continue their advance on all fronts, the Japanese government did not contemplate the military conquest of China. There were still men with calculating minds at the top who realized that even if the Japanese armies occupied the whole of the three million square miles of China and its dependencies, it would be beyond Japanese resources to administer them and to keep the Chinese people in subjection. What Japan had hoped for was that once Chiang Kai-Shek had lost his capital he would be willing to come to terms. What was wanted was a subservient China, open to Japanese economic exploitation. But although negotiations took place, Chiang was unwilling to accept the harsh conditions offered him. The Communist historians insist that it was only the pressure of popular opinion following the Sian Incident which prevented Chiang from coming to terms with Japan, but, whatever the truth, the fact remains that he did not do so and the war continued.

In the summer of 1938 hostilities took place between Japanese and Russian troops in some strength who fought for the possession of a hill on the borders of Korea. It seemed as if war might ensue between the two countries, and indeed there were influential Japanese officers who were quite prepared for a war on two fronts, so convinced were they of Japanese invincibility. But again the Emperor intervened, laying down that henceforth not a single

Japanese soldier should be moved without his express orders. This, no doubt, had a moderating effect for the moment, but Japanese military action, intended to bring Chiang and his refugee government in Chungking to accept their terms, continued. In the autumn of 1938 the Japanese occupied Hankow, and then Canton. The Japanese Premier, Konoye, thereupon issued a declaration that Japan's 'immutable' policy was the establishment of a New Order in East Asia—meaning a political, economic, and cultural union of Japan, Manchukuo, and China (with, of course, Japan in command). He followed this up with renewed offers of peace to the Kuomintang government.

It was at this juncture that the Kuomintang leader, Wang Ching-Wei (who had previously attempted to mediate between Chiang and the Communists), tried to persuade Chiang to accept the Japanese terms. As he saw things, there was no reason why Japan, providing that it avoided war with the United States and Britain or with the Soviet Union, should not in the end impose her will on China. Having failed to bring Chiang over to his point of view, in 1939 he fled from Chungking to Indochina, and in due course he set up a puppet régime under the Japanese at Nanking. This régime was recognized by the latter as the official government of China.

While these events were taking place in Eastern Asia, there had been remarkable developments in Europe. The Germans had enjoyed a series of overwhelming diplomatic victories, and when Berlin proposed a military alliance between Nazi Germany and Japan, the proposal had strong attractions for the Japanese. But since a commitment of this sort might involve Japan in war with Britain and perhaps also with the United States, the Japanese government hesitated before accepting the German Foreign Minister Ribbentrop's overtures. Then came the German–Soviet 'Non-Aggression' Pact in August 1939. This was regarded by the Japanese as a slap in the face as it came at the very moment when Japanese troops were being severely mauled by the Russians on the borders of Manchukuo and Outer Mongolia. Baron Hiranuma, who had succeeded Konoye as Premier, resigned, and his place was taken by a cautious retired general called Abe, who announced that Japan would adhere to a 'middle course' in respect to the hostilities which had now broken out in Europe. In other words, Japan would wait and see what course the war was taking before it committed itself to one side or the other—if indeed it took sides at all.

While these large-scale struggles were in progress to west and east of it, Southeast Asia was not directly concerned in any of them, and early in 1939 there did not seem to be any immediate prospect that the repose of the region would be upset. Certainly the 'appeasement' of Nazi Germany by Britain might well have involved the re-distribution of some British colonies to satisfy renewed German ambitions for a 'place in the sun', but even if the 'appeasement' policy failed to maintain peace and a European war ensued, Germany seemed to lack the means of extending hostilities to South and East Asia on any scale.

Each of the Southeast Asian countries was occupied by its own internal affairs, though their rulers were keeping a wary eye open for possible international development. As has been seen in Chapter 6, the presence of large minorities constituted a major problem in Malaya and Siam, and also one on a smaller scale for Indochina, Indonesia, the Philippines, and the British Bornean territories. Burma had no Chinese problem, but it had an Indian problem, largely owing to the fact that most of the best rice-lands of Southern Burma were in the hands of Indian moneylenders (mostly from South India), and landless Burmese peasants were roaming the country, and often resorting to crime. In Malaya, however, the Indians (mostly South Indian labourers on the rubber-estates) performed an important function in the economy. Another minority was the Arabs, of whom there were about 30,000 in Indonesia and about 3,000 in Malaya (many of the latter landowners in Singapore), but they did not constitute a 'problem'. It was they who had been to the front of the Pan-Islam movement, whose aim was to bring the Muslims of Indonesia and Malaya nearer to their fellow Muslims of the Middle East. The Europeans accounted only for a few thousands in all the Asian countries, mostly merchants and professional men, though they included also the British, Dutch, and French officials in whose hands the government of these countries, except Siam (Thailand), still lay.

As for the Japanese, they, too, numbered only a few thousands in the whole of Southeast Asia, living in small communities of a few hundred each, mostly in the big cities. Here they were occupied in the importation of Japanese goods or in modest occupations, namely as photographers, packers, masseurs, and barbers. They kept very much to themselves, and gave little indication that they were members of a race with imperialist ambitions whose soldiers were over-running China and clashing with Soviet Russia. Yet the authorities suspected many of them of having secret occupations in addition to the ones in which they were openly engaged. This was to prove to be the case when the Japanese invaded Malaya in 1941–2, for the Japanese who owned a few rubber-estates in Malaya turned out to have been preparing the way for the invasion by spying and mapping the jungle-paths, and some 'barbers' and 'masseurs' proved to be Japanese army officers or officials in disguise.

When war broke out in Europe in September 1939 it had little immediate effect on Southeast Asia. Allied strategy relied on France retaining a firm grip on Indochina, and thus protecting the Singapore Naval Base from the landward side. To Malaya and the Borneo territories was allotted the function of producing raw materials essential to Britain's war effort.

Meanwhile Japan was still remaining neutral, as an 'interested spectator'. It had been impressed by the success of the German *Blitzkrieg* ('lightning war') in Poland, but there was an apparent stalemate on the Western Front and it did not seem that Germany was strong enough to take the offensive. But when Norway, Denmark, and the Netherlands were overrun by the Germans, and France had collapsed by the middle of the summer of 1940, the whole situation changed. The Japanese political parties went into voluntary liquidation and the constitution became, in effect, 'totalitarian'. Japan then proceeded to sign the Tripartite Axis Pact of September 1940 (with Germany and Italy). Konoye was once again Prime Minister. Pressure on Southeast Asia was now exerted by the Japanese—the British, in response to this (having no alternative), agreed to close the Burma Road for six months, and France was forced to admit Japanese troops into northern Indochina. The Japanese gave the closing of the supply-routes to the Chungking government as their reason for making these demands—but Malaya and Indonesia now felt ominously unprotected. Indonesia, in particular, possessed the oil and other commodities needed by the Japanese, should they decide to extend their hostilities. The British had withdrawn most of their warships in the East to reinforce their navy in Europe, and the only Power with a fleet strong enough to resist the Japanese, should they attack at sea, was America.

The events of 1939–41 were to provide, so to speak, a 'curtain-raiser' to the main Eastern drama, but the simultaneous Japanese attack on Pearl Harbour, the Philippines, and Malaya on 8 December (7 December, that is, to the east of the 'date line') rang up the curtain on the drama itself. The Pacific War that now took place was to bring Western power in East and Southeast Asia into temporary eclipse, and to influence profoundly the whole future history of the region.

9

THE PACIFIC WAR AND ITS AFTERMATH

THE JAPANESE INVADE SOUTHEAST ASIA

To carry out their carefully prepared plans, the Japanese relied on surprise. The Allies, deeply occupied with the war in Europe, thought that their military and financial resources were too deeply committed in China to allow of adventures elsewhere. This was an impression that the Japanese encouraged. But when their negotiators in Washington failed to obtain the concessions they sought, their bombers suddenly swept down on Pearl Harbour without any declaration of war, they bombed Guam, Hong Kong, and the Philippines, and their troops landed in North-east Malaya and Thailand. Thailand surrendered at once and allowed the passage of Japanese troops through her territory for their invasion of Malaya and Burma.

On 10 December 1941 the Japanese bombed and sank the British battleships *Prince of Wales* and *Repulse* which had been sent to intercept their landings in Kelantan. In a campaign of ten weeks their troops advanced down the Malay Peninsula, infiltrating behind the British lines by the jungle-paths (which their 'civilian' colleagues had mapped in peacetime), and on 15 February Singapore fell. Meanwhile, the Japanese had invaded the Philippines, North Borneo, Indonesia, and Burma. In the Philippines, a strong resistance was put up in the Batan Peninsula by American–Filipino soldiers for over four months against vastly superior forces, but this was overcome by 9 April 1942. By the end of May, a large part of Burma was in Japanese hands, the Burma Road had been cut, and India itself was threatened. To the south, it seemed that an invasion of Australia might soon take place.

In April and May, however, the Japanese suffered two setbacks

which caused them to postpone any plans they may have had for
the invasion of India and Australia. Their aircraft were severely
handled when they attacked Colombo and Trincomalee in Ceylon
in April, and the following month a squadron under Admiral
Nagumo, escorting Japanese troops for a landing at Port Moresby
in Southern New Guinea, was engaged by an American carrier
force. Both sides suffered heavy damage, but the outcome was that
the Japanese gave up their attempt to capture Port Moresby by
naval action. This engagement is known as the Battle of the Coral
Sea.

Nevertheless, in the first six months of their lightning victories
the Japanese had occupied most of Southeast Asia. Their conquest
of Indonesia and Malaya had given them control of rich supplies
of oil, rubber, tin, bauxite, and other raw materials for their war
effort. They had managed all this with comparatively small forces,
only eleven divisions (considerably less than 200,000 men in all)
being used to conquer the Philippines, Malaya, Burma, and the
Dutch East Indies. But the Japanese soldiers and sailors were all
picked, highly trained men, who fought with fanatical self-sacrifice,
regarding surrender, even to superior force, as worse than death.
The Allies had greatly underestimated the Japanese skill in organization and the fighting qualities of their soldiers, sailors, and airmen.
At this stage of the war Japan seemed undefeatable: it was only
later on that her limitations became apparent.

THE JAPANESE OCCUPATION

The Japanese claimed to be bringing the blessings of freedom and
independence to the Southeast Asian countries by liberating them
from the 'Colonial yoke' and including them in their 'Co-Prosperity' sphere. The inhabitants saw them as fellow-Asians, for to
begin with the single-mindedness imperialism of Japan, which sub-
ordinated the freedom and individuality of every country it invaded
to its own glory under its god-like emperor, was concealed behind a
propaganda screen. The growth of Nationalism had made the
peoples of many of these countries impatient of European control,

and the Japanese were therefore assured of a welcome from the militant Nationalists and from disaffected elements in the population. But it soon became clear to these 'ex-colonials' that they had got rid of one master only to find him replaced by another of a more ruthless kind. The Japanese made no attempt to continue the welfare programmes, well advanced in Southeast Asia, since they needed all the local resources of raw materials and man-power for their own war purposes.

When disillusionment set in, it spread to all parts of Southeast Asia. What ensued is strikingly illustrated in the case of Malaya.

The Japanese regarded the Chinese in general as their enemies, but the Chinese Communists as such above all. Therefore, directly Malaya was in their hands, they began to round up all the Chinese Communists they could lay their hands on. Soon after the fall of Singapore, identification parades were held to pick out those Chinese who had been active against the Japanese before and during the Campaign. Informers—men, women, and boys, hooded like members of the Ku-Klux-Klan in the Southern United States—picked out victims by the hundred. There then followed executions lasting for days. Several thousands perished in this way. Some were shot as they stood; others were tortured to death; hundreds more were put onto *tongkangs* (lighters), towed into the harbour, and forced to jump overboard. From launches and other naval vessels the Japanese machine-gunned them as they swam or struggled in the water.

Those town-dwelling Chinese Communists who were able to escape fled into the jungle of the highlands of central Malaya to join their comrades who had formed guerrilla units to resist the Japanese —or, rather, to form the nucleus for a Communist Revolution directly the Japanese were expelled by the Allies (as they expected they would be in due time).

The immediate concern of the Japanese was to squeeze every cent they could out of the local population. Since the Chinese community were the richest, a start was made with them. The leading *towkays* (heads of businesses) were told that a 'gift' from them of 50 million Malayan dollars (£5·8 million) had been decided upon. This was to be handed over by 20 April 1942. Actually only $29 million was forthcoming in cash, and the *towkays* were forced to

The Japanese Occupation

obtain loans from the Yokohama Specie Bank on the security of the Chinese associations to pay the remainder.

But this was only a beginning. The Japanese had plans for tapping Malaya's resources as a whole. The *zaibatsu*[1] soon arrived, and of them the Mitsui and Mitsubishi were the first in the field. Smaller Japanese civilian traders then followed in shoals to share the business the big companies had left. They formed *kumiai*, or syndicates, which were, in effect, government-protected compartments of the black market. They were assisted by unscrupulous elements among the Chinese. The gambling farms, long abolished by the British, were also revived by the Japanese in 1943.

All public works were stopped. Heaps of stone for repairing the roads were still at the road-side when the British returned. The anti-malarial measures were discontinued, with the result that many thousands died. The importation of rice practically ceased (the Japanese could spare no shipping for it), and there was consequently widespread malnutrition.

The Japanese occupation of Malaya was marked by bribery, corruption, and incompetence. Moreover, the conquerors were guilty of much brutality, with bullying and face-slapping, but, what was much worse, they had torture-chambers in every centre in which horrible barbarities were committed.

To begin with, the Malays on the whole did not oppose the Japanese occupation—many indeed openly welcomed it. It was not that they had been on bad terms with the British (far from it) but there was a widespread feeling among them that the British had been too lenient with the Chinese, whose economic pressure on themselves they resented. Therefore a change of 'Colonial Power' might not be a bad thing. But as time went on they became completely alienated from the Japanese, and longed for the return of the British. There was a Malay resistance group called the Wataniah in Pahang from an early period of the Occupation, but, early in 1945, Malay groups were formed under British officers who had been dropped in by parachute in North Perak and Kedah.

As in Malaya, the Japanese in Burma started off with much in their favour. The extreme Burmese Nationalists, the Thakins, as

[1] See p. 169.

179

we have seen, were already in communication with them, had received training from them in subversion, and had helped to prepare a welcome for them.

In 1943, in furtherance of their plans, the Japanese granted 'independence' to Burma, and pledged assistance to it in developing its economy within the 'Co-Prosperity Sphere'. Ba Maw was the puppet Prime Minister, and his government immediately declared war on Britain and the United States. Yet, in spite of this gesture, the Japanese began to lose hold of Burmese popular sentiment in the first few weeks of their occupation. One reason was that the war had resulted in the laying waste of much of Burma, and its continuance brought nothing but privation to the people. By the end of 1943, many Thakins had changed their ground and sought either close relations with the USSR or even reconciliation with Britain.

The Japanese, however, were somewhat more successful in Indonesia. They started off by launching their 'Three A's Movement'. Its general theme was 'Asia for the Asians' (under, of course, Japanese leadership). The movement got its name from 'A', the first letter in Asia, which occurred in each of the following slogans— 'Japan, the Leader of Asia', 'Japan, the Protector of Asia', and 'Japan, the Light of Asia'. But although some Indonesians were found to lead the movement, it soon petered out. But the freedom the Japanese gave the Indonesian Nationalists to organize ensured their collaboration. The Nationalist leaders, who had been interned by the Dutch, were released for this purpose.

Most of the political parties were brought together in a 'People's Strength Concentration', or *Putera*, under the leadership of Sukarno and Hatta and two other Indonesians, one a prominent Muslim. All other parties were forbidden. Putera supported the Japanese in the war, and helped to recruit Indonesians for the Japanese labour battalions, in which many hundreds of thousands perished.

The Japanese, however, did not give self-government to the Indonesians, even of the very restricted kind they had given to the Burmese, until shortly before their surrender in 1945.

On taking over in the Philippines, the Japanese set up a new political party, the *Kalibapi*, and installed a puppet government.

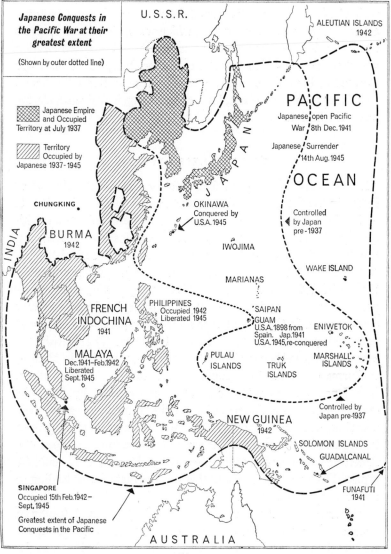

Japanese Conquests in the Pacific War at their greatest extent

(Shown by outer dotted line)

Japanese Empire and Occupied Territory at July 1937

Territory Occupied by Japanese 1937-1945

U.S.S.R.

ALEUTIAN ISLANDS 1942

PACIFIC

Japanese open Pacific War 8th Dec. 1941

Japanese Surrender 14th Aug. 1945

OCEAN

CHUNGKING

JAPAN

OKINAWA Conquered by U.S.A. 1945

Controlled by Japan pre-1937

INDIA

BURMA 1942

IWOJIMA

WAKE ISLAND

MARIANAS

FRENCH INDOCHINA 1941

PHILIPPINES Occupied 1942 Liberated 1945

SAIPAN

GUAM U.S.A. 1898 from Spain. Jap. 1941 U.S.A. 1945, re-conquered

ENIWETOK

MALAYA Dec. 1941–Feb. 1942 Liberated Sept. 1945

PULAU ISLANDS

TRUK ISLANDS

MARSHALL ISLANDS

Controlled by Japan pre-1937

NEW GUINEA 1942

SOLOMON ISLANDS

GUADALCANAL

SINGAPORE Occupied 15th Feb. 1942– Sept. 1945

FUNAFUTI 1941

Greatest extent of Japanese Conquests in the Pacific

AUSTRALIA

Map 7

181

In September 1943, when the Japanese Premier, Tojo, visited the islands he repeated a promise of independence for the Philippines which had already been given, and the same month the constituent assembly approved a constitution which was in important respects similar to that already granted under the Americans. An election was then held at which, on 25 September, Joseph P. Laurel was elected President. The following month the new 'Republic' signed an alliance with Japan—but, for the time being, it avoided declaring war on America.

THE JAPANESE DEFEAT

The basic reason for Japan's final defeat was major miscalculation. It had in the first place relied on a German victory against Russia which did not happen; in the second place, it entered the war with quite inadequate shipping (a mere 7 million tons as compared with the 24 million of Britain and the 12 million of the United States). But its defeat was due also to other errors of knowledge and planning. The Allies were taken at a disadvantage owing to their unpreparedness and their false assumptions regarding Japan's military commitments in China, but they showed a superior resilience and adaptability to the Japanese in the long run. The British, for example, who had been so behindhand in jungle warfare in Malaya, in Burma mastered the Japanese tactics and improved on them. The Japanese, too, were taken at a disadvantage by the swift development of the American submarine campaign against their shipping, and the convoy system they belatedly devised proved inadequate for the purpose. As early as the beginning of 1943, the Americans were sinking ten times as much tonnage as could be replaced by new building, and this was the main factor leading to the collapse of the Japanese economy.

The turning point in the war at sea was the Japanese defeat by an American fleet at the battle of Midway on 4 June 1942 (though it was proclaimed as a victory to the Japanese people). This was the first of the early Allied naval victories—the battle of the Solomons Sea (12–15 November 1942), and of the Bismarck Sea (2–4 March 1943) were others. But these, in a sense, were 'defensive victories,' for the Allies could not hope to take the offensive until they had built up their strength. In the meantime they carried out attacks on Japanese-held islands in the Pacific, which were defended by the enemy with ferocious gallantry, and had to be bombed or shelled flat before they could be occupied.

On land, the Japanese had, so far, suffered no defeat. The first came in June 1942 when, having failed to take Port Moresby from the sea, they advanced towards it overland through the forests of New Guinea. When they were within thirty miles of their objective, they were checked by the Australians, forced back over the Owen Stanley Range, and after bitter fighting the whole of their force was destroyed. Japanese troops, it had been proved, were, after all, defeatable. Soon afterwards they were driven from Guadalcanal in the Pacific, and lost ground in New Britain and elsewhere. Allied air superiority meant that the Japanese garrisons were cut off from any reinforcement or retreat—yet Japanese surrenders were few, and those who were captured were usually too weak, from wounds or starvation, to kill themselves.

Within eighteen months of Pearl Harbour, it was clear to thoughtful Japanese that their country was beginning to lose the war. But no one said so openly—the army would have treated any such opinion as defeatism. Germany's war with the Soviet gave Tokyo much anxiety, and more than once it suggested to Hitler that he should come to terms with the Russians—but without avail. The only effect of Italy's surrender in September 1943 was to make the Japanese armed forces more determined than ever to fight to the death. In 1944 they were still able to undertake the offensive on a limited scale, as against airfields used by the Americans in South China, and in a bid to encircle and destroy British and Indian forces in the Arakan, the Chin Hills, and Manipur, and then to break through into Bengal and Assam. But here superior British generalship defeated this attempt.

Following their landing on Saipan in June 1944 which brought them within bombing distance of Tokyo, the Americans took the Marianas, and drew nearer to the Philippines. In October, a landing was made on Leyte. Thereupon the last great naval battle of the war took place in which the Japanese lost four aircraft carriers, the giant 64,000 ton battleship 'Murashi', and ten cruisers. For a moment the outcome of the battle was touch and go, but resulted eventually in an overwhelming American victory which marked the end of the Imperial Japanese Navy after less than eighty years of existence.

Japanese resistance to the American advance in the Philippines was long drawn out and every step was contested. The same was true at the small island of Iwojima, less than 900 miles from Tokyo, and at Okinawa, where the Japanese suffered enormous casualties before the islands were taken.

In July 1945 the American President and the British Premier issued from Potsdam a proclamation (to which Chiang Kai-Shek, in Chungking, added his voice) calling upon Japan to surrender all its armed forces, declaring that the alternative for Japan was 'prompt and utter destruction'. Meanwhile, Japan was being bombed from the air on an unprecedented scale—the attack on Tokyo being probably the most intense of the whole war. The devastation of the capital city surpassed that caused by the Japanese earthquake of 1923. It was much the same at Osaka, Nagoya, and Kobe (though Kyoto remained untouched—preserved by the Americans on account of its artistic value).

The Japanese were hesitating as to the course they should follow. If Japan were invaded, the Allied casualties would undoubtedly be huge, and the Japanese army and navy leaders felt that they had a chance of inflicting at least one great reverse on the enemy if the invasion came. But many Japanese of influence were now satisfied that Japan must seek peace before the invasion came. A majority in Premier Suzuki's government felt that, whatever else happened, the monarchy must be saved at all costs.

On the morning of 6 August 1945 an American Superfortress dropped a single atomic bomb on Hiroshima. As the world knows, it obliterated the city and killed most of its inhabitants. On 8 August the Soviet declared war and attacked Japan. While the Japanese Cabinet was deadlocked as to the conditions they should attach to surrender, news came that a second atomic bomb had been dropped—this time on Nagasaki. But still the Japanese delayed their reply. On 13 August Tokyo was again raided by fifteen hundred carrier-borne Allied bombers. On 15 August the Japanese surrendered, and the voice of the Emperor was heard announcing the decision over the air. The Pacific War had at last come to an end.

THE SURRENDER, AND THE ALLIED OCCUPATION OF JAPAN

The question at once arose as to whether the Japanese troops in Southeast Asia would accept the Imperial command to surrender to the Allies, or whether they would ignore it and fight on to the death. Imperial Princes, meanwhile, were sent to each Command to explain and enforce the Imperial rescript ordering the surrender. Actually, few cases of defiance of the rescript occurred, and these were among isolated units.

The American occupation of Japan, as accepted by the terms of surrender, proceeded without a hitch. The first American troops arrived by air in Tokyo, and the formal surrender took place on 2 September 1945 on the deck of the American battleship *Missouri*. The man who accepted the surrender on the part of the Allies was General MacArthur, the Supreme Commander for the Allied Powers. He was the man designated as the first ruler of Japan under the occupation, and remained in this position until he was dismissed by President Truman in April 1951 during the Korean War. The Occupation itself continued until 1952.

The Japanese people had had no idea what they were to expect from their new rulers. They themselves were confused, weary of the war, and suffering from shortage of food and other privations. But they accepted the inevitable with good grace. Allied retribution was confined to the Japanese leaders, seven of whom, including two former Prime Ministers, Tojo and Hiroto, were sentenced to death after a trial that lasted two years. The Supreme Commander, who is known as 'SCAP' to history from his office, proceeded on the reform of Japan and the demilitarization of its government, in the attempt to turn the country into a democracy on the Western model.

One of the first tasks of SCAP was to frame a new Constitution for Japan. This was based on the three principles—the retention of the monarchy, subject to the will of the people, the foreswearing of war for ever, and the abolition of 'all forms of feudalism'. Where the Meiji Constitution emphasized *duties*, the new Constitution stressed *rights*. The new rights included freedom of thought, 'the right to maintain the minimum standards of wholesome and cultured living, the right of education, and equal rights of husband and wife'. The new Constitution, which showed obvious signs of being the product of American thinking, was broadly acceptable to the Japanese people. It could not, however, alter their traditional character, and in applying and interpreting it they remained Japanese.

The Occupation was terminated by the San Francisco Peace Treaty of 28 April 1952. The invitation to San Francisco was issued jointly by the United States and Britain to Japan and to the nations that had fought it. Neither Communist nor Nationalist China was invited. By the terms of the Treaty, Japan recognized the independence of Korea and renounced all claims to Formosa and the Pescadores, to South Sakhalin and the Kuriles, and the former mandated islands in the Pacific. The Treaty placed no limitations on Japanese economy and trade, and Japan's right to self-defence in keeping with the United Nations Charter was recognized.

The Soviet delegate, Gromyko, attacked the Treaty, and his country, together with Poland and Czechoslovakia, refused to sign it.

On the same day as the San Francisco Treaty was signed, the United States concluded a security pact with Japan in which the latter requested the retention of American forces in and about its territory as a defence against attack from overseas. In the pact, however, the United States expressed the belief that Japan would increasingly resume responsibility for her own defence.

THE POST-WAR SITUATION IN SOUTHEAST ASIA

The three and a half years of the Japanese occupation of Southeast Asia had transformed the political situation almost beyond recognition. Instead of being in firm control of their territories, the British, the Dutch, the French, and the Americans were faced with the task of re-establishing their control on the basis of the Japanese sur-render—if, that is, they could succeed in doing so.

In Malaya, the British Southeast Asia Command had established contact with the Chinese Communist Malayan People's Anti-Japanese Army (MPAJA), the jungle force, in 1943 through officers sent into Malaya by submarine, and in the latter stages of the war many other officers were parachuted in. When the Allies planned to invade Malaya to liberate it from the Japanese, an agreement was made between the Supreme Allied Commander (Lord Mount-batten) and the MPAJA whereby the latter would assist the invasion by attacking the Japanese lines of communication, etc. The sur-render, however, made the invasion unnecessary.

When the British forces landed in Malaya in September, they found that the MPAJA had emerged from the jungle and had oc-cupied many towns on the mainland as 'liberators'. The agreement with Lord Mountbatten, however, was grudgingly observed by the MPAJA who gave way to the British Military Administration (BMA). The BMA then proceeded to get the pre-war administra-tion on its feet again. Relations between them and the MPAJA were very uneasy, but the latter, nevertheless, agreed to be dis-banded, and in December each man handed in a rifle or other arm and received a gratuity of $350 (Malayan).

The Malayan Communist Party, however, whose military arm had been the MPAJA, was resolved to make the position of the British untenable and to work for a Communist revolution. They were able, in January 1946, to engineer a series of strikes, which temporarily paralysed the southern part of the country. But when on 15 February they attempted to call a stoppage of work to cele-brate the British surrender to the Japanese on that date four years previously, the British were ready for them and the 'stoppage' collapsed. Thereafter the MCP remained underground, infiltrating labour, until they came out in open revolt in June 1948.

The British government had decided during the war that, as a first step towards self-government, upon the liberation of Malaya the nine States of the Peninsula and the Settlements of Penang and Malacca should be formed into a Union. Singapore was to remain a separate Colony. This Union came into being on 1 April 1946 on the termination of the military government. It was, however, boycotted by the Malay Rulers (who had been allocated a purely honorary position in it), and there were mass demonstrations of Malays against it, organized by a new Malay party, the United Malays National Organization (UMNO), led by Dato Onn bin Ja'afar. In consequence of this the British government abandoned the Union and substituted for it a Federation, which came into being in February 1948. In this Federation, the Rulers were given more power than they had possessed since British protection began in the 1870s.

The birth of UMNO marked the effective beginnings of Malay Nationalism. So far, the Chinese had no single organization, though they were influential in several of the political parties that had come into being since liberation.

The Dutch, meanwhile, had vastly more difficulty in resuming possession of Indonesia than the British had had in Malaya. For one thing they were delayed for some weeks in reaching Java by shortage of shipping, thus giving the Indonesian Nationalists time to organize resistance to their return. In 1943 (as we have already seen) the Japanese had nominally given Indonesia its independence, but it was not until shortly before their surrender that they handed over the government to the Nationalists. On 17 August 1945 the Commission of the Independence of Indonesia issued a proclamation of independence in the name of the Indonesian people. Japan had already surrendered to the British on 14 August and in September the Southeast Asia Command took over some key positions in Indonesia, but did not intervene in Indonesian politics.

In the meantime the Dutch had been able to occupy Borneo and other Outer Islands which gave them a base from which to negotiate. An agreement was reached between the Dutch and the Indonesian Republic at a conference held under the chairmanship of the British Special Commissioner, Lord Killearn, at Linggajati (Cheribon) on 15 November 1946. The Indonesian Republic's authority over Java, Madura, and Sumatra was recognized, and both parties agreed to a United States of Indonesia with the Queen of the Netherlands at its head. But the compromise was not successful. The Dutch wished to retain a federal government, which would have left some power in the hands of the Netherlands, while the Nationalists were resolved to control the whole of Indonesia. The Dutch thereupon undertook two military operations which they called 'police actions' (in July 1947 and in December 1948), but which were really attempts to reconquer their past possessions. Both of these actions failed.

Meanwhile, in September 1945 the Japanese surrender in Indochina had been accepted by Chinese forces to the north of the 16th parallel and by British forces to the south of it. Thereupon, in pursuance of the Allied decision to return to France her lost colonies, the British gave way to the French forces which had been parachuted in. But to the north of the parallel it was only after extended negotiations that the Chinese troops withdrew, allowing the French to take over. Even so, the French ships met Vietminh gunfire from the Haiphong forts, causing them heavy casualties.

The French attempt to re-establish themselves in Indochina was very similar to that of the Dutch to regain Indonesia, and it suffered a similar fate. During the war the Vichy French had aided the Japanese, and an underground opposition arose against them. This was organized by the Vietminh, headed by Ho Chi Minh, and the movement was recognized by the Allies. When at the end of the war, French troops arrived and tried to take over, they were faced by the Nationalist Vietminh and were compelled eventually to recognize their Vietnam Republic. To begin with, the Republic was willing to leave its foreign affairs and the protectorate over Cambodia and Laos to France, but negotiations broke down when the French insisted on regarding Cochin-China (historically part of Vietnam) as a French colony. Civil war then ensued and continued for eight years, ending in the withdrawal of the French from the whole of Indochina.

In Burma, Aung San had succeeded Ba Maw as Prime Minister, and in May 1945, soon after the reoccupation of Rangoon by the British, he demanded that the 'Provisional Government' created under him should be treated as an 'Ally'. This request was refused by General Slim, who pointed out that Aung San was, under British law, a traitor, but Lord Mountbatten, the Supreme Allied Commander, defined the British attitude in a directive of 2 June in which he said, 'The guiding principle which I am determined shall be observed is that no person shall suffer for political opinions honestly held, whether now or in the past, even if these may have been anti-British.'

The British government had at first wished to delay Commonwealth status for Burma until 1948, but Aung San's answer to this was to form the Anti-Fascist People's Freedom League (AFPFL) which demanded complete independence at once. A Labour government had in the meantime come into power in Britain, and on 20 December 1946 the Prime Minister, Mr Attlee, announced a new policy for Burma in the House of Commons. In January 1947 Aung San headed a Burmese delegation to London and obtained what he wanted—namely 'full independence within a year'. Large-scale British loans to Burma were to be continued. U Saw, Ba Sen, and the Communists repudiated the agreement as 'selling out to the British'. There was meanwhile the question of the minorities to be settled (the Karens, Shans, Kachins, etc.). But on 19 July 1947 Aung San and six of his ministers were murdered by agents of Aung San's rival, U Saw (who was duly hanged for the crime). U Saw had intended to seize power in the confusion following the murder, but was frustrated in his design by the prompt action of the last British Governor, Sir Hubert Rance. Thakin Nu succeeded Aung San, and proceeded to Britain to complete the negotiations for independence. Burma became fully independent on 4 January 1948 (the date having been selected as a lucky one by the Burmese astrologers).

To the Philippine Nationalists, as to the Burmese and Indonesian Nationalists, the most important issue was that of independence. Therefore the question of 'collaboration' with the Japanese was quite a secondary matter—the 'collaborationists' such as Sukarno, Aung San, and Laurel, were 'patriots' to the Nationalists. The Americans, on their resumption of control in the Philippines, found it expedient to make concessions to Filipino sentiment in this respect. They then fulfilled their pre-war promise, and on 4 July 1946 the Philippines became independent. To keep the islands from ruin, however, large American loans were made to the new government, and provision was made for a very gradual raising of the United States tariff walls against the Philippines.

INDIA AND PAKISTAN BECOME INDEPENDENT

If for Indonesia, Indochina, and Malaya, the Pacific War had speeded up the coming of independence in a surprising way, in the Indian Subcontinent and in Burma, its achievement in the near future had been a foregone conclusion even in 1941. The war had, in fact, delayed the transfer of power. Once again, the Indian army had taken a part on the Allied side, and the Fourteenth Army, largely composed of Indian units, had driven the Japanese step by step out of Burma. During the course of the war, Indian troops (both Hindu and Muslim) had suffered 24,000 fatal casualties (and had incidentally won 31 V.C.s).

But now the war was at an end, the members of the Congress Working Committee who had been imprisoned were released and a political amnesty was declared. An all-party conference was called at Simla, but it broke down owing to the refusal of Congress and the Muslim League to compromise. In the elections held early in 1946, Congress obtained majorities in 8 out of the 11 provinces, while the Muslim League captured practically all the seats reserved for Muslims. The minor political parties were practically eliminated.

The future of the Subcontinent now hinged on the personalities of three men—Gandhi, Nehru, and Jinnah. Where Gandhi and Nehru stood has already been made clear. Jinnah came to the forefront only as the partition of the Subcontinent became more and more inevitable. Muhammed Ali Jinnah (1876–1948), a lawyer from Western India, had begun as a Muslim Nationalist supporter of Congress, and it was only when the Congress leaders made it clear that co-operation between Hindu and Muslims meant the *absorption* of the latter by the former that he went into irreconcilable opposition.

In an attempt to break the deadlock, the British government then sent a Cabinet mission consisting of Lord Pethick-Lawrence, Sir Stafford Cripps, and A. V. Alexander. This commission recommended that there should be a 'three-tiered' constitution—an all-India government at the centre with control over foreign affairs and defence, self-governing provinces and states, and federations of those provinces which agreed to a joint administration. The latter would fall into three administrative groups—the first consisting of the Punjab, the North-West Frontier Provinces, Baluchistan, and Sind, the second of Bengal and Assam, and the third of the rest of British India. If these divisions were agreed upon, the Muslims would be able to control the legislatures in which they had a majority. But the plan fell through as neither side would agree on the details. The British government then decided upon partition.

A bill was passed by Parliament on 5 July 1947 providing for the establishment of the two dominions of India and Pakistan. It was intended that Lord Mountbatten, who had become the last Viceroy on 22 March, should be Governor-General for both these dominions but the Muslim League refused to enter a Hindu state on any terms, and Jinnah became Governor-General of Pakistan with his capital at Karachi. Grave trouble at once arose as to the boundaries between the two dominions, resulting in bloodshed on a vast scale. In particular, the boundary commission of Indians and Pakistanis had not been able to agree on the future of the Punjab and the British chairman of the commission had had to make a decision. The river line of the Sutlej and Ravi he decided upon cut the powerful Sikh community in two, and a savage civil war ensued. Refugees fleeing from India to Pakistan, and Pakistan to India, perished in their millions. Thus, at their birth, the two new dominions were baptized in blood. The formal transfer of power took place on 15 August 1947 and the British empire in India was at an end.

As a postscript to this account it must be added that Mahatma Gandhi, when at the age of seventy-eight he was touring the country urging communal peace, was murdered on 30 January 1948 by orthodox Hindu extremists, whose hatred he had incurred by his liberal attitude towards the 'untouchables' and in other matters of religion.

CIVIL WAR IN CHINA

Though divided, the Indian Subcontinent was at least ruled by two seemingly stable governments, each of which could rely for its administration on a civil service highly trained under the British.

China, on the other hand representing the other of the two great traditional civilizations of Eastern Asia, was to be riven by civil war for several more years to come.

Even during the Pacific War it had been plain to close observers that once it was over there would be a full-scale collision between Chiang Kai-Shek and the Communists. Whilst both sides were supposed to be fighting the Japanese, there had been an attempted liquidation of the Communist army in detail by commanders of certain Kuomintang army corps, and Chiang had set aside a large part of the money and munitions he received from America for fighting the Japanese for use against the Communists after the war.

Immediately after the Japanese surrender in 1945 the civil war started, although it remained undeclared for some months. In September, the Communist leader, Mao Tse-Tung, flew to Chungking to negotiate with Chiang and an agreement was reached, on 10 October, for a Political Consultative Conference. But before the Conference could take place, Communist bases were attacked in many parts of China. In the midst of the confused situation which followed, Nationalist (KMT) forces were landed from American transport-planes with the intention of wiping out all the Communist bases in Manchuria and Hopei. The Nationalists managed to secure control of the cities and larger towns, but the countryside remained in the hands of the Communist guerrillas and the Nationalist garrisons were thus virtually isolated. Meanwhile, the Russians announced that their forces were withdrawing from Manchuria (which they had occupied in accordance with the terms of the Japanese surrender), but although they delayed their departure for three months at Chiang's request in order that his troops might have time to take over, they obstructed the latter when they arrived. A period of warfare between the KMT and the Communists, punctuated by truces, now ensued.

In the summer of 1946 General Marshall arrived in China on the instructions of President Truman to attempt to find a basis of settlement between the two sides—but failed to do so. The civil war continued, and the United States abandoned its attempts to secure peace by negotiation. It, however, urged Chiang once again to fight the Communists by internal reforms as well as with military weapons.

But Chiang, convinced that the Americans had no choice but to support him in whatever he did, made no real attempt to adopt a democratic system and relied on party dictatorship up to the moment of the Communist victory of 1949. In 1947 one more mission, this time under General Wedemeyer, was sent by President Truman to Nanking, which advised that, since a compromise was impossible, the United States should give 'all-out' aid to Chiang. 'All-out' aid, however, would have involved the employment of American ground forces, and for this neither the United States government nor American public opinion was prepared.

China was in 1947 in a terrible state. Inflation, which had started while the Nationalist government was still at Chungking, was now entirely out of control. It had already destroyed the 'white-collar' class which had gradually been emerging in China since 1937 and which might have checked both Communists and Right Wing extremists. Added to the scourge of inflation was Chiang's increasing reliance on his secret police force which infiltrated every corner of Chinese life. When wage-earners were paid in a currency whose exchange value was first hundreds of thousands, then millions of 'dollars' to the pound sterling, and which every two or three days depreciated still further so that there was nothing left from the previous week's wages to pay the increased prices for food-stuffs, it was plain even to the casual observer that the Kuomintang régime was doomed.

IO

SOUTH, EAST, AND SOUTHEAST
ASIA SINCE 1945

The following is a table of outstanding events in the region since the Pacific War:

1947	India and Pakistan independent
1948	Burma independent
1949	Indonesia independent
	The People's Republic of China established
1950–3	The Korean War
1954	Dien Bien Phu and the Geneva Conference
1955	The Afro-Asian Conference at Bandung
1957	Malaya independent
1959–	Sino-Indian boundary question
1963	Malaysia established

The most important events of the post-war years were the successive acquisition of their independence by the one-time imperial dependencies and 'colonies' of the region and the coming into being of the People's China. As a background to these happenings, there was throughout the period the great effort of these countries to develop their resources to the level of the West—an effort complicated in India, China, Japan, North Vietnam, Java, etc., by the unprecedented population increase which threatened to cancel out every advance in production. Behind everything, too, was the great question as to whether co-existence was possible between the two great world blocs to avoid the catastrophe of a global atomic war.

In the preceding chapter the attainment of independence by India, Pakistan, Burma, and the Philippines have been described. That of Indonesia, and of Vietnam, Cambodia, and Laos was delayed for a few years after the war, and an account of the way in which these countries were finally separated from the 'Colonial

Power' must now be added. It will be preferable to do this in chronological sequence, introducing the other important events which supervened.

After the failure of the two 'police actions' by the Dutch in Indonesia, a deadlock ensued during which both sides clung on to the territory of which they were in actual control. It was at this juncture that the Secretary-General of the United Nations intervened at the instance of Australia and India. In consequence, a Committee of Good Offices was set up, with representatives of Australia, Belgium, and the United States and the Republican government to reach an agreement. After a great deal of bargaining and temporizing, a round-table conference was called at The Hague to arrange a transfer of power. Having given up the hope of saving anything of importance from the wreck of their East Indian empire, the Dutch (as Dr van Mook expressed it) had decided to grant independence to Indonesia 'with good grace and liberality'. On 27 December 1949 the provisional government of the United States of Indonesia was constituted with Sukarno as its President and Mohammed Hatta as its Prime Minister. The United States of Indonesia was to be a federal republic of sixteen states enjoying equal partnership with the Netherlands under the Netherlands Crown. This, however, was only a 'face-saving' device for the Dutch, for they knew very well that the Indonesians were determined on complete independence and dissociation from Holland.

But one slip remained between the cup and the lip—one obstacle to the dignified (if sorrowful) withdrawal of the Dutch from the stage on which they had acted so prominently for over three hundred and fifty years. This was due to their insistence on retaining West New Guinea (West Irian, as the Indonesians called it) on the ground that it was not part of Indonesia. Its population (they argued) was of a race quite distinct from that of Indonesia and had never been included in the ancient island empires before the Dutch arrival. What were the real motives of the Dutch in hanging on to this stretch of undeveloped, sparsely inhabited territory is not clear. The West New Guinea budget had an annual deficit of millions of guilders which they had to make up, but apart from their desire to restore their lost prestige in Asia, it is possible that they hoped that the discovery of the oil that was believed to exist in the territory would recoup them for their expenditure.

But independence by itself is not a solution of all internal problems —often indeed it accentuates them. For one thing, the unifying bonds of the Colonial régime having been removed, the newly-independent countries tended to break apart. This was the case in Burma, where the withdrawal of Britain was succeeded by civil war. The AFPFL itself was a coalition of several different elements, and its authority was at once challenged by a succession of enemies. The Red Flag Communists and the *Mujahids* (bands of Muslim marauders from North Arakan) were already in the field, and then there was a threat from the People's Volunteer Army (PVO), the huge private army raised by Aung San, which was living off the country by extortion and refused to be disbanded. Then the White Flag Communists (hitherto co-operating with the AFPFL government) came out in revolt. After this the government was defied first by the frontier peoples and then by the Karens. As one revolt was brought under control, another began, and it seemed as if Burma must break up into fragments. Yet, as if by a miracle, the Premier U Nu (no longer a Thakin, but U, or 'mister') was able to restore some sort of order, and by July 1950 the troublesome PVO was disbanded. But disorder continued—trains and lorries were ambushed, and gangs of robbers pillaged the countryside. The marvel was that Burma held together at all.

In Malaya, in June 1948, a little over three months after the creation of the new Federation, the Communists came out into open rebellion against the government, beginning the period of warfare and terror known as the 'Emergency', which was to last for another twelve years.

But while those new countries of Southeast Asia were suffering the ailments of their infancy, developments on a vast scale were taking place in China.

THE PEOPLE'S REPUBLIC OF CHINA IS ESTABLISHED

When the all-out Civil War started in 1946, the Kuomintang government had reason to be confident of victory. It had an enormous army of over four million men at its disposal, and controlled an area with a population of more than 300 million, all the big cities, and most of the railways. It also had large financial reserves and supplies of war material (obtained mostly from America). Chiang Kai-Shek declared that the issue 'would be settled by military means within five months'.

The Communists, for their part, were also confident of the outcome. The strategy the Communist forces adopted was one developed through long years of experience. When the KMT army launched an all-out attack, the People's Liberation Army (as it was called) went on the defensive. It evacuated many cities and stretches of country in order to induce the enemy to extend his line, and, wherever opportunity offered, attacked him at his most vulnerable point with superior force. This strategy was to prove eminently successful. By the end of 1948, the Communists were the masters of Manchuria, and North China was open to their attack. Kuomintang generals began to surrender as the People's Liberation Army advanced, taking with them all their arms and equipment. After the fall of Hsuchow (near Peking), the result of the civil war was no longer really in doubt. The Communists crossed the Yangtze on 20 April 1949 and entered Nanking on the 23rd. After this, there was a general Kuomintang collapse during which the Governors of the provinces peacefully changed sides.

Chiang Kai-Shek, meanwhile, had fled to Formosa (Taiwan), with a contingent of his troops, and the People's government was set up at Peking on 1 October.

Thus was the Communist Revolution accomplished. The whole balance of power in East and South Asia had been changed and the world situation transformed beyond recognition. The Communist bloc now extended from the North Sea to the China Sea and comprised some eight hundred million people.

The history of the People's Republic in the next two decades was to turn first on Land Reform, and then on an ambitious programme of industrialization, to accomplish which the Communists relied on an increase in agricultural production to provide the necessary capital. The effort to achieve this extra production led to the planning of the 'Great Leap Forward' of 1958, which was followed by three years of set-backs due to bad harvests caused by flood and drought. The outstanding feature of these years was the creation of the 'People's Communes', representing collectivization on a vast scale. But although the Communists accomplished a great deal, China, in the 1960s, still had a long way to travel before it could hope to catch up with the West. Then, in 1962, occurred an open policy split between China and the USSR, in which the People's government attacked 'co-existence' between the USSR and the West on the ground that it involved a surrender to 'imperialism', and themselves made a bid for the leadership of the Communist world.

Such is the background against which the happenings in East and South Asia in the 1950s and 1960s must be examined in greater detail.

The consequences of the Communist victory were strongly reflected in the politics of Southeast Asia. Britain recognized the People's government, as did Indonesia and Burma. The Philippines and Thailand, however, did not—nor did the USA. One source of anxiety to the Southeast Asian Governments, irrespective of recognition or non-recognition of the People's China, was the future intentions of the latter towards its neighbours, and the effect of its establishment on the ten million or so Overseas Chinese. Would the latter become a 'spearhead' for the recovery of territory over which the Chinese Empire at one time had held sway?

THE KOREAN WAR, 1950-3

By the Potsdam agreement, the USSR had accepted the surrender of the Japanese troops north of the 38th parallel. This parallel thus became an 'iron curtain' separating two distinct states—one Communist and the other anti-Communist. Between 1945 and 1950 the United Nations made ineffectual attempts to reunify Korea.

Both North and South Korea aimed at reuniting the country under their respective leaderships. Then (in pursuance of this aim) North Korean forces crossed the 38th parallel on 25 June 1950 (though the Communists, as was to be expected, alleged that it was the South Koreans who first crossed the frontier) and fighting began.

The Security Council of the United Nations at once met and demanded the immediate withdrawal of the North Koreans to the

38th parallel. Only the Soviet bloc dissented, but as Russia itself was boycotting the Council at the time there was no veto. The Council asked all members of UN to help it enforce its demands. President Truman sent American troops to Korea at once, and Mr Attlee promised all available British support. On 7 July General MacArthur (SCAP) was appointed Supreme Commander of the UN Korean forces.

The first part of the war was marked by alternate advances of North and South, but with the arrival of superior American forces the North Koreans were pushed back. MacArthur was anxious to press as far forward as possible, and the UN authorized him to extend the war into North Korea if necessary. Pyongyang, capital of North Korea, fell to the UN forces on 19 October. But even before the UN troops had crossed the 38th parallel, Chou En-Lai had stated that, if North Korea were invaded China would not stand idle. When the UN troops approached the Yalu River (the frontier with China), Chinese troops entered Korea in great force. MacArthur's troops, heavily outnumbered, fell back and the line was not restored until the Chinese were some seventy miles inside South Korea.

A United Nations counter-offensive now began, but on 11 April 1951 General MacArthur was relieved of his commands by President Truman. This was a climax of a series of incidents in which the General had defied the President. He had been willing—indeed anxious—to carry the fighting into Chinese territory, even at the risk of global war.

After this, a stalemate developed. Negotiations between the two sides began on 10 July 1951 but were twice broken off. On 8 June 1953 agreement was reached on the repatriation of prisoners, but at this point the President of South Korea, Sygman Rhee, announced that South Korea would not accept the armistice terms. Pressure, however, was brought upon him by the Americans, and an agreement was reached. But neither the United Nations nor the Communists could agree on the terms for reuniting Korea, and the country remained divided.

One important consequence of the Korean War was the stationing of the United States Seventh Fleet in the Formosa Channel, with

orders to prevent any invasion of Formosa from the mainland—
thus perpetuating the separation of Formosa from the remainder
of China.

DIEN BIEN PHU AND THE GENEVA CONFERENCE

The failure of the French to re-establish their empire in Indochina
was followed by the political disintegration of the whole region.
Meanwhile, the French were engaged in civil war with the Vietminh
and were struggling to keep what power they could by political
expedients. On 9 March 1949 they came to an agreement with Bao
Dai, the last emperor of Annam, whereby the independence of
Vietnam (comprising Annam, Tongking, and Cochin-China) within
the French Union was recognized. With Cambodia, too, the French
sought an arrangement which would preserve as much as possible
of French influence. In 1946 it had agreed to a National Consultative Assembly, and that same year Thailand (Siam) was persuaded
to return to Cambodia the territory of which it had again taken
possession in 1941 with the help of the Japanese. On 8 November
1949 France recognized the kingdom of Cambodia as an independent Associate State in the French Union. Laos, too, became an
independent sovereign state within the French Union (14 July
1949), but here the situation was complicated by the existence of
the Pathet Lao. Pathet Lao was the development of a wartime
underground movement and was headed by Prince Souphannouvong who belonged to a junior branch of the royal family. It was
in association with the Vietminh, and in 1953 it invaded Laos from
Vietnam with considerable popular support inside Laos.

Throughout, the French were working on the assumption that
Cambodia and Laos could be isolated from Vietnam, since, in the
early stages at least, Nationalism had not yet developed in them.
But Nationalism is contagious, and within a short space of time the
French were confronted by its advance in all three countries. As
each successive phase of the conflict ended in failure for the French,
they embarked on the next one with most sanguine expectations,
and each time their optimism was shared by the British and the
Americans. The end came, however, when in April and May 1954

the French High Command decided to make a stand at Dien Bien Phu, a place of no strategical importance situated in the middle of an open plain and vulnerable to attack on every side. Dien Bien Phu fell to the North Vietnamese forces on 7 May, and since the French were unable to send any reinforcements to Indochina, this defeat virtually decided the outcome of the war.

Although the North Vietnamese now seemed to have nothing between them and the occupation of the whole of Vietnam, the fear of involvement in a world war induced the Communist Powers to hold back and to consolidate their position. Foster Dulles, the American Secretary of State, was so alarmed by the Vietminh victory that he was willing to engage in 'limited' atomic warfare to save the situation, but the British Prime Minister, Eden (as he states in his *Memoirs*) refused to give British endorsement to this reckless plan. Instead, a conference was convened at Geneva between the Western Powers and the Communist bloc, and a cease-fire was negotiated by an agreement reached on 20 July 1954. This was signed by the Commander-in-Chief of the French Union Forces in Indochina and on behalf of the Commander-in-Chief of the People's Army of Vietnam. Latitude 17° North, with certain exceptions, was fixed as the line of demarcation between the Northern and Southern zones, and an international commission composed of representatives of Canada, India, and Poland was appointed to supervise the carrying out of the agreement. General elections were to take place in July 1956 to decide the future of the whole of Vietnam—but these elections were not held. Ngoh-dinh-Diem ('Diem'), the Premier of South Vietnam, who had come into power when Bao Dai was forced to abdicate, refused to recognize the agreement as his government had not been a signatory to it.

America virtually succeeded France as the guardian of the *status quo* in South Vietnam and Laos, with all the financial and military commitments that this entailed. The Civil War in South Vietnam went on endlessly, and the complex troubles in Laos between left wing and right wing, with the moderates attempting to hold the balance, threatened at times to bring East and West into head-on conflict over this country of 89,000 square miles with a sparse population of less than two million people, mostly of Thai race.

The Afro-Asian Conference at Bandung

THE AFRO-ASIAN CONFERENCE AT BANDUNG

Those Asian states which had recently obtained their independence, or had been independent in varying degrees all along, now felt that they should establish a closer relationship among themselves in pursuit of their common objectives. They therefore decided to call a conference. 'Anti-Colonialism' was still the common bond, even though it was 'dating' rapidly with the relinquishment of Colonial control, and it was decided therefore to extend the proposal to include Africa, since Africa was supposed still to be embraced in the 'Colonial toils'. This was the idea which was shaping itself in the minds of the Prime Ministers of Indonesia, India, Burma, Pakistan, and Ceylon when they met at Bogor (Buitenzorg) in Java at the end of 1954.

In consequence of the decision then arrived at, a joint invitation was issued to twenty-five 'Sovereign States' to attend an Afro-Asian Conference at Bandung in Java at the end of April 1955. These states extended from the Gold Coast to Japan; all the Arab States were included (their acceptance involving the exclusion of Israel); the Central African Federation, Libya, Egypt, the Sudan, Gold Coast, Ethiopia and Liberia, Iran, North and South Vietnam, and the Chinese People's Republic.

It will be seen that the inclusion of Communist China cut across the division between the two world blocs. It was the assumption of the Conference that common problems could be discussed—or even solved—regardless of this ideological barrier. Some of the participants, indeed, were disposed to ignore its existence.

The matters brought before the Conference were many and various, but the subject of under-development was the dominant theme. This was emphatically an association of the 'have-nots'. The intention was not to dispense with aid from the 'have' countries (notably the United States), but to define the conditions on which this aid could be accepted. 'Aid without strings' was the implied slogan of the gathering. This, of course, was excluding the People's China, which sought no aid from capitalist countries— though it was prepared, on certain conditions, to trade with them.

In retrospect, it cannot be said that the promise of solidarity between the Asian and African countries was fulfilled in the event. There were too many conflicting interests and attitudes to allow the Conference being developed into an alliance, but it did demonstrate the new political awareness of the countries represented and their ambition to stand on their own feet.

There was, however, one important by-product of Bandung which should not be allowed to escape notice. In the pre-war years, when the Kuomintang Nationalism was the guiding principle, the dual nationality of the Overseas Chinese had been the cause of constant friction between the Southeast Asian governments and Nanking. The People's government was not unaware of this, and negotiations between Peking and Jakarta had been in progress for some months before the Afro-Asian Conference met. Then, while the Conference was in session, it was announced that a treaty on nationality had been signed between Indonesia and China.

The treaty was intended to regulate the nationality of the Chinese and Indonesian nationals residing in the territory of the other. Within two years these nationals had to choose which nationality they would adopt, and after that the Chinese and Indonesian governments undertook to use their influence with those who elected to retain their Chinese or Indonesian nationality to dissuade them from engaging in local politics. Since the number of Indonesians resident in China was insignificant, this treaty mainly affected the Chinese in Indonesia. The agreement was not ratified until 1960, but its effect was that those traders who retained Chinese nationality became subject to the laws prohibiting aliens from engaging in retail trade in the country districts, and in certain other occupations, so that a large number of them (estimated at some 300,000) were deprived of the means of earning a livelihood. The People's government protested at this harsh treatment of its nationals, but accepted the situation and undertook to repatriate those Chinese who wished to return to China (even though their ancestors may have left it hundreds of years before). This was in the interest of placating Indonesia, with which the People's China wished to be on good terms.

This sequel to the Bandung Treaty belongs, however, to a later period, and we must, in providing a commentary on the chronological table which heads this chapter, retrace our steps to see what was happening in Malaya after the substitution of the Federation for the Union in 1948.

MALAYA BECOMES INDEPENDENT

Malaya's advance towards self-government was retarded by its 'plural' society. In order that there might be elections, it was first necessary that there should be a common citizenship for members of all races. This had been provided for under the Union constitution, but when the Union was replaced by the Federation, the citizenship regulations made under the latter gave Federal citizenship automatically to all Malays and Other Malaysians (Muslims from Indonesia), but others (e.g. Chinese and Indians) had to satisfy certain requirements (e.g. the birth of both parents in Malaya) before they were eligible for citizenship. Measures, however, were being taken to broaden the regulations to admit more non-Malays to citizenship.

The Communist insurrection of June 1948 put the clock back much further than had the abandonment of the Union. Since the Communist guerrillas in the jungle were over 99 per cent Chinese, their success would have meant that, far from being an independent democracy, Malaya would have become a totalitarian state ruled by a Chinese Communist minority as an appendage to the People's China. The basic reason for the Communist failure was lack of popular support.

Yet, the Communist guerrillas were assisted by a Chinese 'squatter' community—or rather by those squatters who were intimidated by the Communists. These squatters, about half a million in number, had mostly taken to the countryside during the Japanese occupation to grow food. They had settled wherever they found arable land without any regard to their legal title to it. They supplied the guerrillas with food and man-power, and the question of neutralizing them was the first that confronted the government.

The key to the squatter problem, and hence to the eventual defeat of the Communists, was found in 1950 by a committee of civil servants who drew up plans for re-settling the squatters in new villages built for their reception which could be policed so that supplies from them could not reach the guerrillas. This re-settlement was carried out successfully by General Sir Harold Briggs over a period of a year or so. The new villages were provided with water, light, and other amenities. Nevertheless, the Communist guerrillas were able to continue to terrorize the countryside for years to come. The nature of the country gave them the tactical advantage. Their numbers were never more than 3–5,000 (the most suitable number for this kind of warfare) but the jungle gave them instant cover for attack or retirement. The forces deployed against them included several thousands of British, Malay, Gurkha, and other troops, and a large force of police and home guard, mostly Malays. The jungle-fighting entailed the greatest danger and hardship, and the security forces were at a disadvantage as compared with the guerrillas who could choose their points of attack and disappear instantaneously into the forests. So the war dragged on.

In October 1951 Sir Henry Gurney, the High Commissioner for Malaya, was ambushed and murdered by terrorists as he drove in an ordinary, unarmoured car up the road through the jungle to Fraser's Hill. In consequence of this, civilian morale dropped dangerously. To restore this morale a soldier was appointed to succeed Sir Henry Gurney as High Commissioner. This soldier, General Sir Gerald Templer, was also placed in command of the armed forces. He was entrusted with the dual task of stepping up the campaign against the Communists and advancing the country towards self-government. He succeeded in re-establishing civilian morale and in stepping up the military offensive, although the Communist guerrillas continued to be as active and dangerous as ever for several years after his departure. Towards the second task, however, the measures he took under a 'directive' from Mr Lyttelton, the British Secretary of State for the Colonies, were calculated to bring full self-government somewhere about the time of the Millennium. A start was to be made by introducing village councils and then extending democratic responsibility upwards by stages until it eventually reached the legislature—this was called 'sowing the grass seeds of democracy'.

Malaya becomes Independent

But what General Templer did succeed in doing was to unite Malays and Chinese in opposition to official policy. Hitherto the 'Emergency' had driven the two main communities farther apart, but now (quite unexpectedly) the United Malays National Organization (UMNO), under Tunku Abdul Rahman, and the Malayan Chinese Association (MCA), under Sir Cheng-Lock Tan, came together to contest the municipal elections under an arrangement for the allocation of seats between the Communities (including the Indians and Pakistanis). Then when, in 1954, it was proposed to hold elections for the legislature under an official scheme that would retain an official majority, an UMNO–MCA delegation, headed by Tunku Abdul Rahman and Mr T. H. Tan, went to London to demand an unofficial majority in the legislature. Mr Lyttelton refused to meet this demand, with the consequences that all members of the UMNO–MCA Alliance walked out of the legislature and from all boards and committees on which they were serving. But the British government, realizing the impossibility of fighting the Communists and postponing self-government simultaneously, now changed its attitude, amending the constitution so that a political party which obtained *all* the seats at the polls would have a majority over the officials of *five* members. At the elections now held (1955), the UMNO–MCA Alliance obtained 51 out of the 52 seats to be filled by election, thus obtaining a majority of four.

With this small majority the Alliance proceeded quickly towards independence—this time with the full co-operation of the British government, and of the new Colonial Secretary, Mr Lennox-Boyd. On 31 August 1957 the Federation of Malaya became fully independent. This was on *Merdeka* (independence) Day. Thus ended the eighty-three years of British protection.

With the approach of independence, the Communist guerrillas lost ground. As Tunku Abdul Rahman, now Prime Minister of the Federation, said in 1961: 'When we took over with independence in 1957, the Communists had been claiming to be fighting for Malayan freedom. But once we had our freedom their argument lost its force, and by 1960 we were able to end the Emergency.' All that remained was a handful of 'hard-core' Communist guerrillas in the forests of the Malayan-Thailand border.

Since 1945

THE SINO-INDIAN BOUNDARY QUESTION

The two great South and East Asian countries, India and China, had one great problem in common, and that was how to develop their resources to feed their rapidly increasing populations, and how to industrialize to give them a higher standard of living. They were both 'under-developed' countries. Having failed to do these things within a capitalist framework, China had resorted to Communism: India, on the other hand, had chosen to embark on a series of five-year plans within a system of private enterprise. The former system, being 'totalitarian', was the more rapid, but it involved great pressure on the Chinese people with consequent stresses and strains. India, on the other hand, was worried by the slowness of its development time-table, and the question was asked whether it could produce results quickly enough to ward off disorder and revolution.

Both India and China had other troubles on their hands—the former was, for example, involved in the Kashmir question with Pakistan, and the demand of linguistic minorities to break off into separate provinces, and the latter had first its land reform to occupy it, after that the Korean War, and then its experiment with the People's Communes.

For some years India and China, intent on their own problems, kept on good terms. But then, suddenly, in 1959, the two countries came into violent collision over their common frontiers.

The Sino-Indian Boundary question is one of great complexity, the rights and wrongs of which would be outside the scope of this book to discuss, but in short it may be said that it was a legacy of the old British and Chinese Empires. The existing frontiers had been established when the British Empire was at its strongest and the Chinese Empire at its weakest, and it was likely that when China was once again a 'Power' it would reassert some of its ancient claims. The sectors in dispute were widely separated—the western sector between the Karakoram Pass and the east of Ladakh, the middle sector between Ladakh and Nepal, and the third sector far to the east between Bhutan and Burma. For the next few years, there was to be bitter fighting between the Indians and the Chinese over these disputed frontiers, at times threatening to develop into an all-out war.

The effect of the Sino-Indian dispute on the international situation was very great. For one thing, it disposed of the possibility of an *Asian* bloc against the West. For another, it paved the way for the Sino-Soviet policy split (which continued to grow in bitterness in 1963), since Russia was supplying India with war planes, etc.—and continued to do so after the frontier clash. But, as significant as anything else, it re-awakened the apprehensions of the Southeast Asian countries that China was 'expansionist'—a theory which there had so far been little evidence to support.

The Sino-Soviet policy split arose primarily from China's fear that the Russians, in agreeing to 'peaceful co-existence' with the West, would accept the *status quo* in the Formosa Channel whereby China would be permanently deprived of what it claimed to be part of its sovereign territory.

THE ESTABLISHMENT OF MALAYSIA

Throughout history, human societies have been forming themselves into changing political patterns. If you thumb through an historical atlas with coloured maps you get the effect of a kaleidoscope. This is as true of South, East, and Southeast Asia as it is of the Middle East and Europe. The latest pattern may be the design of an indigenous princely conqueror, the extension of a distant empire, or the result of communities being drawn together by similarity of race, interest, etc., and when the breakup of these larger units takes place, it is reflected in the more complex mosaic of the colouring. Rarely, however, do the political boundaries coincide strictly with the ethnic boundaries, for there is nearly always an overlap when a race from one country extends into an adjoining or distant one. Indeed, this is unavoidable, since a political distribution of territory on a strictly racial basis would entail administrative chaos.

With the withdrawal of the European Colonial Powers, Southeast Asian boundaries began to alter. Sometimes, as in the case of Indonesia, Burma, and the Philippines, they retained the area which nature or the Colonial Power had bequeathed to them: in others,

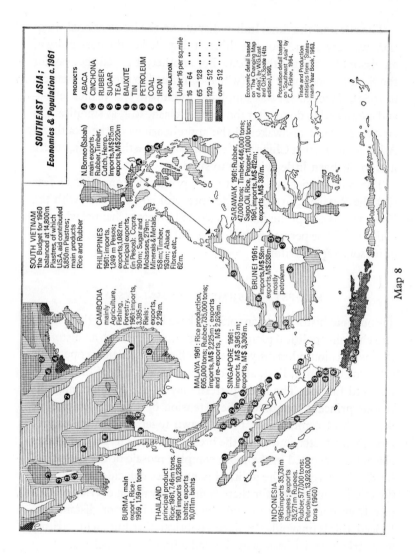

SOUTHEAST ASIA :
Economics & Population c.1961

SOUTH VIETNAM
the Budget for 1960
balanced at 14,800m
Piastres, of which
U.S.A. aid contributed
5,850m Piastres;
main products
Rice and Rubber

PHILIPPINES
1961: imports,
1,249 m Pesos;
exports, 1,082 m.
Principal exports,
(in Pesos): Copra,
190m; Sugar and
Molasses, 279m;
Minerals & Metals,
158m; Timber,
193m; Abaca
Fibres, etc,
62m.

N. Borneo (Sabah)
main exports,
Rubber, Timber,
Cutch, Hemp.
Imports, M$215m
exports, M$220m

SARAWAK 1961: Rubber,
47,000 tons; Timber, 446,000 tons;
Sago, Oil, Rice, Pepper, 11,000 tons;
1961, imports, M$412m;
exports, M$ 397m.

BRUNEI 1961:
imports, M$58m
exports, M$233m
mostly
petroleum

CAMBODIA
mainly
Agriculture,
Fishing,
Forestry.
1961: imports,
3,395m
Riels;
exports,
2,219m.

MALAYA 1961 : Rice production,
605,000 tons; Rubber, 735,000 tons;
imports, M$ 2,225m ; exports
and re-exports, M$ 2,626m.

SINGAPORE 1961:
imports, M$ 3,963 m;
exports, M$ 3,309 m.

BURMA main
export, Rice;
1959, 1.59 m tons

THAILAND
principal product
Rice; 1961 7,746m tons.
1961 imports 10,236m
bahts; exports
10,011m bahts

INDONESIA
1961 imports 35,731m
Rupees; exports
35,271m Rupees.
Rubber, 577,000 tons;
Petroleum, 13,928,000
tons (1960)

PRODUCTS

ABACA
CINCHONA
RUBBER
SUGAR
TEA
BAUXITE
TIN
PETROLEUM
COAL
IRON

POPULATION

Under 16 per sq. mile
16 – 64 " " :: ::
65 – 128 " " :: ::
129 – 512 " " :: ::
over 512 " " :: ::

Economic detail based
on 'The Changing Map
of Asia', by W.G. East
and O.H.K. Spate 4th
edition), 1961.

Population detail based
on Southeast Asia by
C. A. Fisher, 1964.

Trade and Production
statistics from 'States-
man's Year Book', 1963.

Map 8

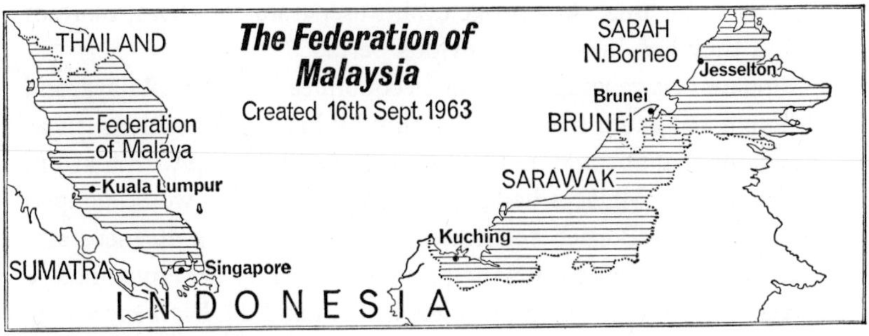

The Federation of Malaysia

THAILAND

Federation
of Malaya

•Kuala Lumpur

SUMATRA ꞏSingapore

SABAH
N.Borneo

Jesselton

Brunei

BRUNEI

SARAWAK

Kuching

I N D O N E S I A

Created 16th Sept.1963

Map 9

MALAYSIA. Head of State: H.H. Sir Putra ibni Al-Marhum Syed Hussan Jamalullail (Raja of Perlis). Capital: Kuala Lumpur. Parliament consisted of a Senate and a House of Representatives. The House of Representatives had 159 members: 105 for the Federation of Malaya, 25 for Sarawak, 16 for Sabah and 15 for Singapore.

The Fourteen States of Malaysia

	Area sq. miles	population (c. 1961)	
Johore	7,360	1,045,000	
Kedah	3,660	772,000	
Kelantan	5,780	562,000	
Malacca	640	330,000	
Negri Sembilan	2,590	416,000	
Pahang	13,920	350,000	Federation of Malaya
Penang	400	635,000	
Perak	8,030	1,363,000	
Perlis	320	100,000	
Selangor	3,150	1,140,000	
Trengganu	5,000	312,000	
Singapore	225	1,670,000	Singapore
Sarawak	48,250	760,000	Borneo States
Sabah	29,000	455,000	
Total	128,325	9,900,000	

Racial Distribution
(in thousands c. 1960)

(adapted from T. E. Smith *The Background to Malaysia*)

	Malays	Chinese	Indians & Pakistanis	Borneo (indigenous non-Malay)	Others	Total
Fed. of Malaya	3,461[a]	2,552	773	—	123	6,909
Singapore	227[a]	1,231	138	—	38	1,634
Sarawak	129	229	2	378	6	744
North Borneo	25	105	3	283	39[b]	455
Total	3,842	4,117	916	661	206	9,742

[a] Includes persons of Indonesian origin who have largely been absorbed into the Malay community.
[b] Includes 25,000 Indonesians.

211

such as Indochina, they broke up into separate countries, more or less as they had been in a previous period.

Singapore is geographically and economically part of Malaya, and although separated from it politically by historical accident it was inevitable that at some time or other it would join up with it again, as Penang and Malacca had already done. But what would happen to the British Borneo territories—Sarawak, North Borneo, and Brunei—when they gained their independence, as they must before so very long? This was a question which had long been exercising the minds of the Malayan leaders.

The credit for originating the idea of Malaysia is generally given to Tunku Abdul Rahman, the Prime Minister of Malaya, and there can be no doubt that the proposal first took practical shape in his mind. His motive was political, and it can be expressed in the following terms. Earlier, the Tunku and his government had been reluctant to seek a closer association with Singapore for fear of influence of Communism spreading through the Peninsula from the centre where it was undoubtedly strongest. Moreover, a merger with Singapore would mean the addition of some hundreds of thousands of fully enfranchised Chinese to the electoral rolls which would threaten, if not destroy, the Malay voting superiority in Malaya as a whole. But if Sarawak and North Borneo, and possibly Brunei, were brought in, the largely indigenous (and supposedly conservative) population of these territories would provide some sort of balance to the Chinese of the area—especially the Chinese of Singapore. The propositions would be roughly six million non-Chinese to four million Chinese in a ten million total. It was true that of the non-Chinese, only about 3,800,000 were 'Malays' (all Muslims), and that 660,000 odd were non-Malay natives of Borneo, and that there were in addition some 900,000 Indians and Pakistanis and 200,000 'others'. But the non-Chinese could be expected to hold together to counterbalance the Chinese in their own interest.

It happened that the Prime Minister of Singapore, Mr Lee Kuan-Yew, also favoured the idea of Malaysia, although, being a Chinese himself, he saw the problem as one of counterbalancing the Communists—not the Chinese as such.

One difficulty, however, arose from the fact that the British

Borneo territories were less advanced politically than Malaya and Singapore, since Nationalism had not so far developed among their peoples, though political parties had been in existence for some time. There was, on this and other accounts, some difference of opinion in those territories as to the terms on which they should join Malaysia, and a great deal of discussion would have to take place when the constitution was drafted.

In November 1961 Tunku Abdul Rahman went to London to negotiate for the federation with the British government. There were no great difficulties so far as Malaya and Singapore were concerned, except for the continuance of the British bases, for which an acceptable formula was found, but the British government was unwilling to agree to the creation of Malaysia until the wishes of the peoples of the Borneo territories had been consulted in the matter. Accordingly, a Commission under Lord Cobbold, with two Malayan members (one a Chinese), was sent to Sarawak and North Borneo (Sabah) to investigate the opinion there. After an exhaustive enquiry, involving thousands of miles of travelling, the Commission reported that, although there were some objections and provisos in certain quarters, the great majority of the people favoured the merger.

There were, however, some unseen rocks ahead. One unexpected one was a revolt in Brunei against Malaysia in December 1962, which had to be suppressed by British military action (Brunei was still under British protection). This revolt was staged with Indonesian support. The Sultan of Brunei later decided that his State would for the time being remain outside the proposed federation—but differences with the other states as to the allotment to federal purposes of Brunei's great riches, arising from oil, were the reason for this decision—not the revolt.

Up to the revolt, all had seemed plain sailing for the birth of Malaysia—but then the horizon began to cloud over. President Sukarno of Indonesia and some of his spokesmen now voiced opposition to the proposed federation. The Philippines also laid claims to Sabah (North Borneo) on historical grounds. Tunku Abdul Rahman then arranged to meet the Philippines President and Dr Sukarno in Manila. From the published reports their conversations seemed to have been amicable on the whole, and there was even an announcement of an agreement in principle to join Malaysia, Indonesia, and the Philippines into a wider association to be known as,'Maphilindo'. But as the agreed day for the declaration of Malaysia (31 August 1963) approached it was clear that the Indonesian president was resolved to continue and to step-up his opposition to Malaysia, which he denounced as a creation of 'neo-Colonialism' inspired by Britain.

In deference to President Sukarno's claim that the opinion of the peoples of Sarawak and North Borneo had not been properly consulted, the declaration of Malaysia was delayed to allow a United Nations Commission to visit these States. This UN commission in due course confirmed the findings of the Cobbold Commission, and Malaysia came into being on 16 September. Indonesia then declared a boycott of all Malaysian trade, and frontier incidents began to increase on the Bornean border between Malaysia and Indonesia. The outlook for Malaysia was thus troubled—but its sponsors were confident that it would weather the storm and become established on an enduring basis.

At this point, this book must end. History is never a completed, rounded-off unity—it is ever in the making.

APPENDIX

A NOTE ON BOOKS FOR FURTHER READING

In the following note the more up-to-date books have been singled out for mention, and 'classics' are not included (the latter, however, will be found listed in the bibliographies). The titles are arranged as far as possible according to the chapters to which they are especially relevant. Only works in the English language are mentioned, though there are numerous authorities in other languages which the more advanced student will have to consult.

CHAPTER 1

For the geography of Southeast Asia, C. A. Fisher, *South-east Asia* (Methuen, 1964) is the most up-to-date and comprehensive work, but E. H. G. Dobby, *Southeast Asia* (University of London Press, 5th edn, 1956) and W. G. East and O. H. K. Spate (editors), *The Changing Map of Asia* (Ithaca, Cornell University Press, 1958) provide the basic information. R. R. Sellman, *An Outline Atlas of Eastern History* (E. Arnold, 1954) provides all the essential information on the historical geography of the region. D. G. E. Hall, *A History of South-East Asia* (New York, St Martin's Press, 1955, new edn, 1964) is the most comprehensive work on the subject. A shorter book giving all the essential facts is Brian Harrison, *Southeast Asia* (Macmillan, 1954). The early history and geography of the Malay Peninsula and the surrounding area before 1500 (with the original Chinese, Sanskrit, Greek, Tamil, and other texts) is set out in Paul Wheatley, *The Golden Khersonese* (Kuala Lumpur, University of Malaya Press, 1961). The bibliography of this work is a guide to the study of the early history of Southeast Asia in general.

CHAPTER 2

At this point a general survey of Indonesian history can be found in B. H. M. Vlekke, *Nusantara, a history of Indonesia* (Chicago, Quadrangle Books, 1960). For Malaya, Sir R. O. Winstedt, *A History of Malaya* (Singapore, Marican & Sons, rev. edn, 1962) is still the standard work and gives the early history and cultural background. Nicholas Tarling, *Anglo-Dutch Rivalry in the Malay World* (Queensland University Press, 1962) describes what its title indicates, and should be read in conjunction with the same author's *Piracy and Politics in the Malay World* (Melbourne, F. W. Cheshire, 1963). For full information relating to Sir T. S.

Appendix

Raffles, there is C. E. Wurzburg, *Raffles of the Eastern Seas* (Hodder & Stoughton, 1954) and as a guide to Raffles' policies during his régime as Lieutenant-Governor of Java there is John Bastin, *The native policies of Sir Stamford Raffles in Java and Sumatra: an economic interpretation* (Oxford University Press, 1957). The story as it relates to Malaya can be followed up in L. A. Mills, *British Malaya 1824–67* (Malayan Branch, Royal Asiatic Society, 1925). Burmese history prior and subsequent to 1800 is to be found in G. E. Harvey, *History of Burma from the Earliest Times to the Beginning of the English Conquest (1824)* (Longmans, 1925) and for the period 1885 onwards, J. S. Furnivall, *The Political Economy of Burma* (Rangoon, 2nd edn, 1938) demonstrates the shortcomings of the 'village' system. Furnivall is also a leading authority on the Dutch East Indies, and his book, *Netherlands India: a Study in Plural Economy* is indispensable for an understanding of Dutch policy. (Furnivall emphasizes the importance of the opening of the Suez Canal as a turning point in South and East Asian history.)

CHAPTER 3

Strictly speaking, Sir F. A. Swettenham, *British Malaya* (Allen & Unwin, new edn, 1948) is a 'classic', and should therefore be omitted, but it provides such a graphic account of Malayan history by one who helped to make it and who lived on long enough to see the past in perspective, that it is included here. British intervention in the Malay States is the subject of two comparatively recent works—namely, C. Northcote Parkinson, *British Intervention in Malaya 1867–1877* (Singapore, University of Malaya Press, 1960), and C. D. Cowan, *Nineteenth Century Malaya, 1867–1877: the Origins of British Political Control* (Oxford University Press, 1961). J. Kennedy, *A History of Malaya A.D. 1400–1959* (Macmillan, 1962) covers a long period of Malayan history, but is particularly useful for its description of the development of the 'Resident' system. As regards Sarawak, Sir Steven Runciman, *The White Rajahs* (Cambridge University Press, 1960) gives the history of the Brooke family from 1841 to 1946. For North Borneo, K. Tregonning, *Under chartered company rule: North Borneo 1881–1946* is the standard authority.

CHAPTER 4

Michael Edwardes, *Asia in the European Age 1498–1955* (Thames & Hudson, 1961) gives a panoramic impression of the Western contacts with the South and East Asian countries over a period of four and a half centuries (with rather more emphasis on India, however, than on China and Japan). Percival Spear, *India: a modern history* (University of Michigan Press, 1961) is a comprehensive work on the Subcontinent. There is not yet a satisfactory history of the Anglo-Chinese War of

Appendix

1839–42, but A. Waley, *The Opium War through Chinese Eyes* (Allen & Unwin, 1958) is an authoritative account based on Chinese sources. An outline survey of Chinese history is given in V. Purcell, *China* (Nations of the Modern World, Benn, 1962), and the same author's *The Boxer Uprising: a background study* (Cambridge University Press, 1963) contains introductory chapters on nineteenth-century China as well as a detailed account of the origins of the Uprising. G. B. Sansom, *A History of Japan* (Cresset Press, Vols. I, II, III, 1957, 1961, 1963) is the standard history of Japan in English, but brings the story only up to 1867, but Richard Storry, *A History of Modern Japan* (Penguin Books, rev. edn, 1963) gives a mass of reliable information on the modern period in a small space.

CHAPTER 5

Swettenham and Kennedy (see under Chapter 3 above) can again be followed with safety for this period, but Rupert Emerson, *Malaysia: a Study of Direct and Indirect Rule* (Macmillan, 1937) subjects the colonial policy of the British and Dutch to critical scrutiny from an American point of view. J. S. Furnivall, *Netherlands India* (see under Chapter 2 above) is again a valuable guide to the Dutch régime in Indonesia in this later period. For the events leading to the 1932 Revolution in Siam and for the sequel to them, K. Landon, *Siam in Transition* is the authority, and Virginia Thompson, *Thailand: the New Siam* (New York, Macmillan, 1941) is a compendious account of the country. Two books on Burma relating to the 'colonial period' can be recommended, namely, J. L. Christian, *Modern Burma* (Berkeley, California, Institute of Pacific Relations, 1942), and G. E. Harvey, *British Rule in Burma, 1824–1942* (Faber, 1956). For French Indochina, Thomas E. Ennis, *French Policy and Developments in Indo-China* (University of Chicago Press, 1936) accurately sets out the situation there before the Pacific War. J. R. Hayden, *The Philippines: a Study in National Development* (New York, Macmillan, 1942) deals minutely with the evolution of the Philippine political parties.

CHAPTER 6

This chapter widens the territorial scope of the book very considerably so that it is necessary to have recourse to generalized and comprehensive works on China, Japan, and the Indian Subcontinent. L. C. Goodrich, *A Short History of the Chinese People* (New York, Harper, 3rd edn, 1959) is an excellent summary, Li Chien-Nung, *The Political History of China, 1840–1928*, translated by Teng Ssu-Yu and J. Ingalls (Princeton, N.J., 1956) is a translation of a standard work in Chinese. For Japan, Richard Storry (see under Chapter 4 above) again provides essential information.

Appendix

These books contain bibliographies which give the key to the vast literature on China and Japan for this period. For the Indian Subcontinent, Spear (see under Chapter 4 above) can again be referred to.

CHAPTER 7

Since the Overseas Chinese figure so prominently in the extension of Nationalism into Southeast Asia, it might be well to make a start in additional reading with V. Purcell, *The Chinese in Southeast Asia* (Oxford University Press for Chatham House, 1951, new edn, 1965). Many studies were published during this phase of the Nationalist movement in the region, but the more up-to-date works (mentioned under Chapters 8, 9 and 10 below) deal with the events of this time in the light of the information that has since become available.

CHAPTERS 8, 9, 10

For the last three chapters, it is preferable to have recourse to the more up-to-date books, since it is only recently that sufficient information has become available to enable the developments to be described with any authority. For the situation in China, the following is a selection of recommended books: C. P. FitzGerald, *Revolution in China* (Cresset Press, 1952) and *Floodtide in China* (Cresset Press, 1958), Kuo Ping-Chia, *China: new age and outlook* (Penguin Books, new edn, 1960), and C. Brandt, B. Schwartz, and J. K. Fairbank, *A Documentary History of Chinese Communism* (Allen & Unwin, 1952). Alastair Lamb, *The China-India Border* (Chatham House Essays, Oxford University Press, 1964) treats effectively in a small space a subject of great contemporary interest. For Japan, there is Sir E. Dening, *Japan* (Nations of the Modern World, Benn, 1960), and, once more, Richard Storry, *A History of Modern Japan* (see under Chapter 4 above). For Southeast Asia, there is V. Purcell, *The Revolution in Southeast Asia* (Thames & Hudson, 1962), J. M. Gullick, *Malaya* (Nations of the Modern World, Benn, 1963), Hugh Tinker, *The Union of Burma* (Oxford University Press for Chatham House, 3rd edn, 1961), Tibor Mende, *Southeast Asia between Two Worlds* (Turnstile Press, 1955), Dorothy Woodman, *The Republic of Indonesia* (Cresset Press, 1955), and D. Lancaster, *The Emancipation of French Indochina* (Oxford University Press for Chatham House, 1961). For the transitional period after the Japanese surrender, Lennox Mills and Associates, *The New World of Southeast Asia* (University of Minnesota Press, 1949) contains authoritative articles on the Philippines, Indonesia, Burma, Malaya, French Indochina, Siam (Thailand), and the Chinese in Southeast Asia. T. E. Smith, *The Background to Malaysia* (Chatham House Memoranda, 1963) is an informative monograph on the subject of its title.

INDEX

Abe, Premier of Japan, 172
Abdullah, 51–3, 57
Abdul Rahman, Tunku, 207, 212–13
Abdur Rahman, Tunku (1818), 30, 42
Acheh, 20, 29
Afghanistan, 72, 77, 131
Africa, Africans, 203
Aguinaldo, 114
Ahmad, of Malacca, 11
Alaungpaya, of Burma, 14–15
Ali, Sultan of Johore, 42
Ali, Sultan of Perak, 51
Allenby, Lord, 130
America, Americans (USA), 40, 61, 68, 69, 81, 83–4, 88, 106, 113–18, 138, 139, 149–51, 175, 182–6, 190, 193–4, 196, 200–1, 202
Amritsar, 131
Ananda Mahidol, Prince, 108
Anfu clique, 134
Angkor, 6, 7–8
Angkor Wat, 7
Anglo-Dutch Treaty (1824), 31–3, 59
Anglo-Japanese Alliance, 121, 138
Anking, 123
Annam, 2, 4, 7, 24, 44, 64, 67, 148–9, 201
Anti-Comintern Pact, 171
Anwhei, 123, 127
Arabs, 8, 173
Arakan, 15, 22–3, 34, 62, 183, 197
Assam, 15, 34, 183, 192
Assaye, 23, 71
Attlee, Clement, 190, 200
Aung San, Premier of Burma, 147, 189–90, 197
Australia, Australians, 3, 176–7, 183, 196
Austria-Hungary, 88
Ava, Court of, 22, 34, 63

Bahadur Shah, Mogul Emperor, 75
Bali, 8, 20
Ba Maw, Dr, 147, 180, 189
Ba Sen, 190
Bandjermasin, Sultan of, 20
Bandung, 142, 203

Bangkok, 15, 20, 40, 101, 108, 156; Treaty of, 38, 106
Bannerman, Col., 29
Bantam, Sultan of, 21
Bao Dai, Emperor of Vietnam, 25, 201–2
Ba Pe, U, 145
Baroda, Gaekwar of, 71
Batan Peninsula, 176
Batang Maru, Battle of, 60
Batavia (Jakarta), 13–14, 21, 26, 30, 37, 105
Batavian Republic, 14
Battambang, 23, 106
Bazin, 149
Beirut, 153
Belcher, Capt., 60
Belgium, 68, 196
Ben, mandarin, 23
Bencoolen, 28, 32
Bengal, 12, 15, 19, 23, 73, 78, 183, 192
Bentham, Jeremy, 73
Bentinck, Lord William, 72, 73–4
Bhamo, 63
Bhutan, 208
Birch, J. W. W., 51–2, 57
Birkenhead, Lord, 133
Bismarck Sea, Battle of, 182
Bithur, 71
'Black Flags, the', 66
Bogor, 203
Bombay, 19, 70, 76; Presidency, 71
Bombay Burmah Trading Co., 62–3
Borneo, 20, 38, 47, 57–61, 157, 173–4, 176, 188, 212
Borneo, North (Sabah), 2, 58, 61, 212–14; British North Borneo Co., 61
Borobodur, 6
Borodin, 163
Bowring, Sir John, 40, 68
Boxer, Protocol, 88, 120
Boxer Uprising, 87–8, 119–20
Brahmanism, 7
Briggs, Sir H., 206
Britain, British, colonial policy (before 1800), 19–20, 24; (in 19th cent.) 43–4, 45–7, 48, 57, 67; (in 20th cent.) 144, 145

British, imperialism (before 1800),
11, 12–13, 17, 18, 22; (in 19th
cent.) 26, 28, 32, 33–6, 41, 43–4,
47–53, 63, 70–8; (in 20th cent.)
91–2, 100, 109–11, 148, 155,
186–7, 214
in China, 86, 88, 127
rivalry with Dutch, 25–8
treaty with Siam, 39
See also under Trade, East India
Company
Brooke, Sir Charles, 61
Brooke, James, 31, 47, 58–61
Brunei, 1, 47, 58, 61, 212, 213
Buddhism, 6, 7, 99, 100, 109, 147
Budi Utomo, 141
Bugis, the, 15, 18–19, 30, 46–7
Bui Quang Chieu, the, 149
Bukit Kuda, 95
Burdett-Coutts, Baroness, 60
Burma, 1, 4, 13, 14, 22–3, 33–6, 62–4,
72, 101, 109–11, 145–7, 173,
176–7, 179–80, 182, 190, 197,
199, 203, 209
Burney, Capt., 38
Buxar, 12

Cach Menh Dang, 149
Cach Menh Thanh Nien Hoi, 149
Cachar, 33
Cairo, 153
Calicut, 10
Cambodia, 1, 2, 4, 7, 8, 15, 23, 44,
66–7, 101, 106, 189, 195, 201
Canning, Lord, 76
Canton, 66, 78, 80, 125, 135–6, 163
Carimon Is., 29, 32
Carnarvon, Lord, 53–4
Carnatic, the, 12, 70
Caste system, the, 6, 75, 161
Catholicism, Roman, 8, 69
Cavanagh, Col. O., 42–3
Ceylon, 70, 94, 177, 203
Chakri dynasty (Siam), 20, 39
Chamber of Princes (India), 131
Champa, 6, 7
Chams, the, 4
Chang Hsueh-Liang, 155, 166
Chang Tso-Lin, 134
Chelmsford, Lord, 130
Chen Chiung-Ming, 135–6
Chen Kuo-Fu, 163
Chen Li-Fu, 163
Ch'en Tsu-Yi, 9

Chen Tu-Hsiu, 135
Cheng Ho, 9
Chiang Kai-Shek, 123, 135–7, 139,
153, 155, 157, 161–6, 171–2, 184,
193–4, 198
Chin, 146; Chin Hills, 183
Chin Pu Tang, 127
China, Chinese, at Bandung, 203–4;
Boxer Uprising, 87–8, 119–20;
boundary dispute with India,
208–9; civil war, 192–4, 197–8;
early contacts and influence, 4–8,
9–10; in Borneo, 20, 59, 60; in
Malaya, 48, 92–4, 97, 99, 151,
153–5, 212–13; in Siam, Burma
and Indonesia, 100–2, 109, 151,
155–7; in the 1930s, 163–7;
isolation in the early 19th cent.,
18, 78, 80; Opium War, 78–80;
overseas nationalism and Communism, 151–2; People's Republic, 197–9; reform movement,
87; reunification, 133–7, 162;
revolution of 1911, 122–9, 152;
war with France, 66–7; war with
Japan, 85–6. *See also under*
Communism; Kuomintang;
Manchuria; Nationalism; Trade
Chit Haing, U, 145
Chittagong, 23
Cholas, the, 7
Chou En-Lai, 200
Christianity, 10, 11, 69, 75, 78–9, 81,
114, 142, 159
Chu Teh, 163–4
Chulalongkorn (Rama V), 39, 68,
106–7
Chungking, 166, 172, 175, 184, 193,
194
Churchill, Sir Winston, 147, 159
'Citizens' Society, the', 127
Clarke, Sir A., 50, 52
Clive, Robert, 12
Cobbold, Lord, 213–14
Cobden, R., 60
Cochin-China, 2, 4, 15, 24, 44, 66–7,
111, 189, 201
Coen, J. P., 13
Colombo, 177
Communism, in Burma, 190, 197; in
China, 129, 135, 153, 162–7, 178,
193–4, 198–9; in Indonesia, 143;
in Malaya, 154–5, 187, 197,
205–7; in Vietnam, 149

Index

Confucianism, 6, 82, 135
Congress Party, Indian, 77, 133, 143, 157, 159–61, 191
'Constitutional Compact, the', 128
Coral Sea, Battle of, 177
Cotton, Sir H., 77
Councils Act, Indian, 76–7, 130
Cox, Capt. H., 23
Crosthwaite, Sir C., 63
'Culture System, the', 37, 103
Curzon, Lord, 77

Daendels, Marshal, 26
Daing Kemboja, ruler of Bugis, 18
Dalhousie, Lord, 36, 74
Dandi, 160
Dansai, 106
Data Bandar, 52
Dato Klana, 52
Dato Onn bin Ja'afar, 188
Davidson, J. G., 52
de Behaine, Pigneau, 15, 24
de Bussy, C. C., 22
de Genouilly, Admiral, 66
de Lesseps, F., 44
de Suffren, Admiral, 22
Deccan, 71
Dekker, E. Douwes, 38, 142
Delhi, 71, 75, 131
Denmark, 68
Deshima, 83
Deva-Raja, 7
Dewry, Commodore, 114
Dien Bien Phu, 202
Disraeli, Benjamin, 44, 48, 77
Dom Muang, 107
Doumer, P., 67
Dufferin, Lord, 63
Dulles, F., 202
Dupleix, J. F., 12
Dupré, Admiral, 66
Dutch, see Netherlands
Dyaks, Land, 59, 61; Sea, 47
'Dyarchy System, the', 110, 131, 145, 160–1
Dyer, General, 131

East India Company, British, 12–13, 19, 21, 25, 27, 28, 30, 36, 38, 41, 42, 75, 76
East India Company, Dutch, 13–14, 15, 21, 37, 46

Eden, Sir A., 202
Education, in Burma, 110, 145; in India, 73–4; in Indochina, 112; in Indonesia, 103, 144; in Malaya, 96–7, 153; in the Philippines, 115; in Siam (Thailand), 101, 107, 157
Egypt, 21
'Emergency, the' (Malaya), 197, 207
En Ming, 123
'Ethical Policy, the', 103, 105, 141

Farquhar, Capt., 60
Federal Council (F.M.S.), 98
Fendall, John, 28
Feng Yu-Hsiang, 164
Foochow, 67
Formosa, 86, 147, 186, 198, 200–1, 209
France, French,
    clashes with China, 81, 88
    collapse of, 174
    colonial policy (before 1800), 24; (in 19th cent.) 43–4, 64, 67; (in 20th cent.) 111–13, 144–5, 148
    imperialism (before 1800), 11, 12, 22; (in 19th cent.) 43–4, 64–7; (in 20th cent.) 112, 186, 189, 201–2
    in Burma, 62
    in Indochinese peninsula, 2, 15, 24, 68, 111–13, 174
    See also under Trade
Franco-Prussian War, 66
Funan, 7, 8
Furnivall, J. S., 64, 105, 146
Fytche, Sir A., 109

Gandhi, Mahatma, 131–2, 142, 159–61, 191–2
Garnier, F., 66
Geneva Conference, 202
Germany, Germans, 86, 88, 114, 127, 170, 172–3
Gia-Long, 23–4, 64
Gladstone, W. E., 44, 48, 60, 61
Goa, 11, 71
Goodnow, F. J., 128
Gordon, General, 81
Government of India Act (1919), 110, 130
Government of India Act (1935), 110, 160

221

Index

Governor-Generals of India, *see* Bentinck; Canning; Dalhousie; Ellenborough; Hardinge; Hastings; Minto; Shore; Wellesley. *See also* Viceroys
Gromyko, A. A., 186
Guadalcanal, 183
Guam, 176
Guinea, New, *see* Irian
Gujarat, 72
Gurkhas, 72, 206
Gurney, Sir H., 206

Ha-Tien, 24
Habibullah Khan, 131
Haifeng, 164
Haiphong, 189
Haji Agus Salim, 143
Hankow, 126, 162, 167
Hanoi, 66, 149
Hanseatic cities, 68
Harbin, 122
Hardinge, Lord, 72
Hare-Hawes-Cutting Bill, 150
Hart, Sir R., 82
Hastings, Marquess of, 29, 71, 72
Hatta, M., 180, 196
Hayashi, Count, 121
Haynau, Gen., 60
Heilungkiang, 165
Heiser, Dr, 114
Hinduism, Hindus, 6, 7, 8–9, 73, 74–5, 131–3, 159, 161, 191–2
Hindustan, 71
Hiranuma, Baron, 172
Hiroshima, 184
Hiroto, Premier of Japan, 185
Hitler, Adolph, 171, 183
Ho Chi Minh, 149, 189
Ho Lung, 163
Hoare, Sir Samuel, 160
Holkar, Maratha chief, 71
Holland, *see* Netherlands
Hon-Dat, 24
Hong Kong, 113, 138, 176
Hoover, H. C., 150
Hopei, 193
Hsiu Ch'eng-Chi, 124
Hsu Hsi-Lin, 123
Hsuan Hsing, 125
Hsuchow, 198
Hu Shih, 135
Hué, 7, 24, 66

Hume, Sir A., 77
Hunan, 123, 135, 164
Hung Hsiu-Chuan, 81
Hussein, of Johore, 30–1, 42
Hyderabad, 70–1

Imperialism, Japanese, 86, 120–1, 128, 137–40, 157, 165–72, 176–82. *See also under* Britain; France; Netherlands
India, Indians, at Bandung, 203; boundary dispute with China, 208–9; British India and the Mutiny, 70–8; civil disobedience, 158–61; early contacts and influence, 4–8, 10; European empires, 12–15, 18; in Burma, 146; in Malaya, 97–100, 212; independence, 191–2, 195; reforms and nationalism, 129–33; relations with Burma, 33–6. *See also under* Communism; Nationalism; Trade
Indies, East, *see* Malay Archipelago
Indische Partij, the, 142
Indochina, 2, 15, 24–5, 64–7, 98, 102, 111–13, 145, 148, 173–5, 189, 201–2, 212
Indonesia, 1, 4, 8, 13, 18, 21, 36–8, 98, 102, 142, 145, 173, 176–7, 180, 188, 195–6, 199, 203, 204, 209. *See also* Java
Indragiri, 18
Indus, River, 72
Industrial Revolution (Europe), 16–7, 46, 92
Inukai, Premier of Japan, 168–9
Irian, West, 3, 196
Irrawaddy, River, 4, 147
Irrawaddy Flotilla Co., 62
Irwin, Lord, 132, 158–9
Iskandar Shah, *see* Parameswara
Islam, 6, 8–10, 69, 75, 142, 153
Ismail, 51
Italy, 68, 88, 183
Iwojima Island, 184

Jakarta, 13, 204. *See also* Batavia
Jambi, 18
Janssens, General, 26
Japan, Japanese, defeat and occupation, 182–6; in Burma, 147; in

Index

Malaya, 96; in Manchuria, 165–6; in Philippines, 151; invasion of S.E. Asia, 176–82; isolation in early 19th cent., 11, 18; progress in late 19th cent., 82–5; relations with China, 127–9; war with Russia, 121–2. *See also under* Communism; Nationalism; Trade

Java, 8, 14, 15, 20–1, 26–8, 31, 37–8, 46, 141, 143, 188, 195

Jayavarman II, of Angkor, 7

Jehol, 165

Jervois, Sir W., 52–3

Jesuits, 79

Jinnah, M. A., 133, 191–2

Jogjakarta, 21

Johnson, C., *see* Brooke, Sir C.

Johore (empire), 18–19, 30, 46

Johore (state), 42, 57

Johore, Sultan of, 30, 42

Johore Bahru, 95

Jones Bill, the, 115

Kachin, Kachins, 63, 146, 190

Kali, 72

K'ang Yu-Wei, 87, 124

Karachi, 72, 192

Karakoram Pass, 208

Karenni, Karens, 146, 190, 197

Kashmir, 208

Kedah, 7, 15, 18, 39, 41, 98, 179; Sultan of, 19

Kelantan, 41, 96, 98, 176

Keppel, Admiral, 59

Kertanagara, King of Java, 9

Khmers, 4, 7

Ki Hadjar Dewantoro, 142

Kiangsi, 123, 127, 163

Kiaochow, 86, 88

Killearn, Lord, 188

Kimberley, Lord, 48–50

Kirin, 128, 165

Klang, 52

Klong Toi, 156

Kobe, 184

Koda-ha, the, 170

Konoye, Premier of Japan, 172, 174

Korat, 23

Korea, 85, 120, 122, 171, 186, 199–200

Krat, 106

Kuala Kangsar, 57, 94, 97

Kuala Lumpur, 51, 57, 95, 96

Kublai Khan, 9

Kuching, 60

Kung, H. H., 163

Kuomintang, 123, 126–8, 135–7, 152, 153–4, 161–7, 193–4, 197–8

Kuriles, 186

Kuyper, Dr A., 103

Kwangchouwan, 86

Kwangsi, 152, 164

Kwangtung, 80, 123, 127, 152, 164, 169

Kwantung (North China), 140

Kyoto, 84, 184

Labuan, 59

Ladakh, 208

Lahore, 130; Congress, 159

Lake, Lord, 71

Lampang, 156

Lampson, Sir M., 154

Langat, 52

Langson, 67

Lansdowne, Lord, 121

Lanun, 47

Laos, 1, 2, 4, 189, 195, 201, 202

Larut, 51, 52

Laurel, J. P., 182, 190

League of Nations, 166, 168–9, 170–1

Lee Kuan-Yew, 212

Lela, Maharaja, 53

Leonowens, Anna, 68

Leyte, 183

Li Hung-Chang, 82

Li Lieh-Chun, 127

Li Ta-Chao, 136

Li Yuan-Hung, 125, 134

Liang Ch'i-Ch'ao, 87, 124

Liaoning, 128, 165

Liaotung Peninsula, 122

Light, Capt. F., 19

Lin Tse-Hsu, 79

Linggajati, 188

Lloyd George, David, 158

Lombok, 20

Louis Bonaparte, King of Netherlands, 25

Louis XVI, 24

Low, Sir H., 55–7, 92, 93, 94

Lu Hsun, 135

Luang Pradist Manudharm, *see* Pridi

Lufeng, 164

Lyttelton, O., 206–7

Lytton, Lord, 77

Macao, 79
MacArthur, General, 185, 200
Macassar, 46
Macaulay, Lord, 74, 76
Macdonald, Ramsay, 158
Madras, 19, 70, 76
Madura, 103, 188
Mahmud, King of Malacca, 11
Majapahit, 7, 8
Malabar, 131
Malacca, 9, 11, 13, 18–20, 27, 30, 32, 38, 41, 46, 187, 212; Straits of, 29
Malaria, 96, 111, 179
Malay Archipelago, 1, 20
Malay Peninsula, 1, 7, 8, 15, 18–20, 32, 42, 70, 92, 102, 187
Malay States, the, 38, 41–3, 44, 46, 47–8, 53–7, 68, 89, 91–2, 94, 96–7, 99, 106
Malay States, Federated, 57, 94, 95, 98
Malaya, 1–2, 4, 13, 44, 91–100, 110, 151, 173–5, 176–7, 178–9, 187–8, 197, 205–7, 212–13
Malaysia, Federation of, 1–2, 18, 212–13
Malolos, 114
Manchukuo, 166, 169, 172
Manchuria, 120–1, 134, 137, 140, 163, 164–6, 168, 193, 198
Manchus, 11, 80–2, 86–8, 119–20, 122–7
Mandalay, 62, 63
Mangunkusomo, Dr, 142
Manila, 25, 114, 213
Manipur, 34, 183
Mantri, the, 51, 54
Mao Tse-Tung, 135, 136, 164, 193
'Maphilindo', 214
Marathas, 23, 33, 71–2, 75
Marianas, 183
Maritime Customs (Chinese), 82, 120
Marshall, General, 193
Martaban, 36
Maung Gyi, Sir J. A., 145
McKinley, President, 114
Mecca, 153
Meerut, 75, 130
Meester Cornelis, Battle of, 26
Meiji Constitution, 85, 186
Mekong River, 7, 111; Delta, 4, 7
Menam Valley, 4
Midway, Battle of, 182
Min-Mang, 64

Min Pao, 123, 124
Minangkabaus, the, 18, 41
Mindanao, 8, 69
Mindon, King of Burma, 36
Minthagi, 34
Minto, Lord, 26
Missionaries, 81, 96, 142
Mitsubishi, 139, 169, 179
Mitsui, 169, 179
Moguls, 45, 75, 161; emperor, 71; empire, 11, 12
Moluccas, 11, 32
Mongkolbaurey, 23
Mongkut, Maha (Rama IV), 39, 68
Mongolia, 128, 134, 137, 172
Mongols, 3, 45
Mons, the, 4, 7, 14
Montagu, Edwin, 130
Moplahs, the, 131
Morant, Sir Robert, 68
Moros, the (Ilanos), 47
Mountbatten, Lord, 187, 189, 192
Mukden, 122, 140, 165
Munday, Capt., 59
Munro, Sir Hector, 12
Muslims, 74–5, 99, 131–3, 143, 160–1, 173, 191–2, 197, 205, 212. *See also* Islam
Mutiny, Indian, 73, 74–5
Muzaffir Shah, 9
'Myochit', 147
Mysore, 23

Nagara Rajasima, 156
Nagasaki, 12, 83, 184
Nagoya, 184
Nagpur, 71
Nagumo, Admiral, 177
Nana Sahib, 75
Nanchang, 163
Nanking, 126, 137, 153, 156, 162–4, 166, 171, 172, 194, 198; Treaty of, 79, 80
Nanshi, 162
Napoleon I, 21, 26, 28
Napoleon III, 44
National Congress, Indian, 77, 129, 131
Nationalism, 102, 119, 122, 133, 161, 177; in Burma, 110, 144–7, 157, 179–80; in China, 119, 125, 134; see also Kuomintang; in India, 129, 130–3, 157; in Indochina,

Index

112, 144, 148–9, 151, 157, 201; in Indonesia, 105, 141–4, 151, 153, 157, 180, 188; in Japan, 119, 139, 168; in Malaya, 152, 155, 187; in overseas Chinese, 151–2; in Philippines, 115, 119, 150–1, 157, 190; in Siam (Thailand), 101, 152, 155–7

Nederlandsche Handelsmaatschappij, 37

Negri Sembilan, 41, 52, 57, 94

Negritos, 3

Nehru, Pandit, 131, 133, 159, 191

Nepal, 33, 72, 208

Netherlands, Holland, Dutch, colonial policy, (before 1800) 21, 24; (in 19th cent.) 26, 37–8, 43, 45, 67; (in 20th cent.) 102, 103–6, 141, 144–5
imperialism (before 1800), 11, 13–14, 18–19, 20–22; (in 19th cent.) 26–8, 32, 36–8, 43; (in 20th cent.) 188, 196
in Japan, 11–12
rivalry with British, 25–8
See also under Trade; East India Company

Ngoh-din-Diem, 202

Nguyen Anh (Gia Long), 15, 23–4

Norway, 68

Nu, U (Thakin), 190, 197

Okada, Admiral, 170

Okinawa, 184

Opium, 79, 102

Orange, Prince of, 13, 25

Osaka, 184

Osmena, Sergio, 150

Oudh, 12, 71, 75

Oundle, 107

Pacific War (1941–5), 140, 158, 175, 182–5, 193

Pagan Min, King of Burma, 36

Pahang, 42–3, 57, 94, 96, 179; Bendahara of, 30, 42

Pak Chang, 156

Pakistan, 77, 78, 192, 203, 207, 208, 212

Palembang, 7, 9

Pangkor Island, 51

Parameswara, 9

Pasai, 9

Pasir Salak, 53

Pasquier, Governor-General of Indochina, 149

Pathet Lao, the, 201

Pearl Harbour, 175, 176

Pegu, 36

Peiping, *see* Peking

Peking, 9, 24, 79, 88, 128, 129, 134, 136, 137, 162, 198, 204

Penang, 13, 15, 19–20, 25, 27, 28, 38, 41, 56, 95, 187, 212

People's Communes, 199

People's Liberation Army, 198

Perak, 18, 39, 50, 52, 54, 92, 94, 179

Perak River, 51, 53

Perlis, 98

Perry, Commodore, 12, 83–4

Persia, Persians, 72

Pescadores, the, 186

Pham Quynh, 149

Phayre, Sir A., 109

Phibun (Pibul), 108, 156

Philippines, 1, 8, 25, 69, 98, 113–18, 138, 141, 149–51, 173, 175, 176–7, 181–4, 190, 199, 209, 213

Phnom-Pen, 8

Pindaris, the, 72

Piracy, 38, 44, 46–7, 48, 58, 59–61

Plassey, Battle of, 12

'Plural Society', 98–102, 205

Poona, 71

Pootung, 162

Port Arthur, 86, 121–2

Port Moresby, 177, 183

Port Swettenham, 95

Port Weld, 95

Portsmouth, Treaty of, 122

Portugal, Portuguese, 10–11, 46, 68

Preanger, the, 14

Premiers of Japan, *see* Abe; Hiranuma; Hiroto; Inukai; Konoye; Okada; Saito; Suzuki; Takahashi; Tojo; Wakatsuki

Presidents of USA, *see* Hoover, McKinley; Roosevelt, F.; Roosevelt, T.; Taft; Truman; Wilson

Pridi, 108–9

Prome, 36

Province Wellesley, 15, 19

Prussia, 68

Pu Yi, 124, 134, 166, 169

Pulo Condore, 24

Punjab, 72, 192

225

Index

Putera, the, 180
Putyatin, Admiral, 83
P'ya Manopakorn, 108
Pyong Yang, 200
Pyus, the, 4

Queen's Commissioners, 53
Queen's Declaration, The, 109
Quezon, Manuel, 115, 150-1
Qui-nonh, 66
Quoc Dan Dong, 149

Raffles, Sir T. S., 27-31, 32-3, 36
Railways, 56, 62, 77, 95-6, 112, 120, 125, 167
Raja Haji, 18
Rama, Kings of Siam, Rama I, 15, 23-4; II, 39; III, 39; IV, 39, 68 (see Mongkut); V, 39, 68, 106-7 (see Chulalongkorn); VI, 106-7, 155; VII, 107
Rance, Sir H., 190
Rangoon, 22-3, 33, 36, 189
Ranjit Singh, 72
'Ratha Niyom', 156-7
Raymond, French officer, 71
Reading, Lord, 131
Red River, 111
Rembau, 52
Resident System, 51-7, 92
Revolution (Chinese) of 1911, 122-9, 141, 152
Rhio (Riau), 18, 30
Rhio-Lingga Archipelago, 30, 32, 47
Ribbentrop, Herr von, 172
Ripon, Lord, 77
Roads (in Malaya), 95
Roberts, Lord, 77
Rodger, J. P., 56
Roosevelt, Franklin, 150
Roosevelt, Theodore, 115, 122
Ross, Sir R., 96
Roxas, Manuel, 150
Rubber, 57, 177. See also under Trade
Runciman, Sir S., 60
Russia, Russians, 72, 77, 78, 83, 86, 88, 120-2, 127, 129, 135-6, 139, 143, 162-3, 171, 180, 183, 184, 193, 199-200, 209
Russo-Japanese War, 121-2, 141

Sabah (N. Borneo), 2, 61, 213
Saigon, 44, 66

Saipan, 183
Saito, Admiral, 170
Sakhalin, 122, 139, 186
Salt Gabelle, the, 120, 134
Sambas Sultanate, 20
Samurai, 84
San Francisco Treaty, 186
Sansom, Sir G., 84
Sarawak, 2, 31, 58-61, 212-14
Sarekat Dagang Islam, 142-3
Sastri Commission, 100
Satara, 71
Saw, U, 147, 190
Scientific Revolution, the, 10, 16-17, 93, 98
Secret Societies, Chinese, 51, 89-90, 154
Selangor, 18, 39, 51, 94; Sultan of, 52
Sepoys, 54, 75
Seringapatam, 23
Seven Years War, 12
Shan, 34, 63, 146, 190
Shanghai, 126, 135, 136, 162, 171
Shantung, 88, 137-8, 164
Shensi, 164
Shimonoseki, Treaty of, 86
Shoguns, the, 82-4
Shore, Sir John, 22
Siam, 2, 4, 15, 20, 23-4, 38-41, 56, 57, 67-9. See also Thailand
Sian, 166, 171
Sikhs, 36, 72, 75, 161, 192
Simla Conference, 191
Simon Commission, 110, 132, 146
Simreap (Angkor), 23
Sind, 72, 192
Sindhia, 71
Singapore, 1, 2, 13, 19, 29-32, 38, 41, 42, 47, 56, 89, 91, 94, 97, 102, 113, 143, 155, 173-4, 176, 178, 187, 212-3
Sino-Japanese War, 85-6
'Sinyetha', 147
Sisophon, 23
Sittang basin, 4
Sivaji, 71
Slavery, 27, 40, 52, 56
Slim, General, 189
Sneevliet, 142
Solomons, Battle of, 182
Soong, T. V., 162-3
Souphannouvong, Prince, 201
Spain, Spaniards, 8, 11, 25, 113-14, 141

Index

Speedy, Capt., 54
Spice Islands, 46
Sri Maharajah, 9
Sri Vijaya, 7, 8
State Councils (Malaya), 56
Straits Settlements, 38, 44, 48, 89, 93, 99, 152
Suez Canal, 44
Sukarno, President, 180, 190, 196, 213–14
Sulu Archipelago, 47
Sumatra, 7, 8, 18, 20, 32, 38, 143, 188
Sun Yat-Sen, 87, 123, 126–7, 135–6, 163
Sungei Ujong, 52, 94
Surabaya, 143
Surakarta, 21
Sutlej, 72, 192
Suttee, 73
Sweden, 68
Swettenham, F., 52–3, 55–6
Symes, Capt. M., 22
Syngman Rhee, 200
Szechwan, 125

Taft, W. H., 114
Tagore, Rabindranath, 142
Taiping, 95; Rebellion, 66, 81, 86, 89
Taiwan, *see* Formosa
Takahashi, Premier of Japan, 170
Tan, Sir C-L., 207
Tan, T. H., 207
Taoism, 6, 88
Temenggong of Johore, 29–31, 42
Templer, Sir Gerald, 206–7
Tenasserim, 15, 34, 62
Thailand, Thais, 1, 2, 4, 7–8, 109, 155–7, 174, 176, 199, 201. *See also* Siam
Thakins, the, 147, 179–80
Thibaw, King of Burma, 62–3
Thirawaddy, King of Burma, 34
Thompson, V., 148
Thugs, the, 72
Tientsin, 88; Treaty of, 81
Tipu Sultan, 23, 70
Tjokro, 142
Tojo, Premier of Japan, 182, 184
Tokyo, 138, 168, 169, 183–4, 185
Tosei-ha, the, 170
Toungoo, 62
Tourane, 66; Bay of, 24

Town Sanitary Boards, 96
Trade, extra-territorial rights, 68, 81, 86, 106; in coffee, 14, 57, 92; in cotton, 76; in indigo, 37, 76; in rubber, 92, 94–5, 96, 112; in spices, 10, 19, 32, 37; in sugar, 14, 95; in tea, 92, 95; in tin, 92–5, 96; of Americans, 83; of Arabs and Indians, 8, 89; of British 11, 17, 22, 32, 33, 37, 39, 46, 59; of and with China, 78–80, 81, 86, 138, 155, 203, 204; of French, 11, 66, 112; of and with Japan, 12, 68, 112, 138–9, 154, 165; of Netherlanders, 11–14, 20, 26, 32, 37, 46, 68, 144; of Portuguese, 10–11, 46; of Spaniards, 11; with Indochina, 112; with Philippines, 118, 150
Trincomalee, 177
Trengganu, 41, 43, 98
Tripartite Axis Pact, 174
Truman, Harry, 185, 193–4, 200
Tsai Feng, 124
Tsai-Tien, emperor, 87
Tsingtao, 128
Tsungli Yamen, the, 82
Tsushima, 122, 123
Tu-Duc, emperor, 66
Tumasik, 9
Tung Meng Hui, the, 123, 125
Tung Wen Kuan, 82
Turkey, 131
Twenty-one Demands, 128–9, 137–8
Tydings-McDuffie Act, 150
Tz'u Hsi, empress, 87–8, 124

Union Indochinoise, 67
United Nations, 186, 196, 199–200, 214
University, Chulalongkorn, 107
University of Hanoi, 112
University of Malaya, 97

van Heutsz, Governor-General, 103
Van Hogendorp, Dirk, 21
Van den Bosch, Governor-General, 37
Van der Capellen, Governor-General, 30, 37
Vasco da Gama, 10

227

Index

Versailles, Treaty of, 130, 137
Viceroys of India, *see* Canning; Chelmsford; Curzon; Dufferin; Irwin; Lytton; Mountbatten; Reading; Ripon; Willingdon. *See also* Governor-Generals
Victoria, Queen, 77
Vienna, Treaty of, 30, 31–2
Vietminh, 189, 201
Vietnam, 4, 6, 24, 99, 148–9, 189, 195, 201–2; North, 1, 15, 195, 202–3; South, 1, 15, 202–3
Volksraad, the, 106, 142, 144

Wakatsuki, Premier of Japan, 168
Wang Cheng-Ting, 154
Wang Ching-Wei, 162, 164, 172
Washington Conference, 138
Wataniah, the, 179
Wedermeyer, General, 194
Weihaiwei, 86
Wellesley, Col. A. (Duke of Wellington), 19, 23, 25, 71
Wellesley, Marquess, 13, 23, 70–1
Whampoa, 136
Wickham, Sir H., 94
Willingdon, Lord, 160

Wilson, Woodrow, 115, 137
Women, status in SE Asia, 3–4, 6
Wood, General, 115
Woosung, 162
World War I, 107, 129, 137, 143
World War II, 149, 152, 155, 161, 174
Wuchang, 125, 126
Wuhan, 137

Yalu River, 121, 200
Yandabo, Treaty of, 34
Yang di-pertuan, the, 41
Yangtze River, 81, 139, 162, 171, 198
Yap Ah Loy, 51, 93
Yedo, 84
Yeh T'ing, 163
Yenbay, 149
Yin Ching, 9
Yokohama, 138
Yuan Shih-K'ai, 87, 120, 124, 125–9, 134, 139
Yusof, 51

Zia'u'd-din, Tunku, 51
Zoological Society of London, 32

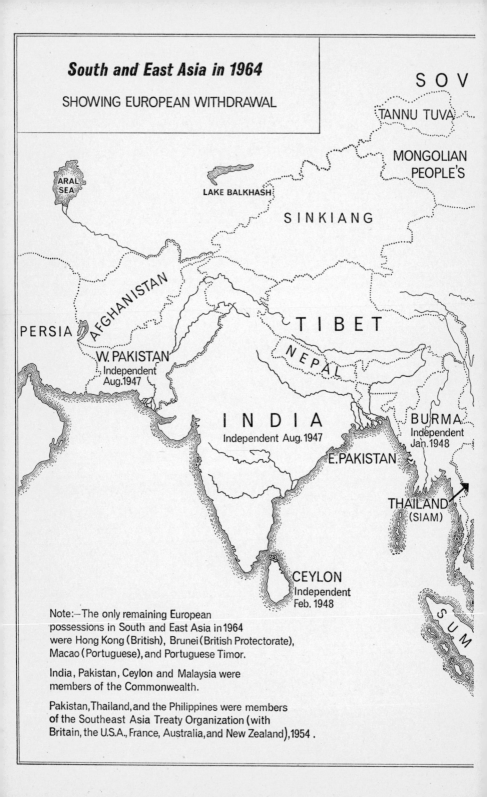

South and East Asia in 1964

SHOWING EUROPEAN WITHDRAWAL

S O V

TANNU TUVA

MONGOLIAN
PEOPLE'S

ARAL
SEA

LAKE BALKHASH

SINKIANG

PERSIA

AFGHANISTAN

T I B E T

N E P A L

W. PAKISTAN
Independent
Aug.1947

I N D I A
Independent Aug. 1947

BURMA
Independent
Jan.1948

E. PAKISTAN

THAILAND
(SIAM)

CEYLON
Independent
Feb. 1948

S
U
M

Note:— The only remaining European
possessions in South and East Asia in 1964
were Hong Kong (British), Brunei (British Protectorate),
Macao (Portuguese), and Portuguese Timor.

India, Pakistan, Ceylon and Malaysia were
members of the Commonwealth.

Pakistan, Thailand, and the Philippines were members
of the Southeast Asia Treaty Organization (with
Britain, the U.S.A., France, Australia, and New Zealand), 1954 .